HB
3730
N395
1985

NEW MATHEMATICAL ADVANCES IN
ECONOMIC DYNAMICS

New Mathematical Advances in Economic Dynamics

Edited by

DAVID F. BATTEN,
CSIRO, Australia and IIASA, Austria

and

PAUL F. LESSE,
CSIRO, Australia

NEW YORK
UNIVERSITY
PRESS

First published in the USA by New York University Press,
Washington Square, New York, N.Y. 10003

Library of Congress Cataloging in Publication Data
Main entry under title:

New mathematical advances in economic dynamics.

　　Papers presented at the Inaugural Conference on the Mathematics of
Economic Forecasting, held at the Royal Melbourne Institute of Technology
in December 1982.
　　Includes bibliographies and indexes.
　　1. Economic forecasting—Mathematical models—
Congresses.　2. Econometrics—Congresses.　3. Economics,
Mathematical—Congresses.　I. Batten, David F.
II. Lesse, Paul F.　III. Conference on the Mathematics
of Economic Forecasting (1st : 1982 : Royal Melbourne
Institute of Technology)
HB3730.N395　　1985　　　338.5'442'0151　　　85-15509
ISBN 0-8147-1084-0

CONTENTS

List of Tables
List of Figures
Preface

1. Introduction 1
    David F. Batten

PART I. STABILIZATION AND CONTROL

---

2. Feedback and Adaptive Control for Uncertain
    Dynamical Systems 15
    George Leitmann

3. Modelling and Optimal Control of Random Walk
    Processes in Economics 37
    John M. Blatt

4. Stabilization and Optimal Management in the Housing
    Industry 47
    Paul F. Lesse and Janislaw M. Skowronski

5. Modelling the Supply-Demand Dynamics of a Slowly
    Renewable Resource 69
    David F. Batten and Paul F. Lesse

PART II. DIFFERENTIAL GAMES

---

6. A Competitive Differential Game of Harvesting
    Uncertain Resources 87
    Janislaw M. Skowronski

7. Identification of Stock and System Parameters in
    a Pareto Harvesting Game of Two Players 105
    Glen J. Crouch and Janislaw M. Skowronski

PART III. DYNAMIC MACROECONOMIC MODELS

---

8. The Solution Procedure for the ORANI Model
    Explained by a Simple Example 119
    Peter B. Dixon

9. Analysis of the Effects of Time Lags and
    Nonlinearities in a Macroeconomic Model
    Incorporating the Government Budget Constraint 131
      Carl Chiarella

PART IV. TIME SERIES ANALYSIS AND ECONOMETRICS

10. Iterative Fitting of a Time Series Model 157
      Bruce D. Craven

11. The State Space Software SARAS Forecasts Better
    than the Box-Jenkins Method 165
      Keshav P. Vishwakarma

12. Electricity Demand Modelling 181
      William A. Donnelly

Contributing Authors 197
Author Index 199
Subject Index 203

LIST OF FIGURES

2.1 Responses of the Uncontrolled System and the System with various Linear Feedback Controls 21

2.2 Responses of the Uncontrolled Nominal System for Two Initial Conditions 22

2.3 Responses of the Uncontrolled System subject to $v(t) = -0.1 \cos t$ 23

2.4 Responses of the Controlled System subject to $v(t) = -0.1 \cos t$ 24

2.5 Simulation Results for $x_1(t)$ under the Constant Disturbance, $d(t) = 5$ 28

2.6 Simulation Results for $x_1(t)$ under the Constant Disturbance, $d(t) = 50$ 29

2.7 Simulation Results for $x_1(t)$ under the Periodic Disturbance, $d(t) = 5 \cos t$ 30

2.8 Optimal Switching Control between Unemployment and Inflation 32

4.1 Typical Relationship between Price and the Rate of Construction in an Industry with Open Access 53

4.2 Typical Relationship between Price and the Rate of Construction in an Industry with Quadratic Cost Functions 54

5.1 A Logistic Model of Forest Growth 72

5.2 The Demand for Forest Products 74

5.3 Supply Curve yielding Zero Return....................80

9.1 Relationship between Transformed (Y') and Untransformed (Y) Output 138

9.2 Jump in ϕ Coefficient with Variations in Output from the Static Equilibrium Value 140

9.3 Sign Switching of Transpose A 142

9.4 Transformation from (y,b) to (x,a) Coordinates 143

9.5 Graphical Determination of the Equilibrium Point $\bar{\rho}$ 145

9.6 Stable Limit Cycle in the (y,b) Plane 146

9.7 Alternative Effects of Changes in ω on the Amplitude of Economic Fluctuations 148

10.1 An Additive Case 157

10.2 A Non-additive Case 157

10.3 An Autocorrelogram 160

11.1 One Quarter Ahead Predictions of the GDP Trend Level over the Sample Period 170

11.2 Estimated Seasonal Factors over the Sample Period ..171

11.3 95% Confidence Intervals of Forecasts during and beyond the Sample Period 172

LIST OF TABLES

8.1 Various Solutions for V_1 and V_2 as V_3 changes in System (2) 125

8.2 Effects on Industry Output of a 100 per cent 'Across the Board' Tariff Reduction Computed using the ORANI Model (main industries affected only).....126

11.1 A Sample of SARAS Output 168

11.2 One Year Ahead Forecasts for 1980, December quarter 174

11.3 Comparison of Mean Forecasts (in billions of Australian dollars) 175

11.4 Comparison of Interval Forecasts (in billions of Australian dollars) 177

12.1 A.C.T. Residential Electricity Demand: Annual Model Data 184

12.2 Box-Cox A.C.T. Electricity Demand 188

12.3 Box-Cox Test Results 188

12.4 Ridge Regression Results 190

12.5 A.C.T. Residential Electricity Demand: Elasticities 190

12.6 Selected Residential Electricity Demand Results 192

PREFACE

Mathematical methods and models to facilitate our understanding of the processes of economic dynamics and economic forecasting have been refined considerably during the past twenty-five years; this field has grown as it has matured in the search for its own identity. A number of innovative new developments have emerged, but many of the resulting techniques involve complexities beyond our simple understanding.

On the other hand, there are many aspects of economic behaviour which can be aptly described, at least to a first approximation, by one or two simple first-order difference or differential equations. Recent studies have confirmed that even the very simplest nonlinear difference equations can possess an extraordinarily rich spectrum of dynamical behaviour. In other words, simple nonlinear systems do not necessarily possess simple dynamical properties.

This book originates from a shared concern with the need to clarify the relationship between our <u>understanding</u> of the process of change within an economic system and our ability to <u>predict</u> or <u>control</u> this dynamic process. The invited papers collected herein were all presented at the Inaugural Conference on the Mathematics of Economic Forecasting, held at the Royal Melbourne Institute of Technology in December 1982. Sessions were devoted to the critical appraisal of recent developments and the identification of potentially productive new research directions. The resulting forum emanating from the fresh interaction between experienced mathematicians, statisticians and economists strongly emphasized the need to pursue more extensive analyses of the relationship between system understanding and predictability. This volume is dedicated to that pursuit.

Part I is concerned with recent approaches to stabilization and control, including deterministic, stochastic and adaptive methods. Part II concentrates on the application of differential game theory involving several players. In Part III, both linear and nonlinear systems of differential equations are used to describe (in simple terms) the dynamics of two macroeconomic models. Part IV discusses new methods for time series analysis and econometric forecasting. The contributions provided by our chapter authors have been carefully edited in an attempt to produce an integrated volume, rather than a collection of autonomous papers.

A work with the scope and diversity of this one naturally owes its existence to many contributors in addition to its authors. Foremost among those to whom the present volume is indebted are Julie Penn, who typed and revised the manuscript with the very capable assistance of Debbie Langdon, and Jennifer Wundersitz, who assisted with editing and coordinated correspondence among the authors. Special thanks are due to Bernie Hawkins for editorial management and Barrie Bilton for the excellent artwork. The financial and organisational support of the Australian Mathematical Society is gratefully acknowledged. In particular, the assistance provided by Rhys Jones and Howard Connell on behalf of the Applied Mathematics Division, Victorian Branch has been invaluable. The original manuscript was assembled at the research home of both editors, namely the Division of Building Research, Commonwealth Scientific and Industrial Research Organisation, Melbourne, Australia. The final version was completed while the first author was a visiting scientist at the International Institute for Applied Systems Analysis, Laxenburg, Austria. The assistance of the Institute's Publications Department is acknowledged. Some of the original research on which certain chapters are based was supported by other organisations, namely the National Science Foundation (Chapter 2) and the Institut des Sciences Economiques, Universite Catholique de Louvain (Chapter 9). The editors wish to express their sincere appreciation to all the above.

David F. Batten
Paul F. Lesse

Chapter One

INTRODUCTION

David F. Batten

ECONOMIC DYNAMICS

Methods and models of economic dynamics describe the motion of an economy, or some part thereof, through time. The basic concept in such models is usually that of a path or trajectory which describes the admissible (feasible) states of economic change. Dynamic models may simply portray the economic trajectory itself, or they may simulate attempts to influence such a path.

Although dynamic behaviour and the broader aspects of economic change have received considerable attention within the last three decades, and though a concern with development has been central to the economic discipline since the classical period of Adam Smith, Malthus and Ricardo, the ruling paradigm is still that of a system in general equilibrium. For the members of this orthodox school, the stationary state is simply replaced by a steady state.

General equilibrium theory has been extended to the realm of dynamics by establishing the existence of intertemporal equilibria in which the behaviour of economic agents is seen to be intertemporally optimal, intertemporally consistent and intertemporally efficient. Corresponding to this notion of economic life is the method of comparative statics, based on the comparison of equilibria that vary with the parameters of the system (such as government control variables). Implicit here is the assumption that the underlying complex dynamic process, which is not actually represented in the equilibrium model, is stable in so much as whenever the state of equilibrium is perturbed the system will begin moving toward and converge to a new equilibrium. In other words, any 'disturbance' to the prevailing conditions is expected to gradually diminish as a new equilibrium path becomes established and transient motion dies out.

The widespread preoccupation by economists with the equilibrium approach has been due in part to its compelling simplicity and elegance, and in part to the prevailing Western experience of steady economic growth in the quarter century following World War II. During this period, economic theorists turned their attention away from the problems of depressions and business cycles to a characterisation of steady growth. A flourishing literature emanated from von Neumann's linear activity analysis model of growth, the Solow-Swan-Tinbergen neoclassical growth model, and the Harrod-Domar model, directing attention towards the existence, stability and intertemporal optimality of balanced growth trajectories.

But growth implies 'more of the same' and not all economic systems follow equilibrium paths. Consequently, a need for complementary theories concerned with the study of economic systems which are not growing smoothly and are not in equilibrium has been recognized by many in the last two decades (e.g. Day, 1975; Nelson and Winter, 1982).

Of course, interest in temporary equilibrium and disequilibrium models is not entirely recent. In addition to our classical mentors, there have been various contributions from historical and instutional economists, business cycle and long wave theorists, simulation modellers, and to single out one individual, Joseph Schumpeter, whose ideas about dynamic competition, technical progress, and other forces of economic change constitute what William Baumol (1970) has called 'the last grand dynamics'. But none of these contributions has filled the intellectual niche sufficiently to sustain the momentum of a main stream of economic thought, and a central unifying theory from a single school of dynamic analysts has yet to emerge.

In the last decade, however, a number of complementary advances have occurred in various fields within and outside economics which seem likely to facilitate a new approach to dynamic theory. Although space limitations preclude any comprehensive discussion of these synergistic avenues of thought, it is important to be aware of the various strands before we explore some of the mathematical tools which could help to provide new insights into how economies change and how society evolves.

We can briefly trace the path of historical thinking relating to dynamic analysis which has led to today's schools of thought in terms of three main strands, namely (i) growth (ii) fluctuation and (iii) development. The early period of classical theories emphasized population growth, capital accumulation and technical progress. During this conceptual period, Malthus in particular showed a fine appreciation of the importance of a distinct and systematic theory of growth.[1] Karl Marx was the first to reveal a deeper understanding of the importance of technological change. With his Theory of Economic Development, Schumpeter travelled even further along the road towards real dynamics. He was particularly aware of the importance of innovation, new technologies and evolution in shaping new pathways of economic development. We may cautiously refer to him as the 'foster father' of economic dynamics.

Any scheme of subdivision chosen for a complex field of endeavour may reveal certain clusters of thought but cannot hope to capture all facets of the endeavour. So it is with economic dynamics. The three channels of analytical thought which we have

Introduction

mentioned are inexhaustive, overlapping and somewhat arbitrary. A few exceptional theorists have contributed substantially to all of these strands. Nevertheless, there are some advantages stemming from such a classificatory approach, particularly when we wish to discuss more recent doctrines and distinctions.

Perhaps the most meaningful way to differentiate between these three schools of thought is not to rely on imprecise distinctions like the equilibrium-disequilibrium scale, but rather to understand the fundamental differences between the three dynamic processes: growth, fluctuation and development. The process of fluctuation or oscillation is largely self evident; resulting cycles may of course be dampened, explosive or stationary. However, the key parameter in any theory of fluctuations is the cycle's <u>duration</u>, since distinctions between the short wave (e.g. 'Kitchin' cycle of 3 to 4 years duration), the medium wave (e.g. 'Juglar' cycle of 7 to 11 years duration), and the long wave (e.g. 'Kondratieff' cycle of 50 to 55 years duration) are of great significance. Research into business cycles and long waves is research into sequences of events or episodes, which are also the subject matter (or part of the subject matter) of macrodynamics.

In order to distinguish between growth and development, we can do little better than quote from Schumpeter (1934, p.63):

> "By <u>development</u>, therefore, we shall understand only such changes in economic life as are not forced upon it from without but arise by its own initiative from within ... Nor will the mere <u>growth</u> of the economy, as shown by the growth of population and wealth, be designated here as a process of development. For it calls forth no qualitatively new phenomena, but only processes of adaptation of the same kind as the changes in natural data".

In short, growth implies 'more of much the same', whereas economic development is a highly evolutionary process. Evolution and development indeed are almost the same word (Boulding, 1981). With his theory of economic development, Joseph Schumpeter was particularly aware of the importance of invention and innovation, as well as the role of new enterprises in shaping future pathways of economic behaviour. Whereas growth is often balanced, development is more than often unbalanced. Whereas growth generally implies a stable or steady state, development may be unstable or unsteady.

The three major strands of economic dynamics call for different analytical approaches to unravel their respective mysteries. Within the last two decades, there has been a rapid acceleration in the use of mathematical tools to study such economic phenomena. Although much of the field of mathematical economics has concentrated historically on the concepts of optimality, market equilibria and social efficiency, attention is gradually shifting from the more orthodox concern with desirable

Introduction

static or steady economic states to a less orthodox emphasis on obtaining an improved understanding of how economies and their parts work dynamically, and how their development over time may be influenced by new policies governing behaviour and organisation. We shall attempt to summarise these advances in the next section.

MATHEMATICAL ECONOMICS

The history of mathematical economics may be divided into three broad and somewhat overlapping periods (Arrow and Intriligator, 1981): the calculus-based marginalist period (1838-1947), the set-theoretic/linear models period (1948-1960), and the current period of integration and nonlinearity (1961-present). However, these dates are really just suggestive, since work in each of the above areas still continues to be significant.

The Calculus-based Marginalist Period

The early period of mathematical economics was one in which economists borrowed methodologies from the physical sciences to develop a formal theory based largely on calculus, using total and partial derivatives and Lagrange multipliers to characterise maxima. The seminal work of Cournot (1838), which has been cited as the starting point of mathematical economics,[2] might also (in a more modest sense) be regarded as the birthplace of mathematical interest in economic dynamics. Although not explicitly dynamic (the variables are time subscripted), Cournot associates the concept of a reaction function with an economic agent. This is the notion of each firm choosing its output in response or reaction to the outputs chosen by others. At this point, Cournot is discussing a multi-period process. The reaction function for a firm is a function which associates a current output choice for the firm with the output levels chosen by other firms at some time in the past. Although Cournot's analysis is not carried far and the dynamics are implicit, his contribution may be seen as the embryo of a mathematical school of economic dynamics.

In general, however, the calculus-based marginalist period did not pay much attention to dynamic analysis. It was a time for laying the mathematical foundations of the modern theories of the consumer, the producer, oligopoly, and general equilibrium. To be sure, there were interesting exceptions, such as the rigorous discussions of the stability of Walrasian general equilibrium by Hicks (1939) and Samuelson (1941), and the studies of optimization over time by Ramsey (1928) and, with special reference to exhaustible resources, by Hotelling (1931). But only at the conclusion of this period did we see the emergence of dynamic analysis as a fundamental issue. In two classic books which continue to be highly influential, Hicks (1946) and Samuelson (1947) both summarized previous theory and developed newer concepts. The former included the useful idea of temporary equilibrium; the latter emphasized a realisation of the fact that

Introduction

even a static theory cannot be fully developed outside an explicit dynamical framework.

It would, however, be remiss not to mention the strong drive near the end of this period toward a numerical economics; an economics that could be statistically operational. This desire sprang largely from a growing interest in more substantial theories of the business cycle and of other economic fluctuations, supported by the associated time-series statistics. Two important contributions in this direction came simultaneously, namely Kalecki (1939) and Tinbergen (1939).

The Set-Theoretic/Linear Models Period

During the postwar period, the earlier calculus basis for mathematical economics was replaced by a set-theoretic approach and by linear models. Using set theory afforded greater generality in that the classical assumption of smooth functions could be replaced by more general functions. Using linear models also extended the treatment of phenomena that could not be represented by smooth functions.

The new apparatus had already been set to work in a highly illuminating approach to the theory of expansion by von Neumann (1937; English version, 1945). His multisector growth model laid the foundations for many later advances in both general equilibrium and growth theory. With the advent of linear programming, a synthesis of all these approaches culminated in Dorfman, Samuelson and Solow (1958) and Gale (1960). Also of fundamental importance was the development of a related model of capital accumulation by Malinvaud (1953). Dorfman, Samuelson and Solow presented the initial formulation of the turnpike theorem, which was to attract attention thoughout the sixties.

Game theory was in the process of development during this period based, in part, on the analysis of linear models.

The Current Period of Integration and Nonlinearity

The present period is one of both integration - in which modern mathematical economics combines elements of calculus, set theory, and linear models - as well as nonlinear analysis - in which new mathematical methods are being sought to further our understanding of nonlinear changes in economic behaviour. A growing interest in mathematical tools for forecasting and prediction has also been evident. The overall breadth of integration has swelled considerably as the field searches for its own identity, but also draws on complementary advances in other scientific disciplines. By necessity, the following summary of developments during the last two decades can only be illustrative. The discussion encompasses each school of enquiry mentioned earlier, but is structured along broader lines.

(1) Optimal growth theory and dynamic equilibria
 The basic problem was initially formulated as one of optimal savings in an article by Ramsey (1928), which was decades ahead of its time. Modern tools of growth theory and

turnpike theorems have been developed by such writers as Samuelson, Uzawa, Koopmans, Cass, von Weizsäcker and Shell. This theory has also been combined with multisector growth models (e.g. Johansen, 1960) to achieve systemwide integration (e.g. Morishima, 1964, 1969; Tsukui, 1979). The mathematical basis of optimal growth theory hinges on the theory of dynamical systems (Varian, 1981). Important publications in this area include Shell (1967), Cass and Shell (1976), Makarov and Rubinov (1977). Later in this volume, both linear and nonlinear systems of differential equations governing the dynamics of macroeconomic models are discussed by Dixon (Chapter 8) and Chiarella (Chapter 9).

(2) Control theory

The mathematical basis of optimal growth theory also includes control theory, whose methods are used to find optimal stabilization policies or desirable trajectories over time for a deterministic or stochastic system. In deterministic methods, there are no uncertain elements; in stochastic approaches, there are random elements but there is no purposeful effort to learn about these elements; in adaptive control, there is an attempt to learn actively the value of uncertain elements. Stochastic elements are common in economics (e.g. equation errors, unknown parameters, and measurement errors), so the methods of stochastic or adaptive control are finding increased application areas (Kendrick, 1981).

Some of the principal books in the field of economics and control theory include Murphy (1965), Åström (1970), Chow (1975), Aoki (1976), Pitchford and Turnovsky (1977) and Leitmann (1981). Surveys of applications of control theory to economics have been written by Arrow (1968), Aoki (1974), Intriligator (1975), and Kendrick (1976). In this volume, methods of adaptive control are discussed by Leitmann in Chapter 2, and modelling and control of stochastic processes are examined by Blatt in Chapter 3; whereas interesting applications involving deterministic/stochastic control are presented in Chapter 4 (by Lesse and Skowronski) and Chapter 5 (by Batten and Lesse). The use of stochastic models (in the state space form of control theory) for time series analysis is discussed by Vishwakarma in Chapter 11.

(3) Game theory

A close link also exists between optimisation methods and the theory of games. The foundations of this mathematical theory were laid by von Neumann (1928), whose minimax theorem later provided the stimulus for the analysis of duality properties in optimal growth models. In the context of dynamic systems, differential games among several players have been studied seriously by mathematicians only during the last two decades. For an introduction to the field, see Intriligator (1971). Some of the principal advances can be found in Luenberger and Rhodes (1969), Kuhn and Szegö (1971), and Shubik and Sobel (1979). Applications of differential game theory to economics have been limited, although various subgroups - such as (i) competitive or cooperative; (ii) zero-sum or non-zero sum; (iii) deterministic or stochastic, and (iv) discrete or continuous - have been actively explored.

Among the more interesting economic applications of differential games are those dealing with the harvesting of renewable resources (Vincent and Skowronski, 1980). Two papers in this field are included in this volume: (i) Skowronski's work on a nonlinear competitive (Nash) differential game involving several players harvesting several resources (Chapter 6); and (ii) his joint work with Crouch on the identification of stock and system parameters in the Pareto-optimal case (Chapter 7). Both these chapters adopt the Liapunov formalism and the nonlinear theory of adaptive identifiers.

(4) Nonlinear models and evolutionary theory

Recent attempts to work across several disciplines in dynamics turn on the modern theory of differential equations and, in particular, on nonlinear dynamical systems. Strands of mathematical topology which are gradually being drawn together include descendents of Pontryagin's structural stability analysis (for good summaries, see Nitecki, 1971; Hirsch and Smale, 1974), the bifurcation theory of Poincare and Lyapunov, differential topology, qualitative dynamics and catastrophe theory (Thom, 1975; Zeeman, 1974, 1982). The goal of the latter is to study and classify ways in which the qualitative properties of a system change as the parameters describing the system vary.

A closely related school of economic thought may be classified under the heading of nonlinear theories of economic evolution. As defined earlier, evolution refers to the gradual development, through progressive and systematic changes, of new technologies and new pathways of economic behaviour. Mathematical tools which belong in this class include self-organizing models of competition and industrial evolution emanating from Prigogine's work (Batten, 1982; Schieve and Allen, 1982), synergetics (Haken, 1983), phenomenological theory (Lesse, 1983), evolutionary theory (Nelson and Winter, 1982), recursive programming and adaptive economics (Day, 1975; Day and Cigno, 1978), and product cycle theory (Andersson and Johansson, 1984).

The common thread running through all of the abovementioned theories is a recognition of disequilibria, instabilities and lifecycle phenomena, along with the role of innovation as the nonlinear engine of structural change and economic development. To this extent, these methods largely stem from a Schumpeterian view of economic dynamics as a study of qualitative changes, and may hold considerable promise for

Introduction

> unravelling many economic mysteries which are nonlinear in nature. The various tools of dynamic analysis discussed herein could assist with this endeavour.

(5) Time series analysis and econometric forecasting
> Although strictly in the realm of statistical methods and probability theory, time series analysis and econometric forecasting are included here to complement our earlier discussion of fluctuations and the business cycle. As a guide to early developments in time series analysis, the reader is referred to Hannan (1960), Box and Jenkins (1970), and Nelson (1973). Two recent analytical developments are discussed in this volume (i) an iterative method devised by Craven (Chapter 10) and (ii) a state-space method based on control theory developed by Vishwakarma (Chapter 11). Econometric forecasting is represented by Donnelly's article on electricity demand modelling (Chapter 12).

SIMPLICITY AND COMPLEXITY

In order to further synthesize the collection of ideas presented in the following chapters, a brief comment is in order concerning simplicity and complexity. Although many new mathematical methods and models to facilitate our understanding of the processes of economic dynamics and prediction have emerged during the last two decades, some of the resulting techniques involve complexities which are beyond our powers of simple interpretation. A case in point is the system dynamics approach introduced in the early sixties by Jay Forrester (1961). Through the introduction of arbitrary negative feedback loops, servomechanisms, thresholds and discrete switching rules, these simulation models were capable of producing an extraordinary range of behavioural modes during the course of a single analysis. Growth, oscillation and decay could all appear in turn, with many endogenous shifts in structure emanating from the complex system of feedback loops involved.

The problem with models of this type is, of course, that when complexity is introduced as an _input_ instead of evolving as an _output_, there is a tendency to accumulate errors and to produce unstable behaviour with respect to very small changes in data. Although such instabilities may imply that a qualitative understanding rather than any quantitative prediction should be the proper objective in dynamic analysis, we can never be certain of this interpretation. Owing to the complications introduced a priori, it is generally difficult to draw any sound conclusions from models of this type.

On the other hand, there are many aspects of economic behaviour which can be aptly described, at least to a first approximation, by one or two simple first-order difference or differential equations. Recent studies confirm that the very simplest nonlinear difference equations can possess an extraordinarily rich spectrum of dynamical behaviour, from stable

Introduction

points, through cascades of stable cycles, to a regime in which the behaviour (although fully deterministic) is in many respects 'chaotic', or indistinguishable from the sample function of a random process (May, 1976). In other words, simple nonlinear systems do not necessarily possess simple dynamical properties.

The collection of papers in this volume subscribe to the rationale that simplicity itself can generate complexity. Accordingly, they pursue various lines of enquiry with the objective of unravelling the relationship between system understanding and predictability. Complexity is actively avoided as an input to the formulation process, but a rich panorama of dynamic behaviour may nevertheless be generated as an output. Thus the volume is dedicated to the pursuit of simple tools to study quite complex mathematical aspects of the structure of economic trajectories.

NOTES

1. We have in mind his Principles of Political Economy and, to a lesser extent, his Essay on the Principles of Population.
2. There are always predecessors; for a study of the prehistory of mathematical economics, see Theocharis (1961).

REFERENCES

Aoki, M. (1974) 'Stochastic Control Theory in Economics: applications and new problems', IFAC Symposium on Stochastic Control, Prague

Aoki, M. (1976) Dynamic Economic Theory and Control in Economics, American Elsevier, New York

Andersson, A.E. and Johansson, B. (1984) 'Industrial dynamics, product cycles, and employment structure', Working Paper WP-84-9, International Institute for Applied Systems Analysis, Laxenburg

Arrow, K.J. (1968) 'Application of control theory to economic growth', in Lectures in Applied Mathematics, Part 2, Vol.12, American Mathematical Society, Providence, Rhode Island.

Arrow, K.J. and Intriligator, M.D. (1981) Handbook of Mathematical Economics, (Volume 1), North Holland, Amsterdam

Batten, D.F. (1982) 'On the Dynamics of Industrial Evolution', Regional Science and Urban Economics, 12, 449-462

Baumol, W.J. (1970) Economic Dynamics, Macmillan, London

Boulding, K. (1981) Evolutionary Economics, Sage Publications, Beverly Hills

Box, G.E.P. and Jenkins, G.M. (1970) Time Series Analysis: Forecasting and Control, Holden-Day, San Francisco

Cass, D. and Shell, K. eds (1976) The Hamiltonian Approach to Dynamic Economics, Academic Press, New York

Chow, G.C. (1975) *Analysis and Control of Dynamic Systems*, Wiley, New York
Clark, C.W. (1976) *Mathematical Bioeconomics*, Wiley, New York
Cournot, A. (1838) *Researches into the Mathematical Principles of the Theory of Wealth*, Paris (in French; English version by Macmillan, 1897)
Day, R.H. (1975) 'Adaptive Processes and Economic Theory' in R.H. Day and T. Groves (eds) *Adaptive Economic Models*, Academic Press, New York
Day, R.H. and Cigno, A. eds (1978) *Modelling Economic Change: The Recursive Programming Approach*, North-Holland, Amsterdam.
Dorfman, R., Samuelson, P.A. and Solow, R. (1958) *Linear Programming and Economic Analysis*, McGraw-Hill, New York
Forrester, J. (1961) *Industrial Dynamics*, MIT Press, Cambridge, Massachusetts
Gale, D. (1960) *The Theory of Linear Economic Models*, McGraw-Hill, New York
Haken, H. (1983) *Synergetics*, Springer-Verlag, Berlin
Hannan, E.J. (1960) *Time Series Analysis*, Methuen, London
Hicks, J.R. (1939) *Value and Capital*, Oxford University Press, New York.
Hicks, J.R. (1946) *Value and Capital*, 2nd Edition, Oxford University Press, New York
Hirsch, M. and Smale, S. (1974) *Differential Equations, Dynamical Systems and Linear Algebra*, Academic Press, New York
Hotelling, H. (1931) 'The Economics of Exhaustible Resources', *Journal of Political Economy*, 39, 137-175
Intriligator, M.D. (1971) *Mathematical Optimization and Economic Theory*, Prentice-Hall, Englewood Cliffs, N.J.
Intriligator, M.D. (1975) 'Applications of Optimal Control Theory in Economics', *Synthese*, 31, 271-288
Johansen, L. (1960) *A Multi-Sectoral Study of Economic Growth*, North-Holland, Amsterdam
Kalecki, M. (1939) *Studies in the Theory of Business Cycles: 1933-1939*, Kelley
Kendrick, D.A. (1976) 'Application of Control Theory to Macroeconomics', *Annals of Economic and Social Measurements*, 5, 171-190
Kendrick, D.A. (1981) *Stochastic Control for Economic Models*, McGraw-Hill, New York
Kuhn, H.W. and Szegö, G.P. eds (1971) *Differential Games and Related Topics*, North-Holland, Amsterdam
Leitmann, G. (1981) *Calculus of Variations and Optimal Control*, Plenum Press, New York
Lesse, P.F. (1983) 'Economics in Time and Space: A Mathematical Theory', *Papers, Regional Science Association*, 51, 81-116
Luenberger, D.G. and Rhodes, I.B. (1969) 'Differential Games with Imperfect State Information', *I.E.E.E. Transactions*, AC-14, 29-38

Makarov, V.L. and Rubinov, A.M. (1977) *Mathematical Theory of Economic Dynamics and Equilibria*, Springer-Verlag, New York

Malinvaud (1953) 'Capital Accumulation and the Efficient Allocation of Resources', *Econometrica*, 21, 233-268

May, R.M. (1976) 'Simple Mathematical Models with Very Complicated Dynamics', *Nature*, 261, 459-467

Morishima, M. (1964) *Equilibrium, Stability and Growth*, Oxford University Press, New York

Morishima, M. (1969) *Theories of Economic Growth*, Oxford University Press, New York

Murphy, R.E. (1965) *Adaptive Processes in Economic Systems*, Academic Press, New York

Nelson, C.R. (1973) *Applied Time Series Analysis for Managerial Forecasting*, Holden-Day, San Francisco

Nelson, R.R. and Winter, S.G. (1982) *An Evolutionary Theory of Economic Change*, Harvard University Press, Cambridge, Massachusetts

Nitecki, Z. (1971) *Differentiable Dynamics*, MIT Press, Cambridge, Massachusetts

Pitchford, J. and Turnovsky, S. eds (1977) *Application of Control Theory to Economic Analysis*, North-Holland, Amsterdam

Ramsey, F.P. (1928) 'A Mathematical Theory of Saving', *Economic Journal*, 38, 543-559

Samuelson, P.A. (1941) 'The Stability of Equilibrium: Comparative Statics and Dynamics', *Econometrica*, 9, 97-120

Samuelson, P.A. (1947) *Foundations of Economic Analysis*, Harvard University Press, Cambridge, Massachusetts

Schieve, W.C. and Allen, P.M. eds (1982) *Self-Organization and Dissipative Structures: Applications in the Physical and Social Sciences*, University of Texas Press, Austin

Schumpeter, J. (1934) *The Theory of Economic Development*, Harvard University Press, Cambridge, Massachusetts

Shell, K. ed. (1967) *Essays on the Theory of Optimal Growth*, MIT Press, Cambridge, Massachusetts

Shubik, M. and Sobel, M.J. (1979) 'Stochastic Games, Oligopoly Theory and Competitive Resource Allocation', Discussion Paper No.525, Cowles Foundation for Research in Economics, Yale University

Theocharis, R. (1961) *Early Developments in Mathematical Economics*, Macmillan, London

Thom, R. (1975) *Structural Stability and Morphogenesis*, Benjamin, Reading, Massachusetts

Tinbergen, J. (1939) *Statistical Testing of Business Cycle Theories*, Agathon

Tsukui, J. (1979) *Turnpike Optimality and Input-Output Systems*, North-Holland, Amsterdam

Varian, H.R. (1981) 'Dynamical Systems with Applications to Economics' in Arrow, K.J. and Intriligator, M.D., eds *Handbook of Mathematical Economics*, North-Holland, Amsterdam, pp.93-110

Introduction

Vincent, T.L. and Skowronski, M.M. eds (1980) <u>Renewable Resources Management</u>, Lecture Notes in Biomathematics, Volume 40, Springer-Verlag, Berlin

von Neumann, J. (1928) 'Zur Theorie der Gesellschaftsspiele', <u>Mathematische Annalen</u>, 100, 295-320

von Neumann, J. (1937) 'Uber ein Ökonomisches Gleichungssystem und eine Verallgemeinerung des Brouwerschen Fixpunktsatzes', <u>Ergebnisse eines Mathematischen Kolloquiums</u>, 8, 73-83. In 1945 translated as: 'A Model of General Economic Equilibrium', <u>Review of Economic Studies</u>, 13, 1-9

Zeeman, E.C. (1974) 'On the Unstable Behaviour of Stock Market Exchanges', <u>Journal of Mathematical Economics</u>, 1, 39-50

Zeeman, E.C. (1982) 'Bifurcation and Catastrophe Theory', <u>Contemporary Mathematics</u>, 9, 207-272

Åström, K.J. (1970) <u>Introduction to Stochastic Control Theory</u>, Academic Press, New York

PART I

STABILIZATION AND CONTROL

Chapter Two

FEEDBACK AND ADAPTIVE CONTROL FOR UNCERTAIN DYNAMICAL SYSTEMS[1]

George Leitmann

INTRODUCTION

In order to predict or control the behaviour of a system in the 'real' world, be it physical, biological or socio-economic, the system analyst seeks to capture its salient features in an abstraction, a mathematical model. Such a model always contains elements which are uncertain. These uncertain elements may be parameters, constant or time-varying, which are unknown or imperfectly known, or they may be unknown or imperfectly known inputs into the system. Despite such imperfect knowledge about the chosen mathematical model, one often seeks to devise controllers which will steer the system response in a desired fashion, for example so as to obtain stable behaviour. Here, two main avenues are open to the system analyst. He may choose a stochastic approach in which information about the uncertain elements as well as about the system behaviour is in statistical terms; loosely speaking, he is content with desirable behaviour on the average. For stochastic treatments in this category, see Kushner (1966) and Aström (1970). On the other hand, he may opt for a deterministic approach and attempt to construct controllers which assure the desired behaviour; loosely speaking, he wishes to guarantee that every possible response of the mathematical model possesses the desired features. Here we shall eschew the stochastic approach and discuss briefly some deterministic ones.

In deterministic treatments of uncertainties in mathematical models which are dynamical systems, information about the uncertain elements may be of two kinds; the analyst knows (or assumes) some functional properties as well as the possible sizes of the uncertain elements, or he may assume only some of their functional properties. In either case the control designer must have access to information about the system response, for example, the state (or possibly only the output) of the system. When the range of the possible values of all uncertain elements is known (assumed), it is often possible to devise state (or estimated state) feedback controls which guarantee desired behaviour of every possible response; e.g., see Monopoli (1966), Krasovskii

(1974), Gutman and Leitmann (1976), Ananev (1977), Leitmann (1979), Molander (1979), Gutman (1979), Leitmann (1980), Leitmann (1981), Monopoli (1981), and Corless and Leitmann (1981). When information about the possible sizes of the uncertain elements is not assumed, control must be based on estimates of uncertainty bounds, and the consequent control laws are adaptive, that is, change as these estimates evolve; e.g., see Salukvadze (1962), Johnson (1968), Lindorff and Carroll (1973), Narendra and Valavani (1978), Morse (1980), Porter and Grujic (1980), Peterson and Narendra (1982), Kreisselmeier and Narendra (1982), and Corless and Leitmann (1983).

In the subsequent discussion we review briefly (but not exhaustively) some results concerning deterministic control of uncertain dynamical systems in the form of ordinary differential equations. The method of devising controls which assure desired behaviour, usually stability in some sense, is based on the constructive use of Lyapunov theory, an approach suggested in a somewhat different context by Lurie (1951), Letov (1955), and Kalman and Bertram (1960).

UNCERTAINTIES WITH KNOWN BOUNDS

Consider a system modelled by

$$\dot{x}(t) = f(x(t),t) + \Delta f(x(t),t,r(t))$$
$$+ [B(x(t),t) + \Delta B(x(t),t,s(t))]u(t)$$
$$+ C(x(t),t)v(t), \qquad (1)$$
$$x(t_0) = x_0,$$

where $x(t) \in R^n$ is the state, $u(t) \in R^m$ is the control, and $r(t)$, $s(t)$ and $v(t)$ are uncertain elements. Thus, $\Delta f(\cdot)$, $\Delta B(\cdot)$ and $v(\cdot)$ account for imperfect knowledge relative to the 'nominal' system

$$\dot{x}(t) = f(x(t),t) + B(x(t),t)u(t),$$
$$x(t_0) = x_0 \qquad (2)$$

and in the input, respectively.

The uncertain elements are assumed to range in known compact sets; namely,

$$r(t) \in \mathbf{R}, \; s(t) \in \mathbf{S}, \; v(t) \in \mathbf{V} \qquad (3)$$

Thus, all information about uncertainty resides in $\mathbf{R}$, $\mathbf{S}$ and $\mathbf{V}$.
Now we consider the following salient conditions:
I. The zero solution ($x(t) = 0$) of the uncontrolled ($u(t) = 0$) nominal system (2) is globally uniformly asymptotically stable. In particular, there exists a Lyapunov function, $V(x,t)$, for that system.
II. The system uncertainty lies in the range of the input. More precisely, there exist a vector $h(t,x,r)$, and matrices $E(x,t,s)$

Feedback and Adaptive Control for Uncertain Dynamical Systems

and $F(x,t)$, such that for all x, t, r and s

$$\Delta f = Bh, \quad \Delta B = BE, \quad C = BF$$

where

$$\max_{s \varepsilon S} ||E(x,t,s)|| < 1.$$

Conditions I and II are the main assumptions for the existence of a feedback control

$$u(t) = p(x(t),t) \tag{5}$$

which assures 'practical stability'; namely, for every initial x_0 and for all possible uncertainties $r(t)$, $s(t)$ and $v(t)$, the solutions of (1) are uniformly bounded and there is a calculable neighbourhood of the zero state, which is uniformly stable, and in which all solutions are ultimately uniformly bounded. This neighbourhood can be made arbitrarily small, so that one can approach global uniform asymptotic stability.

As shown by Corless and Leitmann (1981), this control is a Caratheodory[2] function such that, for given $\varepsilon > 0$,

$$p(x,t) = -\frac{\mu(x,t)}{||\mu(x,t)||} \rho(x,t) \quad \text{if } ||\mu(x,t)|| > \varepsilon$$

$$||p(x,t)|| \le \rho(x,t) \quad \text{if } ||\mu(x,t)|| \le \varepsilon \tag{6}$$

where

$$\mu(x,t) = B^T(x,t) \nabla_x V(x,t) \rho(x,t),$$

and

$$\rho(x,t) = [1-\max_{s \varepsilon S}||E(x,t,s,)||]^{-1}[\max_{r \varepsilon R}||h(x,t,r)|| + \max_{v \varepsilon V}||F(x,t)v||]$$

Thus, the class of guaranteed stability controls defined by (6) depends only on the range sets R, S and V, and the knowledge of a Lyapunov function of the uncontrolled nominal system. This class of 'saturation' controls approximates the class of switching controls corresponding to $\varepsilon = 0$. By taking $\varepsilon > 0$, one avoids the mathematical complications associated with discontinuous differential equations; e.g., see Gutman and Leitmann (1976), Gutman (1979), and Gutman and Palmor (1982). At the same time, one models practical situations which do not allow for switching (infinite nonlinear gain); e.g., see Aizerman and Pyatnitskii (1978). By letting $\varepsilon \to 0$, one approaches guaranteed uniform asymptotic stability.

Before turning to linear systems, a few words concerning matching condition II are in order. By introducing a 'measure of

17

mismatch', one can forego the requirement for matching, albeit at the expense of being able to approach asymptotic stability arbitrarily closely; see Barmish and Leitmann (1981). It should also be noted that matching, while sufficient, is not necessary to assure practical stability; e.g., see Thorp and Barmish (1981). However, it has been shown (Petersen (to appear)) that matching is necessary if a Lyapunov function of the uncontrolled nominal system (2) is employed in feedback control (6) for the uncertain system (1).

If the nominal system is linear and time-invariant, equation (1) is replaced by

$$\dot{x}(t) = [A + \Delta A(r(t))]x(t) + [B + \Delta B(s(t))]u(t) + C v(t) , \quad (7)$$

$$x(t_0) = x_0,$$

and the matching condition II requires the existence of matrices $D(r)$, $E(s)$ and F such that for all r and s

$$\Delta A(r) = BD(r)$$

$$\Delta B(s) = BE(s)$$

$$C = BF$$

and

$$\max_{s \in S} ||E(s)|| < 1.$$

The requirement of a stable uncontrolled nominal system can be relaxed by requiring merely that the pair (A,B) be stabilizable, namely, that there exists a matrix K such that $\bar{A} = A + BK$ is a stable matrix. In that event, one employs linear feedback Kx in conjunction with nonlinear feedback of type (6). Thus, practical stability is assured by

$$u(t) = Kx(t) + p(x(t))$$

where, for instance, for given $\varepsilon > 0$

$$p(x) = \begin{cases} -\dfrac{B^T Px}{||B^T Px||} \rho(x) & \text{if } ||B^T Px|| > \varepsilon \\ -\dfrac{B^T Px}{\varepsilon} \rho(x) & \text{if } ||B^T Px|| \leq \varepsilon , \end{cases} \quad (8)$$

where P is the solution of the Lyapunov equation

$$P\bar{A} + \bar{A}^T P + Q = 0 \quad (9)$$

Feedback and Adaptive Control for Uncertain Dynamical Systems

for a positive definite (symmetric) Q, and

$$\rho(x) = [\max_{s \in S} ||E(s)|| - 1]^{-1}[\max_{r \in R}||D(r)x|| + \max_{s \in S}||E(s)Kx|| + \max_{v \in V}||Fv||].$$

For such linear systems, the treatment of guaranteed stability can be generalized by admitting uncertain output (rather than state) information. Thus, if only uncertain output

$$y(t) = Hx(t) + w(t)$$

is available, where measurement error $w(t)$ can range in a known compact set $\mathbf{W}$, then one may employ a state estimate $\hat{x}(t)$ in place of the actual state $x(t)$. This topic is explored in detail in Leitmann (1981) and Breinl and Leitmann (1983).

Thus far we have been concerned with controls which assure practical stability in the presence of uncertainty. These controls (or slightly modified ones) have the additional property of rendering a neighbourhood of the 'switching manifold'

$$\mathbf{N}_\varepsilon = \{x \in R^n \mid ||B^T Px|| \leq \varepsilon\}$$

attractive and invariant; that is, all solutions of (7) tend, at least asymptotically, towards $\mathbf{N}_\varepsilon$, and those starting in $\mathbf{N}_\varepsilon$ remain in it; see Gutman and Palmor (1982). This property can be exploited for the purpose of achieving 'robustness', namely, to reduce the sensitivity of the solutions of (7) to variations in the uncertainties. In Breinl and Leitmann (1983), this is accomplished by 'tuning' the matrices K and P.

Finally, we note that other than saturation controls can be employed to bring about practical stability of uncertain systems; e.g., see Barmish, Corless and Leitmann (1983).

Example 1:

The following example is taken from Leitmann (1980). Let us consider a linear system subject to input uncertainty, namely, the linear oscillator

$$\dot{x}_1(t) = x_2(t) \tag{10}$$

$$\dot{x}_2(t) = - ax_1(t) - bx_2(t) + u(t) + v(t)$$

where a,b = constant > 0, and the uncertain input is bounded by

$$|v(t)| \leq \rho = \text{constant} > 0.$$

For Q = I in (9), control (8) is given by

$$p(x) = -\rho \text{ sgn } (\frac{1}{a} x_1 + \frac{1+a}{ab} x_2)$$

for $|\frac{1}{a} x_1 + \frac{1+a}{ab} x_2| > \varepsilon$.

Figure 1 shows the system response
$||x(t)|| = \sqrt{x_1^2(t) + x_2^2(t)}$ for initial conditions $x_1(0)=x_2(0)=0$, and with $v(t) = \rho \sin t$. For comparison, the response of the uncontrolled system as well as of the system with linear feedback is shown also in Figure 1.

Example 2:

Here we consider a nonlinear system which is intended to model an optimally harvested population subject to uncertain disturbances. Thus we have

$$\dot{x}(t) = \frac{r}{K} x(t)(K - x(t)) - h^*x(t) + u(t) + x(t)v(t) \quad (11)$$

where r, K = constants > 0 and $h^* = r/2$. The uncertain parameter $v(t)$ is supposed to be bounded by a known constant, that is,

$|v(t)| \leq \alpha$ = constant > 0.

We desire a feedback control that assures practical stability of the positive equilibrium $x(t) = x^* = \frac{K}{2}$ of the uncontrolled nominal system $(u(t) = v(t) = 0)$. Such a control of class (6) is given by

$$p(x) = -\alpha \ x \ \text{sgn } (\frac{x}{x^*} - 1)$$

for $|\frac{x}{x^*} - 1| \alpha > \varepsilon$. This control also guarantees that $x(t) > 0$ if $x(t_0) > 0$. Figure 2.2 shows the responses of the uncontrolled nominal system for two initial conditions. Figure 2.3 illustrates the responses of the uncontrolled $(u(t) = 0)$ system subject to $v(t) = -0.1 \cos t$. Finally, the responses of the controlled system subject to this periodic disturbance are shown in Figure 2.4.

UNCERTAINTIES WITH UNCERTAIN BOUNDS

If a dynamical system contains uncertain elements which are bounded but whose bounds are unknown or not fully known, then control based on its current state (or output) does not suffice, in general, to assure stable behaviour. Various classes of such systems have been explored in the literature. Here we present results for one of the classes of systems treated in Corless and

Fig. 2.1

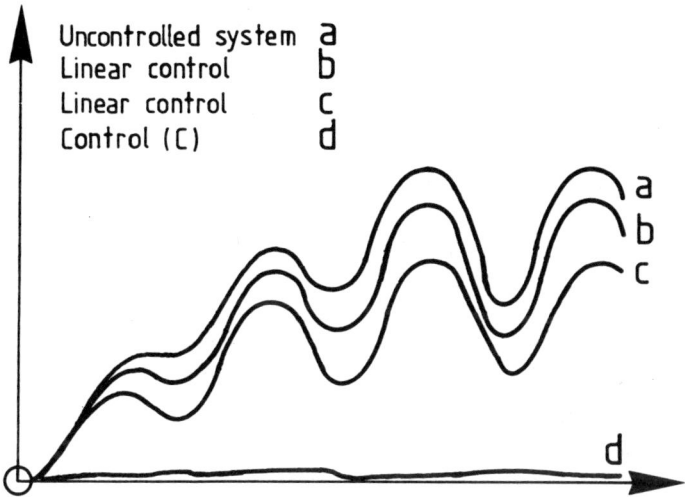

Fig. 2.2

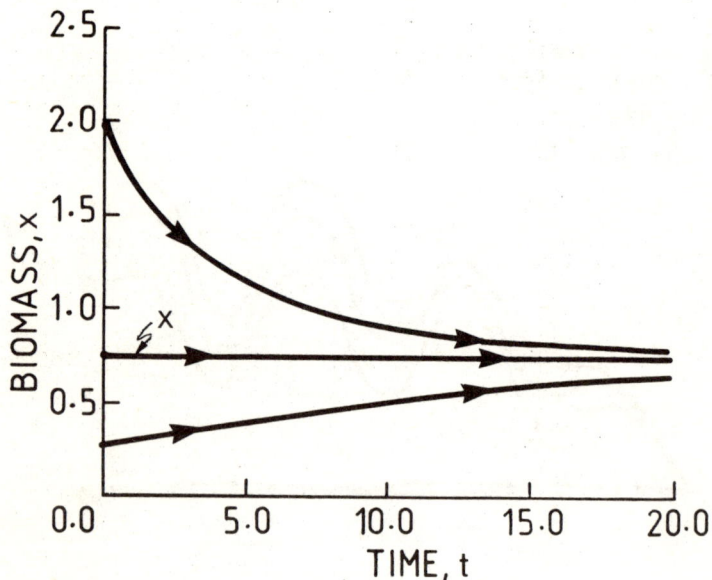

Fig. 2.3

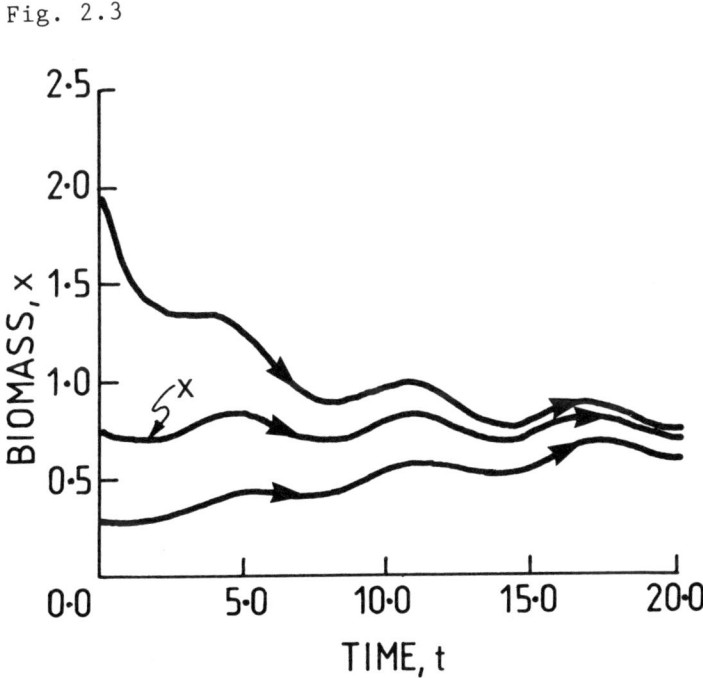

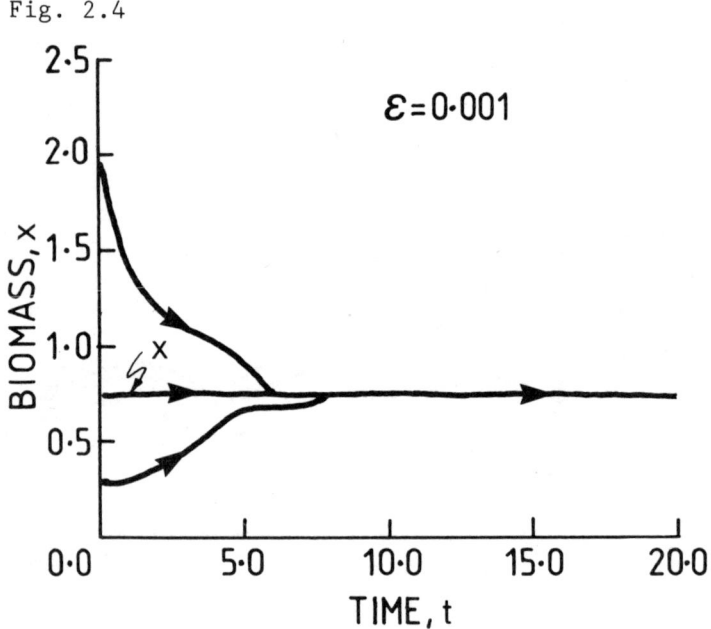

Fig. 2.4

Feedback and Adaptive Control for Uncertain Dynamical Systems

Leitmann (1984).
Consider a dynamic system modelled by

$$\dot{x}(t) = f(x(t),t) + B(x(t),t)g(x(t),t,u(t)) \quad (12)$$
$$x(t_o) = x_o$$

As before, $x(t) \in R^n$ is the state and $u(t) \in R^m$ is the control. Now, however, the functions $f(\cdot)$, $B(\cdot)$ and $g(\cdot)$ are not fully known, that is, they are uncertain. The information about these functions is embodied in the following conditions:

I. The zero solution of the system

$$\dot{x}(t) = f(x(t),t)$$

is globally uniformly and asymptotically stable. In particular, there exists a Lyapunov function, $V(x,t)$, for this system.
II. There exist a function $\rho(\cdot): R^n \times R \to R_+$ and a constant $\beta_o > 0$ such that for all t, x, u

$$u^T g(x,t,u) \geq \beta_o ||u|| [||u|| - \rho(x,t)].$$

III. There exist a constant $\beta \in R_+^s$ and a known function $P(\cdot): R \times R^n \times R_+^s \to R_+$ such that for all x and t

$$\rho(x,t) = P(t,x,\beta).$$

IV. For all x and t, the function $P(t,x,\cdot)$ is of class C^1 and nondecreasing with respect to each component of its argument, β, and $-P(t,x,\cdot)$ is convex.
V. The functions $f(\cdot)$, $B(\cdot)$, $g(\cdot)$, $P(\cdot)$ and $\nabla_\beta P(\cdot)$ are Caratheodory and, in addition, $g(\cdot)$, $P(\cdot)$ and $\nabla_\beta P(\cdot)$ are bounded on compact sets.
VI. For all $t \geq t_o$, $\alpha(x(t),t)$ is known
where $\alpha(x,t) = B^T(x,t) \nabla_x V(x,t)$.

In conditions (I)-(VI), only those quantities specifically noted as known need indeed be available for the construction of the proposed control which assures, among other properties, that every solution of (12) is uniformly bounded and approaches the zero state asymptotically ($\lim_{t \to \infty} x(t) = 0$).

The proposed control is

$$u(t) = p(t,x(t), \hat{\beta}(t), \varepsilon(t))$$

such that $p(\cdot)$ is a Caratheodory function given by

$$p(t,x,\hat{\beta},\varepsilon) = -P(t,x,\hat{\beta})s(t,x,\hat{\beta},\varepsilon) \quad (13)$$

where
$$s(t,x,\hat{\beta},\varepsilon) = \frac{\alpha(x,t)}{||\alpha(x,t)||} \text{ if } ||\mu(t,x,\hat{\beta})|| > \varepsilon$$

$$s(t,x,\hat{\beta},\varepsilon)||\alpha(x,t)|| = ||s(t,x,\hat{\beta},\varepsilon)||\,\alpha(x,t)$$

$$\mu(t,x,\hat{\beta}) = P(t,x,\hat{\beta})\alpha(x,t) ,$$

and the following adaptive rules apply:

$$\dot{\hat{\beta}}(t) = \iota_1 ||\alpha(x(t),t)|| \; \nabla_\beta P(t,x(t),\hat{\beta},(t)),$$

$$\hat{\beta}_i(t_o) > 0, \quad i = 1,2,\ldots,k, \qquad (14)$$

$$\dot{\varepsilon}(t) = -\iota_2 \varepsilon(t) , \quad \varepsilon(t_o) > 0$$

with ι_1, ι_2 = constants > 0.

Thus, in view of condition (VI) and rules (14), knowledge of the current state $x(t)$ is required to determine the proposed control for $t \geq t_o$.

EXAMPLE 3

Consider a simple pendulum of mass m and length ι, subjected to a control torque M and disturbance $|d(t)| \leq \beta\iota$ in the form of a horizontal acceleration of its support point; this disturbance is bounded, but the magnitude of the bound is <u>not known</u>. The same system with a <u>known</u> β is considered in Corless and Leitmann (1981).

Letting $\bar{u} = M/m\iota^2$ and x_1 denote the angle between the pendulum arm and a vertical line, the equations of motion are

$$\dot{x}_1(t) = x_2(t) \qquad (15)$$

$$\dot{x}_2(t) = -a \sin x_1(t) + \bar{u}(t) - \frac{d(t) \cos x_1(t)}{\iota}$$

where $a > 0$ is a known constant.

Since the uncontrolled disturbance-free system is not globally uniformly asymptotically stable, the proposed control is modified to yield a stable uncontrolled nominal system; namely,

$$\bar{u}(t) = -bx_1(t) - cx_2(t) + u(t) \qquad (16)$$

with

$$c > 0, \; b + am > 0, \; m = \min_{x_1 \in R} \frac{\sin x_1}{x_1} .$$

The control portion $u(t)$ will be specified subsequently.

With $\bar{u}(t)$ given by (16), system (15) may be stated in the form of system (12) with

Feedback and Adaptive Control for Uncertain Dynamical Systems

$$f(x,t) = \begin{bmatrix} x_2 \\ -bx_1 - cx_2 - a \sin x_1 \end{bmatrix}$$

$$B(x,t) = \begin{bmatrix} 0 \\ 1 \end{bmatrix}, \quad g(x,t,u) = u - \frac{d(t) \cos x_1}{\iota}.$$

It is readily shown that condition (I) is met with a Lyapunov function given by

$$V(x,t) = (b + \frac{c^2}{2})x_1^2 + cx_1 x_2 + x_2^2$$
$$+ 2a(1 - \cos x_1).$$

Conditions (II) and (III) are satisfied with

$$\beta_0 = 1, \quad P(t,x,\beta) = \beta |\cos x_1|.$$

Conditions (IV) - (VI) are clearly fulfilled. Thus, in accord with (13) and (14),

$$u(t) = - \hat{\beta}(t)|\cos x_1(t)|\tilde{s}(t)$$

where

$$\tilde{s}(t) = \frac{\tilde{\alpha}(t)}{|\tilde{\alpha}(t)|} \quad \text{if } \hat{\beta}(t)|\cos x_1(t)||\tilde{\alpha}(t)| > \varepsilon(t)$$

$$\tilde{s}(t)|\tilde{\alpha}(t)| = |\tilde{s}(t)|\tilde{\alpha}(t),$$
$$\tilde{\alpha}(t) = cx_1(t) + 2x_2(t),$$

and

$$\dot{\hat{\beta}}(t) = \iota_1 |\cos x_1(t)||\tilde{\alpha}(t), \quad \hat{\beta}(t_0) > 0,$$
$$\dot{\varepsilon}(t) = -\iota_2 \varepsilon(t) \quad , \quad \varepsilon(t_0) > 0.$$

Figures 2.5 through 2.7 present simulation results for $x_1(t)$ for the system under the proposed control. In all cases, $x_1(0) = x_2(0) = 3$, $\iota_1 = 1$ and $\iota_2 = 0$ (with $\varepsilon(0) = 0$)[3]. For Figure 2.5, $d(t) = $ constant = 5, while for Figure 2.6, $d(t) = $ constant = 50. Since the gain ι_1 for $\dot{\hat{\beta}}(t)$ is the same in both cases, it is not unexpected that the settling time is much longer in the case of the much larger disturbance. Finally, for Figure 2.7, $d(t) = 5 \cos t$.

Example 4:

In as much as this volume is devoted to problems of economic forecasting, we include an application of the feedback control proposed in Leitmann (1979) to a very simple uncertain

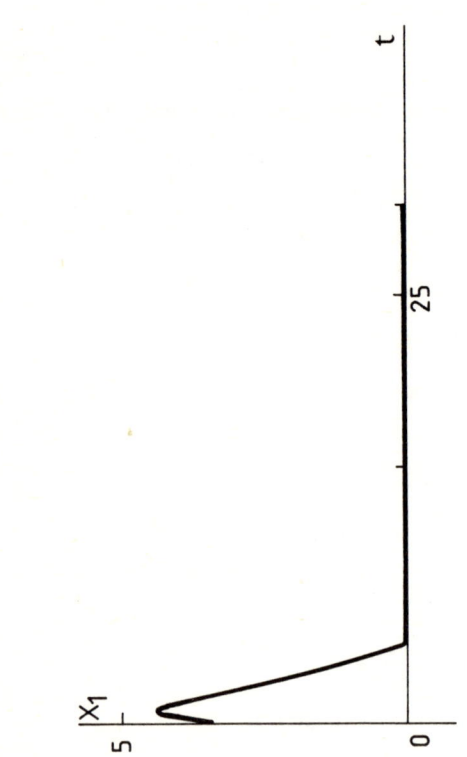

Fig. 2.5

Fig. 2.6

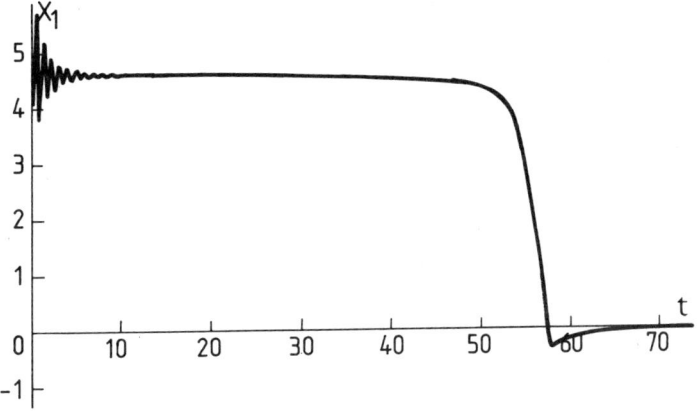

Fig. 2.7

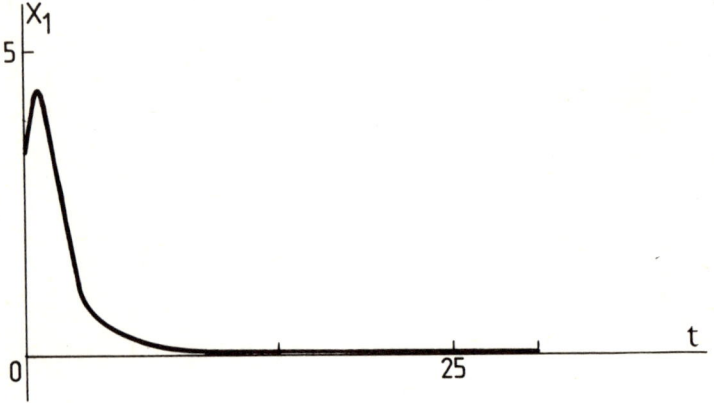

macroeconomic model. The detailed derivations may be found in Leitmann and Wan (1978; 1979).

The model specifies the time history of a 'target effective demand' y(t), that is, the optimal compromise between current unemployment and inflation. In order to allow for both expansion and a limit to growth, this target demand is taken as

$$y(t) = y^\infty(1 - e^{bt}) \qquad (17)$$

where y^∞ is the limit level and $b > 0$ is the constant (relative) rate at which the expansion potential $y^\infty e^{-bt}$ is realized.

The model for change in effective demand y(t) is taken to be

$$\dot{y}(t) = -ay(t) + k_\mu \mu(t) + r_g(t)g(t) + r_y(t) \qquad (18)$$

$$y(t_0) = y_0$$

where

$\mu(t)$ = index of 'smoothed' monetary control,
$g(t)$ = fiscal control,
a = constant > 0,
k_μ = constant 'policy multiplier' for $\mu(t)$,
$r_g(t)$ = uncertain 'policy multiplier' for $g(t)$,
$r_y(t)$ = external disturbances.

In order to reflect the fact that the effect at time t of past monetary control $m(\tau)$, $\tau \leq t$, is cumulative, we take

$$\mu(t) = \int_{-\infty}^{t} [r_\mu(\tau)\exp(-\int_\tau^t r_\mu(s)ds)m(\tau)]d\tau \qquad (19)$$

Upon combining (17)-(19), one arrives at the system equations

$$[y(t)-y(t)]^\cdot = -a[y(t) - y(t)] + k_\mu \mu(t)$$
$$+ r_g(t)g(t) + [r_y(t) - by^\infty$$
$$+ (b-a)(1-e^{-bt})y^\infty], \qquad (20)$$

$$\dot{\mu}(t) = -r_\mu(t)\mu(t) + r_\mu(t), m(t),$$

$$y(t_0) - y(t_0) = y_0 - y_0, \; \mu(t_0) = \mu_0.$$

Here, the state of the system is $(y-y, \mu)$ and the control is (g,m). There are three uncertain elements, $r_g(t)$, $r_\mu(t)$ and $r_y(t)$, subject to known (assumed) constant bounds; namely,

$$\underline{r}_g \leq r_g(t) \leq \bar{r}_g \quad , \quad 0 < \underline{r}_g < \bar{r}_g < \infty \; ,$$

$$\underline{r}_\mu \leq r_\mu(t) \leq \bar{r}_\mu \quad , \quad 0 < \underline{r}_\mu < \bar{r}_\mu < \infty \; ,$$

Fig. 2.8

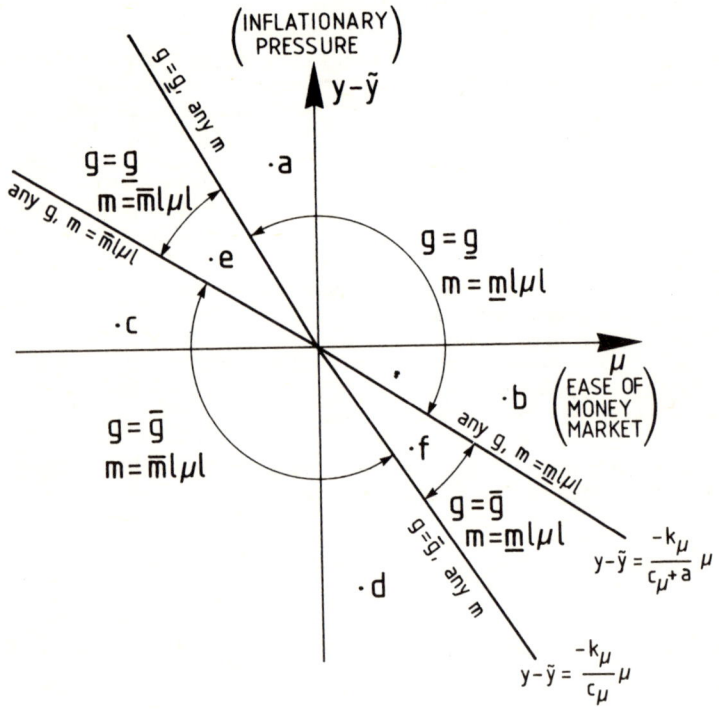

Feedback and Adaptive Control for Uncertain Dynamical Systems

$$\underline{r}_y \leq r_y(t) \leq \bar{r}_y \quad , \quad -\infty < \underline{r}_y < \bar{r}_y < \infty .$$

The proposed control, guaranteeing global uniform asymptotic stability of the zero state ($y = \tilde{y}$, $\mu = 0$) is (ideally) of the switching type and is shown on Figure 2.8, where $c_\mu = \frac{1}{2}(\underline{r}_\mu + \bar{r}_\mu)$, and $\underline{q}$, $\bar{g}$, $\underline{m}$ and $\bar{m}$ are constants satisfying

$$\underline{g} < 0 < \bar{g} , \underline{m} < 0 < \bar{m} ,$$

and 'controllability conditions'

$$\max \{|\underline{r}_y - by^\infty| + |b-ay^\infty|, |\bar{r}_y - by^\infty| + |b-ay^\infty|\}$$

$$< \underline{r}_g \min \{|\underline{g}|, \bar{g}\} ,$$

$$\frac{\underline{r}_\mu - \bar{r}_\mu}{2\underline{r}_\mu} < \min \{|\underline{m}|, \bar{m}\}.$$

It is interesting to note that the switching lines (discontinuity manifolds) of the control do not depend on the uncertainty bounds but only on the average c_μ. In regions e and f of Figure 2.8, where inflationary pressure is relatively high but money supply low, and conversely, fiscal and monetary policies act in oppostion; elsewhere they act to support each other, that is, to 'heat up' or 'cool off' the economy. Of course, in the assumed model, fiscal policy affects demand rate without delay whereas monetary control acts with an uncertain delay. Other properties assured by the employment of this control, as well as economic interpretations of the results, may be found in Leitmann and Wan (1978; 1979).

NOTES

1. This chapter is based on research supported by the National Science Foundation and carried out while the author was recipient of a US Senior Scientist award of the Alexander von Humboldt Foundation.
2. A Caratheodory function $p(\cdot): R^n \times R \to R^m$ is continuous on R^n for all $t \in R$ and Lebesgue measurable on R for all $x \in R^n$.
3. Strictly speaking one should have $\iota_2 > 0$ and $\varepsilon(0) > 0$. However, for 'large' ι_2, $\varepsilon(t)$ approaches zero 'rapidly'.

REFERENCES

Aizerman, M.A. and Pyatnitskii, E.S. (1978) Theory of Dynamic System which Incorporates Elements with Incomplete Information and its Relation to the Theory of Discontinuous Systems. Journal of the Franklin Institute, 306, 379-408
Ananev, B.I. (1977) Minimax Quadratic Problems of Motion

Correction. *Prikladnaya Matematika i Mekhanika*, 44, 436-445

Åström, K.J. (1970) Introduction to Stochastic Control Theory. Academic Press, New York

Barmish, B.R., Corless, M. and Leitmann, G. (1983) A New Class of Stabilizing Controllers for Uncertain Dynamical Systems. *Society for Industrial and Applied Mathematics Journal on Control and Optimization*, 21, 246-255

Barmish, B.R. and Leitmann, G. (1981) On Ultimate Boundedness of Uncertain Systems in the Absence of Matching Conditions. *IEEE Transactions on Automatic Control*, 27, 152-158

Breinl, W. and Leitmann, G (1983) Zustandsrückführung für Dynamische Systeme mit Parameterunsicherheiten. *Regelungstechnik*, 31, 3

Corless, M. and Leitmann, G. (1981) Continuous State Feedback Guaranteeing Uniform Ultimate Boundedness for Uncertain Dynamic Systems. *IEEE Transactions on Automatic Control*, 26, 1139-1144

Corless, M. and Leitmann, G. (1983) Adaptive Control of Systems Containing Uncertain Functions and Unknown Functions with Uncertain Bounds. *Journal of Optimization Theory and Applications*, 41, 155-168

Gutman, S. (1976) Uncertain Dynamical Systems - Lyapunov Min-Max Approach. *IEEE Transactions on Automatic Control*, 24, 437-443

Gutman, S. and Leitmann (1979) Stabilizing Feedback Control for Dynamical Systems with Bounded Uncertainty. *Proceedings of IEEE Conference on Decision and Control*, 94-99

Gutman, S. and Palmor, Z. (1982) Properties of Min-Max Controllers in Uncertain Dynamical Systems. *Society for Industrial and Applied Mathematics Journal on Control and Optimization*, 20, 850-861

Johnson, C.D. (1968) Optimal Control of the Linear Regulator with Constant Disturbances. *IEEE Trans. Autom. Control*, 13, 416-421

Kalman, R.E., and Bertram, J.E. (1960) Control System Analysis and Design via the Second Method of Lyapunov. *Journal of Basic Engineering*, 82, 371-393

Krasovskii, N.N. (1974) Game-Theoretic Control and Problems of Stability. *Problems of Control and Information Theory*, 3, 171-182

Kreisselmeier, G. and Narendra, K.S. (1982) Stable Model Reference Adaptive Control in the Presence of Bounded Disturbances. *IEEE Transactions on Automatic Control*, 27, 1169-1175

Kushner, H.J. (1966) On the Status of Optimal Control and Stability for Stochastic Systems. *IEEE International Convention Record*, 14, 143-151

Lee, C.S. and Leitmann, G. (1983). Optimal Long-Term Management of Ecological Systems Subject to Uncertain Disturbances. *International Journal of Systems Science*, 14, 979-994

Leitmann, G. (1979) Guaranteed Asymptotic Stability for Some

Linear Systems with Bounded Uncertainties. *Journal of Dynamic Systems, Measurement and Control*, 101, 212-216

Leitmann, G. (1980) Deterministic Control of Uncertain Systems. *Astronautica Acta*, 7, 1457-1461

Leitmann, G. (1981) On the Efficacy of Non-Linear Control in Uncertain Linear Systems. *Journal of Dynamic Systems, Measurement and Control*, 103, 95-102

Leitmann, G. and Wan, Jr., H.Y. (1978) A Stabilization Policy for an Economy with Some Unknown Characteristics. *Journal of the Franklin Institute*, 306, 23-33

Leitmann, G. and Wan, Jr., H.Y. (1979) Macro-Economic Stabilization Policy for an Uncertain Dynamic Economy. *New Trends in Dynamic System Theory and Economics*, Academic Press, N.Y., 105-136

Letov, A.M. (1955) *Stability of Nonlinear Regulating Systems*. GITTL, Moscow

Lindorff, D.P. and Carroll, R.L. (1973) Survey of Adaptive Control Using Liapunov Design. *International Journal of Control*, 5, 897-914

Lurie, A.I. (1951) *Some Problems in the Theory of Automatic Control*. Gostekhizdat, Moscow

Molander, P. (1979) *Stabilization of Uncertain Systems*. Lund

Monopoli, R.V. (1966) Engineering Aspects of Control System Design via the Direct Method of Lyapunov. *NASA Report CR-654*

Monopoli, R.V. (1981) Model Following Control of Gas Turbine Engines. *Journal of Dynamic Systems, Measurement and Control*, 103, 285-289

Morse, A.S. (1980) Global Stability of Parameter-Adaptive Control Systems. *IEEE Transactions on Automatic Control*, 25, 433-439

Narendra, K.S. and Valavani, L.S. (1978) Stable Adaptive Controller Design - Direct Method. *IEEE Transactions on Automatic Control*, 23, 57-583

Petersen, I.R. (to appear) Structural Stabilization of Uncertain Systems: Necessity of the Matching Conditions. *Society for Industrial and Applied Mathematics Journal on Control Optimization*

Peterson, B.B. and Narendra, K.S. (1982) Bounded Error Adaptive Control. *IEEE Transactions on Automatic Control*, 27, 11161-1168

Porter, B. and Grujic, Lj.T. (1980) Continuous Time Tracking Systems Incorporating Lwi's Plants with Multiple Nonlinearities. *International Journal of Systems Science*, 11, 837-840

Salukvadze, M.E. (1962) The Analytical Design of Optimal Controls in the Use of Constantly Acting Disturbances. *Avtomatika i Telemekhanika*, 23, 721-731

Thorp, J.S. and Barmish, B.R. (1981) On Guaranteed Stability of Uncertain Systems via Linear Control. *Journal of Optimization Theory and Applications* 35, 559-579

Chapter Three

MODELLING AND OPTIMAL CONTROL OF RANDOM WALK PROCESSES IN ECONOMICS

John M. Blatt

INTRODUCTION

In a much-quoted paper, Paul Samuelson (1965a, 1965b) suggested that an efficient speculative market behaves very much like a random walk process. Intuitively, a 'random walk' consists of steps which may be forward or backward, in random order, with no correlation between one step and the next. At the end of some given fixed time interval (during which he takes many separate steps), our random walker is as likely to find himself forward as backward compared to his initial position. Thus his average displacement from his starting position may be zero. However, the mean square (the variance) of this displacement is positive. It can be shown that at the limit of a large number of steps, N, the variance becomes proportional to N, so that the root-mean-square displacement increases as the square root of N.
    The simplest random walks have steps of the same size, but this is unrealistic in the economic context. There, some statistical distribution of step sizes (for example, a Gaussian normal distribution with zero mean) appears to be more appropriate.
    Another distinction can be made, between random walks in which the steps occur at discrete time intervals which are known in advance (for simplicity, equal time intervals between steps), and other random walks in which the time interval between one step and the next is itself a random variable obeying some distribution law (for example, a Poisson distribution of these time intervals). In the economic context, the latter assumption, often called 'modelling in continuous time', is preferable.
    However, the way random walks are usually modelled in continuous time is by means of so-called 'white noise' or Wiener processes. The technical definition of such a process is exceedingly complex, for a reason which we shall explain later. Intuitively, it is easy enough to explain what is meant. Imagine a random walk in continuous time, in which the average size of the

individual steps is very small, and so is the average time between steps. Now go to the limit of infinitesimal step size, and infinitesimal time between steps, in such a way that the variance of the displacement in some fixed time interval remains constant.

The result of this limiting procedure is called a 'Wiener process', after the pure mathematician Norbert Wiener, who succeeded (in 1923) in setting up a formal axiomatic basis for this process. Engineers call it a 'white noise' process. Much later, Ito (1951) developed a formal theory of 'stochastic differential equations'. This theory is based on exactly the same ideas, but makes the practical handling of the stochastic process somewhat easier though by no means really simple.

Random noise in engineering systems is not precisely identical to pure mathematical white noise, but it is close enough so that white noise provides an acceptable approximation. The entire engineering literature on stochastic systems and stochastic control is based on the white noise assumption for the underlying process, and quite rightly so. When economists and econometricians became concerned with modelling economic systems subject to random shocks, they naturally turned to this existing literature. As a result, the white noise assumption has been adopted in economic modelling and in pure economic theory.

It is our contention that this is entirely inappropriate. Random shocks in economic systems cannot be approximated well by white noise. White noise represents the limit of very many small shocks. Small shocks do occur in economics, of course. However, economic analysts are more often confronted with large, less frequent, shocks.

It is precisely the large shocks (for example, failure of a major bank, bankruptcy of a large corporation, onset of a war, or a revolution in a country with which we trade extensively) which have the most dramatic impacts on business confidence, and through it, on the real economy. To assume that all that needs to be taken into account is the cumulative effect of very many, extremely small shocks is unrealistic.

An illustration of the problem is the well-known option pricing model of Black and Scholes (1973), as reviewed for example by Smith (1976). This model is based upon a white noise random walk assumption for money market behaviour. Although this model is used very widely and quoted even more widely, economists are sometimes unaware that the model does not provide a good fit to the data. Merton (1976) investigated the changes in predictions which result when 'large' steps are allowed in the random walk. To quote from Merton's own introduction (page 127):

> "In essence, the validity of the Black-Scholes formula depends on whether or not stock price changes satisfy a kind of 'local' Markov property, that is, in a short interval of time, the stock price can only change by a small amount. The antithetical process to this continuous stock price motion would be a 'jump' stochastic process defined in continuous

time. ... since empirical studies of stock price series tend to show far too many outliers for a simple, constant-variance log-normal distribution, there is a 'prima facie' case for the existence of such jumps."

The stock price dynamics assumed by Merton are somewhat special and will not be reproduced here. However, the essential result of Merton is, as one would expect, that jump processes do make a significant difference to the option pricing model, and this difference is in a direction to improve the fit between theory and observation (or, conversely, the misfit between the white noise option pricing model and observation is attributable largely to the neglect, through the white noise assumption, of finite jump processes).

In the literature of theoretical physics, more specifically of non-equilibrium statistical mechanics, one can find a 'master equation' which allows for such jump processes in a rather general fashion. The next section is devoted to presenting, without proof, a similar equation for economic modelling. In a later section, we summarise (again without proof) some entirely new work; namely, an extension of these ideas which involves optimal control theory. Our exposition is, of necessity, rather condensed. Further details, as well as suitable heuristic proofs, can be found in Blatt (1981).

STOCHASTIC PROCESSES IN CONTINUOUS TIME

Although Norbert Wiener is often quoted as the founder of the theory of Brownian motion (or white noise), the subject originated in a famous paper by Einstein (1905). In that year, Einstein also published a path breaking paper on the photoelectric effect (this paper was a fundamental step towards the quantum theory of matter). Einstein was awarded the Nobel Prize for these two papers. The Nobel Prize Committee hesitated to mention a third paper, also published in the same year, since that paper was considered too controversial. This third paper announced the theory of special relativity. Einstein was 26 years old at the time!

The intuitive picture underlying Einstein's treatment of Brownian motion is as follows. Consider a 'foreign' particle inside a gas. On a gross scale, the gas exerts a pressure on the particle, but since the pressure acts from all sides, there is no tendency for the particle to move in any direction.

On a microscopic scale, however, the picture looks rather different. The gas consists of very many gas molecules in rapid and random motion, colliding with each other, with the walls of the container, and (occasionally) with the foreign particle. The macroscopic 'gas pressure' is a result of innumerable individual collisions of gas molecules with a foreign body. In what follows, we shall refer to such collisions as 'shocks', in keeping with the usual terminology of economics.

Between shocks, the foreign body moves as if the gas molecules should be entirely absent, that is, the only forces acting between shocks are such general forces as gravity. Thus, between shocks, the motion of the system is deterministic, being predictable from Newton's laws of motion. But the shocks themselves are random events. We do not know precisely when the next shock will happen, nor what will be the energy and momentum of the colliding gas molecule at that time. All such matters are defined only in terms of probability distributions.

Let the n-vector $\underline{x}$ denote the state of the system at some given time t. Consider the infinitesimal time interval between time t and t+dt. If no shock occurs during this time interval, then the state variable develops according to the purely deterministic equation of motion

$$d\underline{x}/dt = \underline{f}(\underline{x},\underline{v},t) \qquad (1)$$

In this equation, we have allowed for the possibility of a control variable (vector) $\underline{v}$ which may influence the time development of the state $\underline{x}$ of the system between shocks. This control variable may be ignored for the time being. We will return to it in the next section.

The natural way to describe the random effects of shocks is by means of a <u>transition probability per unit time</u>, defined as follows:

$$Q(\underline{x},\underline{y},\underline{v})d^n\underline{x}dt \qquad (2)$$

is the conditional probability of the system undergoing a shock during the time interval from t to t+dt, in such a way that the system is found, at time t+dt, in state $\underline{x}$ within the n-volume element $d^n\underline{x} = dx_1dx_2...dx_n$, given that the system was in state $\underline{y}$ at time t and that control $\underline{v}$ was active during the small time interval.

The basic assumption of the subsequent theory is the Markov process assumption: <u>The stochastic process is described uniquely by the transition probability (2); no further information is necessary</u>. Another way of saying the same thing is that the shocks are assumed to be independent events, statistically speaking. The system 'forgets' anything which may have happened prior to the last shock, so information going back farther than that shock is simply irrelevant.

This is the usual assumption for a Markov process. It is, in our view, the stochastic analogue of the well-known 'state space description' of a deterministic system. This description forces the system equations to be differential equations of <u>first</u> order in the time variable t. The Markov process assumption for a stochastic system forces the stochastic process to have at most first order memory. It is well-known that a system with equations of motion not already in state space form (for example, with second order differential equations) usually can be transformed into space state form by introducing additional state variables (additional components of the state vector). Stochastic systems not originally Markov can often (though not always) be transformed into Markov systems by the same method. Thus the Markov assumption is usually a constraint upon the method we use to describe the system, rather than a significant limitation on what systems are covered by the theory.

The probability of any shock at all during the time interval dt is the integral of (2) over all possible final states $\underline{x}$. We call this shock probability σ:

$$\sigma(\underline{y},\underline{v}) = \int Q(\underline{x},\underline{y},\underline{v}) d^n\underline{x} \qquad (3)$$

The reciprocal $1/\sigma$ is called the 'mean free time between shocks'. We make the explicit assumption that the integral (3) is not infinite.

In the 'white noise' limit, the integral (3) does become infinite. This is a highly counterintuitive result. The mean free time between shocks becomes strictly zero in this peculiar limit. As a result, the system suffers infinitely many shocks in any given time interval, no matter how small the interval. No wonder then that the Wiener-Ito theory is so difficult to understand! Instead of proceeding to set up the basic equations for a sensible process, and going to the limit afterwards, Wiener and Ito postulate a set of entirely abstract, pure mathematical axioms to describe this very peculiar limit.

As a result of σ being finite in the present theory, it is always possible to find a time interval dt small enough so that the probability of more than one shock in that time is infinitesimally small, compared to the probability σdt of exactly one shock. It is then possible to expand everything to order dt, ignoring terms of order $(dt)^2$ and higher. We refer to Blatt (1981) for the detailed derivation and merely quote the result, which we call the <u>equation of change</u>.

Let $W(\underline{x},t)d^n\underline{x}$ be the probability, at time t, that the system state $\underline{x}$ is found inside the n-space volume element $d^n\underline{x}=dx_1...dx_n$. Then this probability develops with time according to the equation:

$$\partial W/\partial t = -\sum_{k=1}^{n} \partial/\partial x_i [f_i(\underline{x},\underline{v},t)W(\underline{x},t)] - \sigma(\underline{x},\underline{v})W(\underline{x},t)$$

$$+ \int Q(\underline{x},\underline{y},\underline{v})W(\underline{y},t)d^n\underline{y} \qquad (4)$$

The <u>structure</u> of this equation is of interest. It is a partial differential equation as far as the deterministic part is concerned. However, it is an integro-differential equation with respect to the stochastic part. The integral in (4) represents 'scattering in' of systems in state $\underline{y}$ at time t, into state $\underline{x}$ at time t+dt. The term preceding the integral is the 'scattering out' term, representing systems in state $\underline{x}$ at time t, which have been removed from that state because of a shock during time dt.

The integral equation structure of the equation of change is in the very nature of things. Random shocks lead to sudden shifts in the state of the affected system. A mere differential equation cannot do justice to this situation. A differential equation is quite incapable of describing finite 'jump processes' in which $y-x$ is not infinitesimally small. Astrom (1970) proved that a straightforward differential equation fails to account for stochastic processes. However, he proceeded to draw an erroneous conclusion from this, namely that one is <u>forced</u> to introduce a 'stochastic differential equation'. This conclusion does not follow from the argument. Rather, the correct conclusion is that one must adopt an integro-differential equation like (4).

Under certain very special assumptions it is possible to <u>approximate</u> the integro-differential equation (4) by a partial differential equation, known as the 'Fokker-Planck' or 'Kolmogorov' equation. We refer the reader to Blatt (1981) for the precise assumptions and the derivation of the Fokker-Planck equation.

The Wiener axioms lead to the Fokker-Planck equation as an <u>exact</u> consequence of the axioms. Since one can, and in our view one should, obtain the Fokker-Planck equation only as an approximation, valid under some circumstances (all shocks are very small) and not in other cases, we consider an axiomatic basis for the Fokker-Planck equation a mistaken path. This path is neither necessary nor desirable. It does comparatively little harm in engineering, where the approximations involved are acceptable. It has, however, much less appeal in the case of economic modelling.

STOCHASTIC CONTROL THEORY

Let us proceed from mere description to control. The control variable $\underline{v}$ in equation (4) will now be chosen so as to optimise some criterion of merit. For example, we may wish to minimise total expected (discounted) disutility over a planning period starting at time t_1 and ending at some later time t_2.

In stochastic optimal control, a 'feedback control' law, also called 'closed loop' control, is usually preferred. Such a law decides on the control to be used at time t in the light of the measured state $\underline{x}$ of the system at that time. Its converse, an 'open loop' control law, sets up the entire future control path $\underline{v}(t)$ at the moment the process starts (at time $t=t_1$). With random shocks in the system, the future path of the system cannot be predicted precisely. Thus the closed loop control law makes use of informaton (the actual state of the system at time t) which is simply not available to the controller at time $t=t_1$. For this reason, a properly chosen closed loop control law is superior to any open loop control.

Note, however, that closed loop control in this sense requires that the state of the system at time t be known, i.e., that

Optimal Control of Random Walk Processes

we observe the state fully at all times. For a complicated system, this is a severe requirement. In the economic context, one may measure some of the relevant economic variables of state, but most probably not all of them. The complications introduced by incomplete measurements are well beyond the scope of this paper. Indeed, the extension of the Kalman filter theory to stochastic control of jump processes is still a subject for future research. From a practical point of view, we feel that any attempt to control an economic system when information about the state of this system is rather incomplete should not be handled via optimal control theory. Rather, more robust methods of control which may not be optimal, but are likely to be less extreme and/or hazardous, must then be preferred. Thus, the restriction to fully observable systems, though admittedly severe, is not an unreasonable requirement for optimal control calculations.

We are interested, therefore, in developing an equation which yields an optimal closed loop control law for a stochastic process obeying the equation of change (4). We assume that our purpose is to minimise the integral of some function $f_0(\underline{x},\underline{v},t)$ over the 'planning time' interval from $t=t_1$ to $t=t_2$. Since the future path cannot be predicted precisely, we minimise the mathematical expectation of this integral. Usually, the function f_0 is thought of as a disutility per unit elapsed time.

The procedure underlying the derivation (given in Blatt, 1981) is called 'dynamic programming'. Let us denote the interval between some arbitrary time t and the end t_2 of the planning period by the symbol T; that is, $T=t_2-t$ is the unelapsed time. This time interval is divided into two separate time intervals: an initial, very short time interval of length ε, followed by the remainder of the time, $t_2-t-\varepsilon=T-\varepsilon$. The time interval ε is chosen to be small enough so that the probability of more than one shock within that time can be ignored. Thus terms of higher order in ε may be omitted systematically. (None of this is possible in the Wiener-Ito theory, for the reasons given earlier).

Let us state the final equation which is reached by this procedure. The 'optimum value function' $F(\underline{x},t,t_2)$ is defined as the best (minimal) achievable value of the criterion, if the state of the system at time t is known to be $\underline{x}$ and the planning period ends at time t_2. This function satisfies the following equation:

$$- \partial F/\partial t = \min_{(\underline{v})} [f_0(\underline{x},\underline{v}) + \underline{f}(\underline{x},\underline{v}) \cdot \nabla_{\underline{x}} F - \sigma(\underline{x},\underline{v})F(\underline{x},t,t_2) + \int Q(\underline{y},\underline{x},\underline{v})F(\underline{y},t,t_2)d^n\underline{y}] \quad (5)$$

The control $\underline{v}$ which leads to the minimum value in this equation is the optimal closed loop control:

$$\underline{v}^* = \underline{v}(\underline{x},t,t_2) \quad (6)$$

It depends on the (measured) current state $\underline{x}$ of the system, on the present time t, and on the final time t_2 of the planning period.

Although equation (5) has been derived without the white noise assumption, and indeed with assumptions which are not valid in the limit of white noise, it is still possible to recover the standard white noise results by going to the appropriate limit. All that is necessary is to assume that $Q(\underline{y},\underline{x},\underline{v})$ is zero unless $\underline{y}-\underline{x}$ is very small, and that $F(\underline{y},t,t_2)$ within the integral in (5) can be expanded in a power series around $F(\underline{x},t,t_2)$, in which series we retain only the lowest few powers of $\underline{y}-\underline{x}$. It follows that <u>the Wiener-Ito theory can be bypassed altogether</u>. It is not required to obtain the essential results, at least not as long as there is complete observability of the system being controlled.

It is apparent that (5) is a rather complicated equation, which is likely to be hard to solve in a general case. It turns out, however, that the situation is not nearly as bad as it appears at first sight. The main, indeed almost the only, example of a stochastic control solution in the standard Wiener-Ito theory is the 'LQP' problem, where 'L' stands for 'linear equations of motion' and 'Q' for 'quadratic criterion'. For this same problem, equation (5) allows an explicit solution under quite mild assumptions about the transition probability function $Q(\underline{x},\underline{y},\underline{v})$. This solution leads to exactly the <u>same</u> feedback control law as one obtains in the Wiener-Ito theory, thereby showing that the Wiener-Ito solution of the LQP problem cannot be used as a test of the underlying statistical hypothesis of white noise for the shocks. On the contrary, for the LQP problem the optimal control is of the same (certainty-equivalent) form no matter what assumptions are made about the shocks, within very wide limits. Indeed, the optimal control is exactly the same as if there were no shocks whatever. The presence of shocks affects the final expected value of the criterion, but does <u>not</u> affect what one must do to control the system optimally.

This somewhat surprising, and perhaps even disconcerting, result arises because of the particular problem formulation (LQP). It is <u>not</u> an inherent or universal feature of stochastic optimal control laws. The LQP formulation is used very widely both in engineering and in economics. It is of doubtful value in engineering, and is clearly of no value whatsoever in economics.

The various limitations under which economic policy must labour are highly inconsistent with the LQP formulation. For example, we may wish to minimise the unemployment rate, or some function of several state variables, one of which is the unemployment rate. Now, unemployment is an intrinsically positive variable. With the exception of unusual circumstances (e.g. restricted to war times), unemployment does not go negative. Yet there is no way in which the LQP formulation of economic optimization can handle variables which must stay positive. The essence of that formulation is that all quantities are allowed to vary freely over the full range of values from minus infinity to plus infinity.

The reason that engineers and economists use the LQP formulation so frequently is nothing but mathematical convenience. In our view, the chase after mathematical convenience is particularly dangerous in the optimal control area. What is 'optimal' depends very much on just what criterion we are optimising, and on just what are the equations of motion of the system. Using the LQP formulation means, almost invariably, that we violate both the criterion and the equations of motion. We replace some sensible criterion by a very doubtful one whose only merit is that it is quadratic; and we replace economically meaningful system equations of motion by artificial linearised equations whose only merit, if one can call it merit, is that they are linear. The optimal control calculation then leads to an 'optimal' policy for a rather mutilated and senseless problem. There is no reason to believe that the resulting policy prescription is optimal (in any sense) for the actual economic system.

If we want to obtain a minimal degree of realism from our optimal control calculations, it is necessary to depart from the LQP formulation of the problem. When we do that, it is likely that the nature of the shocks (white noise or finite jumps, for example) becomes important for optimal control. At that point, the theory presented in this paper may be of some assistance.

REFERENCES

Astrom, K.J. (1970) Introduction to Stochastic Control Theory, Academic Press, New York

Black, F. and Scholes, M. (1973) 'The pricing of options and corporate liabilities', Journal of Political Economy, 81, 637-659

Blatt, J.M. (1981) An Elementary Introduction to Optimal Control, Computer Systems P/L, Sydney

Einstein, A. (1905) Investigations on the Theory of Brownian Motion, Reprinted: Dover Publications, New York

Ito, K. (1951) 'On Stochastic Differential Equations', Memorandum of the American Mathematical Society., no.4

Merton, R.C. (1976) 'Option pricing when underlying stock returns are discontinuous', Journal of Financial Economics, 3, 125-144

Samuelson, P.A. (1965a) 'Rational theory of warrant pricing', Industrial Management Review, 6, 13-31

Samuelson, P.A. (1965b) 'Proof that properly anticipated prices fluctuate randomly', Industrial Management Review, 6, pp.41-49

Smith, C.W. Jnr. (1976) 'Option pricing: A review', Journal of Financial Economics, 3, 3-51

Wiener, N. (1923) 'Differential space', Journal of Mathematical Physics (Massachusetts Institute of Technology), 2, 131-174

Chapter Four

STABILISATION AND OPTIMAL MANAGEMENT IN THE HOUSING INDUSTRY

Paul F. Lesse and Janislaw M. Skowronski

INTRODUCTION

Understanding the dynamic changes in the housing market and its stabilisation is becoming increasingly important to the building industry; to planning and municipal authorities and to the public in general. The fluctuations affecting the rate of population growth, inflation, interest rates, prices, and migration rates tend to confuse both consumers and producers. Existing planning techniques usually concentrate on forecasting the demand for housing while treating the fluctuating factors as exogenous variables. Some studies focus on the financial aspects (Lujanen, 1979; Tucker, 1980, 1981) or on the accessibility and affordability of housing (Bromilow 1979). A wide spectrum of techniques can be found in the forecasting studies commissioned by industry (e.g. AIRG-CSIRO, 1980) endeavouring to provide estimates of future demand based on various scenarios. The economics of these problems was covered by Needleman (1965), and an extensive simulation study was carried out by Botman (1981).
 In this paper, we construct a theoretical model of housing dynamics which includes the basic aspects of supply, demand, demography and finance. The model is used as a tool for analysing the notion of industrial instability, and for designing means to prevent it.
 The paper is organized as follows: in the next Section, we introduce a model of housing dynamics in its standardised (nondimensional) form. Thereafter, we define the "instability of building industry" and "construction strategy" in terms of the model, and we design construction strategies which guarantee the economic feasibility of housing construction provided that the fluctuations of demand, and the disturbances due to industrial unrest, are kept within certain limits. The last part of this section is devoted to the design of strategies, which are both safe and profit maximizing.
 From the mathematical point of view this paper deals with a differential game against nature, where the active player

(builder) steers the system towards a target against the opposition of a bounded noise (demand). The target is defined as a set of economically feasible states in the neighbourhood of a moving equilibrium.

THE MODEL

The model consists of four parts:
1. dynamics of supply
2. dynamics of demand
3. dynamics of valuation (price adjustment)
4. objectives and constraints

Our first aim is to gain insight into the nature and causes of instabilities affecting the housing market. To do so, we keep the model simple: We avoid complications caused by heterogeneity of the market by dealing with an average house belonging to a given class. The class is left arbitrary, however, it may be defined in any convenient way (e.g. as a set of houses of a given type of construction limited by size and price constraints). Similarly, the demand is due to a class of buyers suitably defined, so that the buyers form a group homogenous as to their wealth, taste, etc. Locational aspects and influence of competition are ignored.

Dynamics of supply

The number of houses belonging to a given class in a region under consideration being $h = h(t)$, we postulate the dynamics of supply in a simple form

$$\frac{dh}{dt} = -\kappa h + r, \qquad (1)$$

where $\kappa > 0$ is the rate of depreciation, and r is the construction rate, which will be our control parameter.

Dynamics of demand

The demand for housing in a given class can be treated as given by the number of households from a corresponding class y, which in turn is related to the number of people x by

$$y = \frac{1}{\psi} x,$$

where $\psi > 0$ is household size, which may depend on price of housing and on other factors.

For a given population dynamics

$$\frac{dx}{dt} = F(x,t),$$

it is possible to construct the corresponding demand dynamics

Stabilisation and Optimal Management in the Housing Industry

$$\frac{dy}{dt} = \frac{1}{\psi} F(\psi\, y) - \left[\frac{d}{dt}(\ln \psi)\right] \cdot y \,. \qquad (2)$$

The solutions of (2) are dependent on the form of the function $\psi(t)$. The dynamics of household size appears to be very complicated and therefore, to keep the model as general as possible, we shall merely assume that (2) has a solution, which is continuous and bounded.

Dynamics of valuation

We assume that the average price of housing p ([p]=\$/house) is given by

$$\frac{dp}{dt} = k\,(y-h) \qquad (3)$$

with constant k>0.

Objectives and constraints

Objectives:
We introduce economic revenue I_R=pr and cost C, which in general depends on the construction rate, thus C=C(r). Economic rent or net-revenue I_E is given by

$$I_E = I_R - C \,.$$

The objective of the builder is to maximize the discounted economic rent over a period of time, i.e.

$$\max \int_0^T I_E\, e^{-\delta t}\, dt$$

(δ = discounting rate).

Constraints:
(i) The buyers are limited by their budget limitations, i.e. price must not exceed a certain value P:

$$p \leq P$$

(ii) The cost function C(r) is nonnegative for all $r \geq 0$.

(iii) The feasibility of construction is determined by economic rentability, i.e. $r: I_E \geq 0$.

This condition imposes a constraint on the relationship between price and the rate of construction, which depends on the character of C(r).
    We shall distinguish two cases
a)   C(r) is linear $C(r) = c_0 + c_1 r$
b)   C(r) is quadratic in the rate of construction $C(r) = c_0 + c_1 r + c_2 r^2$

Economic rentability demands that $p \geq \frac{c_0}{r} + c_1 + c_2 r$, where the constants c_0, c_1, c_2 are interpreted as overhead cost per unit time, cost of materials, labour, and energy per house constructed, and extra costs associated with fast work (i.e. the cost of materials, labour and energy per house per unit construction rate). All costs, in particular c_1 and c_2, are understood as real costs to the builder, less any payments received from the customer during construction.

The constraint (ii) prescribes $C(r) \geq 0$, for $\forall\, r \geq 0$ and hence the constants c_0, c_1, c_2 must satisfy

$$c_1 < 2\,(c_0\, c_2)^{\frac{1}{2}}.$$

Non-dimensional form of the model
It is convenient to introduce the following nondimensional (normalized) variables:

nondimensional time $\quad\hat{t} = t\,\frac{(Kc_0)^{1/2}}{c_1}$

nondimensional demand $\quad\hat{y} = y\left[\frac{k}{c_0}\right]^{\frac{1}{2}}$

nondimensional supply $\quad\hat{h} = h\left[\frac{k}{c_0}\right]^{\frac{1}{2}}$

nondimensional price $\quad\hat{p} = \frac{p}{c_1}$

cost parameter $\quad\beta = \frac{c_0 c_2}{c_1^2}$

nondimensional rate of depreciation $\hat{\kappa} = \kappa \cdot \frac{c_1}{(kc_0)^{1/2}}$

nondimensional rate of construction $\hat{r} = r\,\frac{c_1}{c_0}$.

The equations (1) and (3) now take the form

$$\frac{d\hat{h}}{d\hat{t}} = -\kappa\,\hat{h} + \hat{r} \tag{4}$$

$$\frac{d\hat{p}}{d\hat{t}} = \hat{y} - \hat{h}\,. \tag{5}$$

The nondimensional economic rent is now

$$\frac{I_E}{c_0} = \hat{p}\,\hat{r} - (1 + \hat{r} + \beta\,\hat{r}^2)\,. \tag{6}$$

Stabilisation and Optimal Management in the Housing Industry

and the constraints :
$$P \geq \hat{p} \geq \beta \hat{r} + \frac{1}{\hat{r}} + 1 \quad . \tag{7}$$

where $\beta=0$, if $C(r)$ is linear, otherwise $\beta > \frac{1}{4}$ due to the constraint (ii).

The magnitudes of the nondimensional parameters are important for evaluation of the relative size of various effects predicted by the model. We have endeavoured to estimate these values on the basis of data published by the Australian Bureau of Statistics (1980). Using the data for Victoria we have arrived at the following rough (order of magnitude) estimates: $\beta \cong 10^{-1} - 10^{-2}$; $\hat{\kappa} \cong 10^{-1}$. The rate of construction is of the order 10^1, the nondimensional price, demand and supply (number of houses) are measured in units. The model equations (4), (5) thus appear to be sensible with all terms of approximately the same size. The relatively high values of the rate of construction indicate that in the range of rates of construction encountered, the linear cost function is an inadequate approximation, and the quadratic function appears to be barely tolerable. This points to a need for more research into cost acceleration in the building industry. Until now, to our knowledge, there has been no interest in gathering data for the more complicated cost functions describing the behaviour of the industry at the higher rates of construction.

STABILITY ANALYSIS

The words "instability of building industry" usually refer to the fluctuating rate of construction, which may be attributed to several factors such as:
a) rapid changes of demand
b) industrial unrest and shortages
c) changing numbers of builders in business due to factors determining the economic feasibility.

It is useful to distinguish two extreme cases
a) Building industry with an open access
b) Building industry operated by sole owner.

In the former case the industry attracts new firms so long as the economic rent remains positive. The firms leave the market as soon as the rent becomes negative. In the latter case the building industry is operated as a single entity with the aim to maximize profit.

We shall treat the two cases separately.

Building industry with open access
Building industry with open access is an idealized model of reality characterized by the condition

$$p = \frac{C(r)}{r},$$

Stabilisation and Optimal Management in the Housing Industry

where the cost function C(r) is to be interpreted as an opportunity cost.

Convex cost functions with non zero overhead cost satisfy
$$\frac{dC(r)}{dr} > 0, \quad \frac{d^2C(r)}{dr^2} \geq 0, \quad \lim_{r \to 0} C(r) = c_0 > 0,$$
and hence there is always a minimum price p_m, and a corresponding rate of construction $r_m > 0$, which satisfies $C(r) = r\frac{dC(r)}{dr}$.

A typical relationship between price and rate of construction in an industry with open access is shown on Figure 4.1. It can be seen that a building industry with an (average) rate of construction $r > r_*$ reacts to a decrease in price (perhaps due to smaller demand y) by slowing down. This is interpreted as a result of some firms leaving the market or limiting their operations. Further decrease in price leads to gradual reduction in r until the level p_* is reached, after which the industry suddenly ceases to operate. The reverse process is more complicated, however. Let us assume that an increase in demand brings the price back above the level p_*. The industry starting anew can employ one of two different rates of construction (r_1, r_2 on Figure 4.1) which are consistent with the price level. The larger rate of construction (r_2) leads to a reversal of the contraction described previously. The smaller rate of construction corresponds to an unstable situation: an unsatisfied demand leading to an increase in price is answered by a reduction in the rate of construction. According to our model, a building industry, once destroyed by falling demand, refuses to start operating again in response to increasing price, unless the initial rate of construction exceeds the critical value r_*. The values r_*, p_* are thus of considerable interest. The magnitude of the critical values depends on the form of the cost function, however, for small values of the (nondimensional) rate of construction the quadratic cost function could be accepted as a tolerable approximation.

A building industry with open access and with quadratic cost function is characterized by the function $\hat{p} = 1 + \beta\hat{r} + \frac{1}{\hat{r}}$ (see Figure 4.2). The critical values in this case are $\hat{r}_* = \beta^{-\frac{1}{2}}$; $\hat{p}_* = 1 + 2\sqrt{\beta}$. Taking into account the inequality $\beta > 0.25$ we obtain $\hat{r}_* < 2$, $\hat{p}_* > 2$.

These inequalities divide the positive quadrant into four regions: A : $\hat{r} < 2$; $\hat{p} > 2$

B : $\hat{r} > 2$; $\hat{p} < 2$

C : $\hat{r} > 2$; $\hat{p} > 2$

D : $\hat{r} < 2$; $\hat{p} < 2$.

Fig. 4.1

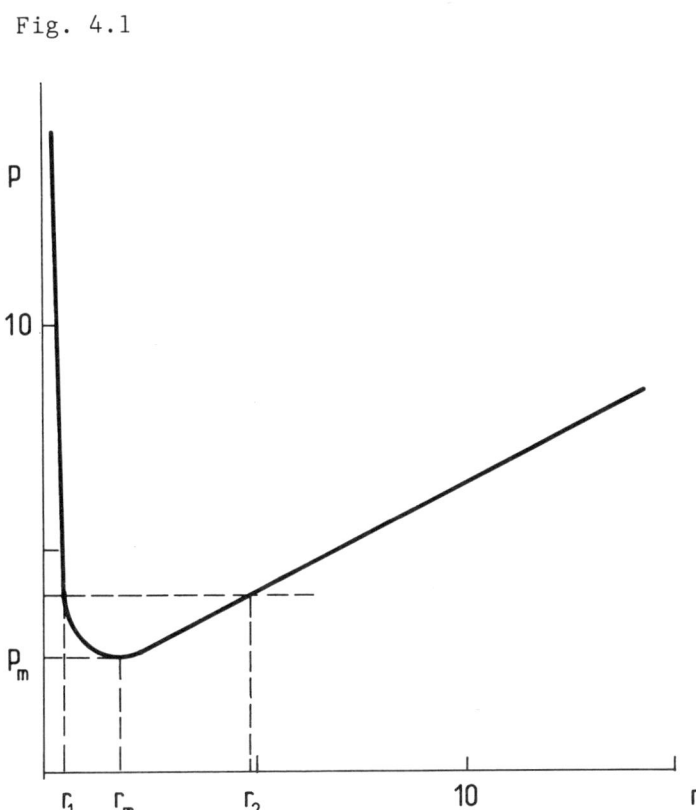

Fig. 4.2

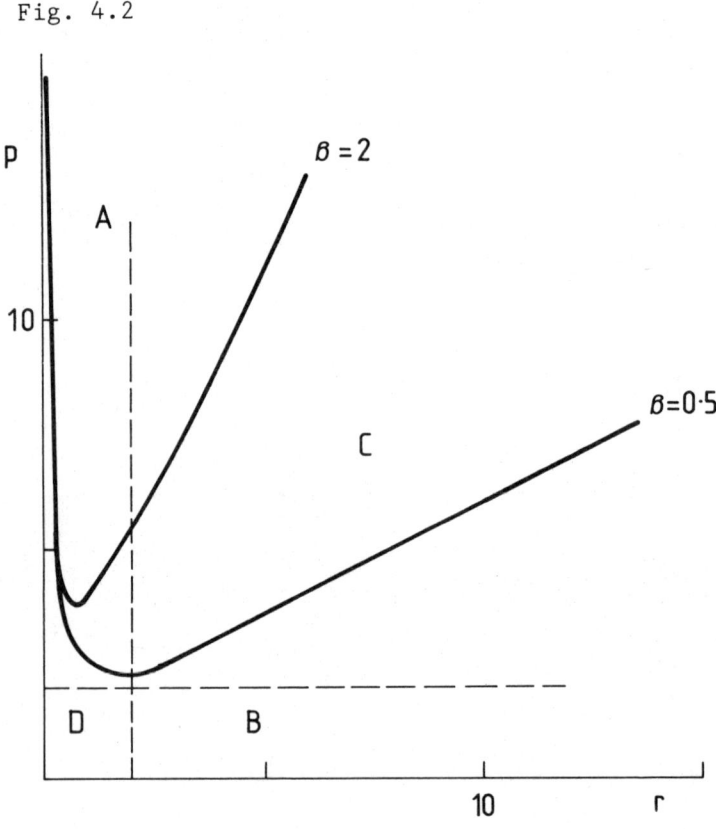

The region A contains the minima of the one parametric family of curves $\hat{p}(\beta, \hat{r})$, and region C contains the stable parts. The definition of region C thus provides a rough estimate of the safe domain in which a building industry with open access will be free from the instabilities described above. We note that this estimate is valid for any industry with a quadratic cost function, no matter what are the values of constants c_0, c_1, c_2. However, the actual (as distinct from nondimensional) values of the critical parameters could be useful for suggesting measures needed to prevent a collapse of the building industry.

As $r_* = (c_0/c_2)^{\frac{1}{2}}$, and $p_* = c_1 + 2(c_0 c_2)^{\frac{1}{2}}$ it can be seen that the industry could be saved from extinction if the actual safe domain could be increased (at least temporarily) by reducing fixed cost c_0 and the operation cost c_1 whenever (r, p) approaches (r_*, p_*). This would be achieved, e.g. by providing suitable taxation relief.

The building industry with open access tends to an equilibrium determined by the r.h.s. of the equations (4), (5): $\hat{y} = \hat{h}$, $\hat{h} = \hat{r}/\kappa$, where $\hat{r}$ is obtained from (7):

$$\hat{r} = (\tfrac{1}{2}\beta)\,[\hat{p} - 1 + ((\hat{p} - 1)^2 - 4\beta)^{\frac{1}{2}}].$$

The last equation determines a construction strategy characteristic for the industry with open access. This construction strategy can be approximated in the vicinity of an arbitrary point $\hat{r}_0, \hat{p}_0$ in the safe domain by

$$\hat{r} = \hat{r}_0 + \frac{d\hat{r}}{d\hat{p}}(\hat{p} - \hat{p}_0),$$

where $\dfrac{d\hat{r}}{d\hat{p}} = \tfrac{1}{2}\beta\,[1 + ((\hat{p} - 1)^2 - 4\beta)^{-\frac{1}{2}} \cdot (\hat{p} - 1)].$ \qquad (8)

We observe that $\dfrac{d\hat{r}}{d\hat{p}} = \infty$ if $\hat{p} = \hat{p}_m$, and

$\dfrac{d\hat{r}}{d\hat{p}} \to \dfrac{1}{\beta}$ if the industry is in a 'healthy' state far from the critical point.

To obtain a qualitative picture of the dynamics, it is possible to linearize the construction strategy, and obtain $\hat{r} = a + b\hat{p}$, where the slope varies from infinity at the critical point to $\tfrac{1}{\beta}$ as $\hat{p}$ increases. The constant a changes from $-\infty$ to $-\tfrac{1}{\beta}$. Below the critical point, i.e. on the part of the $\hat{r}, \hat{p}$ curve we called unstable, $a \geq 0$, $b \leq 0$.

We are interested in the dynamic behaviour of the system in the vicinity of the moving equilibrium point $(\hat{h}_{eq} ; \hat{p}_{eq}) = (\hat{y} ; (\hat{\kappa} \hat{y} - a)/b)$. It is useful to introduce new variables $\eta = \hat{h} - \hat{h}_{eq}$, $\Pi = \hat{p} - \hat{p}_{eq}$. The equations (4), (5) now become:

$$\frac{d\eta}{dt} = -\kappa \eta + b \Pi \tag{9}$$

$$\frac{d\Pi}{dt} = -\eta , \tag{10}$$

where we have dropped the hats above κ and t. The constant b acquires values from the intervals $(\frac{1}{\beta} ; \infty)$ and $(-\infty ; 0)$.

In the former case, corresponding to the behaviour of the system above the critical point, the equilibrium is asymptotically stable. Using elementary arguments, it is possible to deduce that the equilibrium is a node if $\kappa \neq 0$, $\kappa^2 > 4b$, and it is a focus if $\kappa^2 < 4b$. If $\kappa = 0$, the equilibrium is a centre. For b < 0, the equilibrium is unstable. The dynamic analysis thus confirms the earlier introduced qualitative arguments concerning the behaviour of building industry above and below the critical point. It is worth noting that a slope b, which locally satisfied $b < \frac{1}{4} \kappa^2$, can grow if demand decreases, and hence a node can become a focus. This is to be contrasted with the situation, when $b > \frac{1}{\beta} \geq \frac{1}{4} \kappa^2$.
In this case the inequality cannot be reversed, and, therefore, a focus maintains its character irrespective of changes in demand.

Summing up:
1. When analysing the behaviour of building industry with open access we have to distinguish between the stable region with the rate of construction above the critical value, and the unstable region. The critical value separating the two regions is determined by the cost function. In the stable region supply responds positively to changing demand. In the unstable region supply and demand diverges, and the industry faces extinction.

2. In the stable region we can distinguish two types of behaviour according to the relative magnitude of the nondimensional rate of depreciation, and the local slope of the rate of construction b.
   (i) if the rate of depreciation is large, and the slope small, the supply follows demand monotonically (the equilibrium is a node). The situation is more likely to be encountered when demand is high, i.e. when both prices and rates of construction are high (small b), when the price adjustment is slow (small k), and when the fixed overhead cost is relatively

large, and the operation cost is low.
(ii) When the converse conditions apply, the supply periodically exceeds demand, and the industry undergoes cyclical behaviour (the equilibrium is a focus). The cyclical behaviour should occur more frequently in the vicinity of the critical point (large b), and hence when the demand is falling.

3. The rate of depreciation plays the role of damping: should it be zero, the supply would oscillate around demand with constant amplitude. The nondimensional rate of depreciation is large in an industry with low overhead cost, high cost of labour and materials, and with a slow price adjustment.

4. 'Stabilization' of building industry with open access is to be interpreted primarily as reducing the chance of extinction due to a fluctuating demand. This can be achieved by increasing the size of the safe domain, in which both rate of construction and price exceed the critical value. The corresponding measures aim at changing the form of the cost function in an appropriate manner. When the cost function is quadratic, the industry is made more stable by reducing the fixed and operation cost, e.g. by temporary tax relief or subsidy. A 'stabilisation' may have a secondary objective, to avoid an oversupply, and the associated fluctuation of prices and rates of construction. This can be formulated as a preference for a monotonic convergence between supply and demand which is characteristic for a nodal equilibrium. The fluctuations thus could be reduced by suitable changes (listed above), which assist the occurence of a node. 'Stabilisation' of building industry with open access thus can be viewed as a task to be performed by an authority, external to the industry which has an access to the requisite fiscal instruments.

Building industry operated by a sole owner
Building industry operated by a sole owner is an idealised model corresponding to a coordinated, monopolistic or centrally planned industry, which can vary the rate of construction to maximise profits. In the context of industry operated by a sole owner, 'stabilisation' means design of construction strategies which produce construction rates enabling the builders to stay in business, and to make profits despite the disturbances caused by external factors. For practical reasons, these strategies must be simple, and rely only on information readily available. We shall concentrate on strategies linearly dependent on prices.

The problem we address is broadly a design of linear feedback strategy, which would keep the builders in business no matter what bounded fluctuations of demand they encounter. 'Stabilisation' is thus treated as an exercise in finding linear feedback strategies solving certain games against bounded uncertainty, whose dynamics is determined by the model just described. To avoid confusion with the well defined mathematical concepts, we

Stabilisation and Optimal Management in the Housing Industry

shall use the terms I-stability (or economic feasilibity), I-stabilisation, etc. whenever referring to the industrial stability in the sense just described.

Economic Feasibility
From a builder's point of view, the building activity in a region can be viewed as a relation connecting r and p. All pairs r≥0, p≥1 can be labelled as profitable if $I_\varepsilon \geq 0$, or unprofitable if $I_\varepsilon < 0$. The states r,p: $I_\varepsilon = 0$ determine the zero rent supply curve (see Figure 4.1). A construction strategy is a continuous mapping f: p→r, pε(1,P), rε(0,∞). A construction strategy and a corresponding solution of (4), (5) emanating from a point $h(0)=h_o$, $p(0)=p_o$ is said to be I-stable (or economically feasible) in a time interval [0,T] iff $I_\varepsilon \geq 0$ for tε[0,T].

Some construction strategies are always I-stable (economically feasible), e.g. if C(r) = 1 + r, an ε-family of strategies: $\frac{1+\varepsilon^2}{p-1}$ is always I-stable.

It is considered normal for a builder not to reduce the construction activity if prices rise. Consequently, the construction strategies with the property $\frac{dr}{dp} \geq 0$ will be called normal.

Normal construction strategies are in general not always economically feasible. The determination of the conditions, which guarantee the economic feasibility of normal construction strategies, is thus of considerable practical interest.

Linear feedback construction strategies
The construction firms may attempt to avoid unprofitable operation by using a simple (linear) feedback strategy based on prices. Prices are relatively easy to monitor, and, therefore, the linear strategy is certainly practicable. The question is how efficient such a strategy can be made, when facing an unpredictably fluctuating demand function.

Define the set Ω of economically feasible rates of construction for which $I_\varepsilon > 0$. In the case of quadratic cost function

$$\Omega = \{r: \frac{1}{2\beta} [p-1-((p-1)^2-4\beta)^{\frac{1}{2}}] < r < \frac{1}{2\beta} [p-1+((p-1)^2-4\beta)^{\frac{1}{2}}]\}, \quad (11)$$

where $\beta > 1/4$.

Consider the equations (4) and (5) with the rate of construction r being a function of price

$$r = r(p) . \qquad (12)$$

Provided r(p) is sufficiently smooth, it can be expressed as a power series around an arbitrary price pε(0,P).

Stabilisation and Optimal Management in the Housing Industry

Ignoring the nonlinear terms, we have $r = a+bp$, whence the construction strategy is determined by the two constants (a,b).

The equations (4), (5) become

$$\frac{dh}{dt} = -\kappa h + a + bp \qquad (13)$$

$$\frac{dp}{dt} = y - h, \qquad (14)$$

with an equilibrium point $h_{eq} = y$, $p_{eq} = \frac{\kappa y - a}{b}$. We consider now the system (13), (14), with the state vector $(h,p) \in \Delta \subset \mathbb{R}^2$, Δ defined by $h \geq 0$, $p \geq 0$. The demand y plays the role of the uncertainty parameter. The demand is said to be admissible if it generates solutions of (13), (14), $S_{ab}(h_o, p_o, y, t) : \mathbb{R} \to \Delta$ for given $(h_o, p_o) \in \Delta$, $h_o = h(t_o)$, $p_o = p(t_o)$, and strategy (a,b).

Let $S_{ab}(h_o, p_o)$ be the y-family of such solutions over all admissible functions $y(t)$ and denote $S_{ab}(\Delta) = \{S_{ab}(h_o, p_o)/(h_o, p_o) \in \Delta\}$.

A solution $S_{ab}(h_o, p_o, y, t)$ is said to be economically feasible with respect to a given cost function during a time interval $[t_1, t_2]$, $0 \leq t_1 \leq t_2$ if $r \in \Omega$ for $p(t) \in S_{ab}(h_o, p_o, y, t)$, $t \in [t_1, t_2]$.

Denote $\Phi(t_1, t_2)$ the set of economically feasible solutions in $S_{ab}(h_o, p_o)$ on $[t_1, t_2]$.

Given a quadratic cost function $C(r) = 1 + r + \beta r^2$, the set of economically feasible rates of construction generating the economically feasible solutions in $S_{ab}(\Delta)$ satisfies

$\beta r^2 - r(p+1) - 1 \geq 0$
$r = a + bp$, $b \geq 0$
for some $p \geq p_*$.

Eliminating p we obtain

$$r^2 (1/b - \beta) - r(a/b + 1) - 1 \geq 0. \qquad (15)$$

Thus the economically feasible rates of construction must satisfy

$$r_1 \leq r \leq r_2 \quad \text{if } 1/b - \beta < 0 \qquad (16)$$

and $r_1 \leq r \quad \text{if } 1/b - \beta > 0. \qquad (17)$

Here r_1, r_2 are the roots of quadratic equation obtained from (15).

The roots r_1, r_2 represent sensible restrictions on r if they are real and nonnegative. These requirements are translated into

$$D = (\frac{a}{b} + 1)^2 + 4(\frac{1}{b} - \beta) \geq 0 \qquad (18)$$

and either

$$(\frac{a}{b} + 1 + \sqrt{D})(\frac{1}{b} - \beta) \geq 0, \qquad (19)$$

Stabilisation and Optimal Management in the Housing Industry

or $(\frac{a}{b} + 1 - \sqrt{D})(\frac{1}{b} - \beta) \geq 0,$ (20)

It can be readily seen that if $\frac{1}{b} - \beta \geq 0$, there is one nonnegative root. In the opposite case, there are two nonnegative roots if $\frac{a}{b} + 1 > 0$, and two negative roots otherwise. The strategies (a,b) corresponding to economically feasible rates thus must satisfy (18), and a+b≥0 if 1≤βb.

For a given strategy generating an economically feasible rate of construction, we can write (16), (17) in the form

$r_1(a,b) \leq a + bp \leq r_2(a,b)$, (if $\frac{1}{b} - \beta < 0$)

$r_1(a,b) \leq a + bp$, (if $\frac{1}{b} - \beta > 0$).

These inequalities define a nonempty set $\theta(a,b)$ of economically feasible prices corresponding to the strategy (a,b).
The strategies (a,b) satisfying (18)-(20) generate economically feasible solutions in the interval t∈[t₁,t₂] so long as p(t) ∈ $S_{ab}(h_0, p_0, y, t)$ and also p(t) ∈θ(a,b), i.e. so long as p(t) is simultaneously economically feasible, and part of a solution. Whether this is so, and how long is the interval [t₁,t₂], depends, of course, on the initial conditions (h₀, p₀), and on the demand function y(t). We shall show that if the demand is bounded, it is always possible to produce a construction strategy which generates an economically feasible solution in the interval [T;∞], where T≥t₀. More precisely, for any y which is admissible and bounded from below, there exists a normal strategy (a,b), such that $S_{ab}(h_0,p_0,y,t) \in \Phi(T,\infty)$, for all $(h_0,p_0) \in \Delta$, and some T≥t₀.

To prove this statement we need to demonstrate first that it is possible to select a normal strategy for which the zero solution (equilibrium solution) of the system (13), (14) will be uniformly asymptotically stable in Δ. We recollect from the previous paragraph dealing with free access bulding industry that the zero solution of the system (13), (14) is asymptotically stable everywhere in Δ, provided b>0, i.e. if the strategy is normal.

Further, given (a,b), the zero (equilibrium) solution is attained at $h_{eq}=y, p_{eq} = \frac{\kappa y-a}{b}$, and hence when $r_{eq} = \kappa y$.

If the unknown demand function is bounded from below, i.e. if $y(t) \geq \frac{K_-}{\kappa}$, (where K_- is an arbitrary constant $K_- > 0$), the inequality $r_{eq} = a+b\, p_{eq} \geq K_-$ defines a set of equilibrium prices $\theta_{eq}(a,b)$ {p_{eq}: a+b $p_{eq} \geq K_-$}.

To complete the proof we must select (a,b), b > 0 in such a way that $\theta_{eq}(a,b)$ $\theta(a,b)$ for given K_-. This requirement guarantees that the system (13), (14) asymptotically approaches an

Stabilisation and Optimal Management in the Housing Industry

economically feasile equilibrium solution. The corresponding strategies thus must be chosen in such a way that (18)-(20) are satisfied and $r_1(a,b) \leq K_-$. Using (15) we obtain

$$a < K_- - (b/K_-) (K_-^2 \beta + K_- + 1) \qquad (21)$$

$$b \varepsilon (0, 1/\beta) . \qquad (22)$$

As $b>0$, these strategies generate solutions $S_{ab}(h_0,p_0,y,t)$ approaching the zero solution (h_{eq}, p_{eq}) for all (h_0, p_0) $\varepsilon \Delta$ and $\kappa y(t) \geq K_-$.

The equilibrium prices are thus always economically feasible. So long as $\theta_{eq}(a,b)$ is a proper subset of $\theta(a,b)$, every equilibrium price has an economically feasible neighbourhood, and hence a system approaching the zero solution must become first (at some time T) economically feasible, which was to be proven.

According to (22), the slope of the construction strategy b cannot exceed $1/\beta$ lest the system should become economically unfeasible. This limitation can be removed if the unknown demand function y(t) can be assumed to be bounded both from above and from below, i.e. if $K_- \leq \kappa y(t) \leq K_+$, $K_- > 0$.

In this case, the construction strategies (a,b) which guarantee $S_{ab}(h_0, p_0, y, t)$ take the form

$$a = (1/K_-^\varepsilon K_+^\varepsilon \beta - 1) (K_-^\varepsilon + K_+^\varepsilon - K_-^\varepsilon K_+^\varepsilon) \qquad (23)$$

$$b = (1/K_-^\varepsilon K_+^\varepsilon \beta - 1) K_-^\varepsilon K_+^\varepsilon , \qquad (24)$$

where K_-^ε, K_+^ε are arbitrary constants satisfying

$$0 < K_-^\varepsilon < K_- , \quad K_+^\varepsilon > K_+$$

$$K_-^\varepsilon K_+^\varepsilon \beta - 1 > 0 .$$

Equations (23), (24) can be derived in the following way:

We seek strategies (a,b) with $b > \frac{1}{\beta}$ generating rates of construction which are economically feasible between K_-, K_+, i.e. $K_- < r(a,b) < K_+$, with $r(a,b)$ satisfying (15), (18)-(20). Consider two constants K_-^ε, K_+^ε and a, b satisfying (23), (24). It is easy to see that

$$K_-^\varepsilon + K_+^\varepsilon = \frac{a/b+1}{1/b-\beta}$$

$$K_-^\varepsilon K_+^\varepsilon = - ((1/b) - \beta)^{-1} ,$$

and hence that K_-^ε, K_+^ε are the roots of a quadratic equation

$$r^2 (1/b-\beta) - r(a/b+1) - 1 = 0,$$

which is to be compared with (15). The relations (18)-(20) are satisfied automatically. Any r: $K_-^\epsilon < r < K_+^\epsilon$ is thus economically feasible. To complete the proof, we define $\theta(a,b)$, and show that $\theta_{eq}(a,b)$ in $\theta(a,b)$.

We have thus established the existence of strategies which keep the industry profitable from a certain time T on no matter what (bounded) fluctuations of demand are encountered. The time T depends on (a,b), (h_0,p_0) and $y(t)$. From a practical point of view it is important to ensure that T is as close to the present as possible. To do so, it is convenient to introduce the notion of economically safe states corresponding to fixed demand y_0, $\Sigma(a,b,y_0) = \{(h_0, p_0): S_{ab}(h_0,p_0,y_0,t) \varepsilon \Phi(0,\infty)\}$ where y_0 is a positive constant. $\Sigma(a,b,y_0)$ is thus a locus of points from which under strategy (a,b) emanate solutions of the system (13), (14) which are always economically feasible. A subset of $\Sigma(a,b,y_0)$ can be constructed using Lyapunov function $V=V(h-h_{eq}, p-p_{eq})$ associated with (13), (14), i.e. a function satisfying in Δ

(i) $V(h-h_{eq}, p-p_{eq}) \geq 0$, $V(0,0) = 0$

(ii) $\frac{dV}{dt} < 0$ for $(h,p) \varepsilon S_{ab}(h_0,p_0)$

It is easy to verify that

$$V = \frac{1}{2}(h-h_{eq})^2 + \frac{1}{2}b(p-p_{eq})^2 \tag{25}$$

is a Lyapunov function.

The properties of Lyapunov functions guarantee that any ellipse

$$V_o = \frac{1}{2}(h-h_{eq})^2 + \frac{1}{2}b(p-p_{eq})^2, \quad V_o > 0$$

defines a neighbourhood of the equilibrium point $h_{eq} = y_o$, $p_{eq} = \frac{\kappa y_o - a}{b}$ which, once entered by a solution of (13), (14) contains the solution for ever. According to our previous considerations for y_o: $K_- \leq \kappa y_o \leq K_+$, (a,b) can be chosen in such a way that the equilibrium point has an economically feasible neighbourhood. Then, if V_o is sufficiently small, the corresponding ellipse is a part of $\Sigma(a,b,y_o)$. Clearly, V_o corresponding to economically feasible neighbourhoods is restricted by the inequalities

$$p_{eq} - (2V_o/b)^{\frac{1}{2}} \geq (r_1(a,b) - a)/b$$

Stabilisation and Optimal Management in the Housing Industry

$$p_{eq} - (2V_0/b)^{\frac{1}{2}} \geq (r_2(a,b) - a)/b,$$

where $r_1(a,b)$, $r_2(a,b)$ are the roots of (15).

It follows that the maximum value of V_0 is

$$V_m = \frac{b}{2} \left(\frac{r_1(a,b)-a}{b} - p_{eq} \right)^2 \text{ if } p_{eq} < \frac{r_1+r_2}{2}$$

$$V_m = \frac{b}{2} \left(\frac{r_2(a,b)-a}{b} - p_{eq} \right)^2 \text{ if } p_{eq} \geq \frac{r_1+r_2}{2}.$$

Substituting V_m for V in (25) we obtain

$$\left(\frac{r_i(a,b)-a}{b} - p_{eq} \right)^{-2} \left[\frac{1}{b} (h-h_{eq})^2 + (p-p_{eq})^2 \right] = 1, \quad (26)$$

where $i=1$ if $p_{eq} < \frac{r_1+r_2}{2}$, and $i=2$ otherwise.

These ellipses represent subsets of $\Sigma(a,b,y_0)$ denoted $\Delta(a,b,y_0)$. The intersection $\Delta(a,b) = y_0 \Delta(a,b,y_0)$, where $y_0 \in [\frac{K_-}{\kappa}, \frac{K_+}{\kappa}]$, contains the economically safe points (h_0,p_0), i.e. the points from which under the strategy (a,b) emanate solutions

$$S_a(h_0, p_0, y), y \in [K_-/\kappa, K_+/\kappa]$$

satisfying $S_{ab}(h_0, p_0, y) \in \Phi(0, \infty)$.

$\Delta(a,b)$ thus represents a set of points for which a strategy, exists which will prevent the system from becoming economically unfeasible no matter what fluctuations of demand (provided that they are bounded) may be encountered.

It is not immediately clear whether the set $\Delta(a,b)$ is nonempty, and how its size depends on the strategy. To construct $\Delta(a,b)$, it is useful to eliminate h_{eq}, p_{eq} from (26).

We obtain

$$\frac{1}{b}(h-y_0)^2 + \left(p - \frac{\kappa y_0 - a}{b}\right)^2 = \left(\frac{r_i(a,b)-a}{b} - \frac{\kappa y_0 - a}{b} \right)^2$$

$$y_0 \in [K_-/\kappa; K_+/\kappa] \quad (27)$$

Considering y_0 as a parameter, (27) corresponds to a family of ellipses with centres at points $[y_0; \frac{\kappa y_0 - a}{b}]$, which touch the lines $p = \frac{r_i(a,b)-a}{b}$. The set $\Delta(a,b)$ is determined by the overlap of the two ellipses which have their centres situated at $[K_-/\kappa_i \frac{K_- - a}{b}]$ and $[K_+/\kappa_i \frac{K_+ - a}{b}]$.

Optimum Management of building industry operated by a sole owner

In the previous sections, we have dealt with the problem of stabilising the building industry by avoiding the unprofitable operation. In this section, we turn to the problem of designing linear feedback strategies, which maximise discounted profits over a period of time. The design of the profit maximising strategies can be seen as a logical extension of the work already done: having determined the strategies, which make the industry economically feasible in the long run, we have tackled the problem of shortening the interval between the present state, and the time in the future, when the system becomes permanently profitable. However, insisting on permanent profitability may be less appealing to a building industry operated by a sole owner if the profits accumulated in this way were much lower than those obtained while employing a more adventurous strategy. In particular, a strategy leading to periods of unprofitable operation, which would be followed by long intervals of highly lucrative activity, could be expected to exercise a certain seductive power. Such a strategy, if implemented, would be a powerful destabilizing (I-destabilizing) factor, intrinsic in the industry, as distinct from the influence of the more or less random fluctuations of demand, due to external causes. As a consequence, any theoretical attempt to stabilise the system with respect to unpredictable change of demand, would be frustrated in practice by the owner preferring higher profits to I-stability. To avoid this drawback, we endeavour to design a linear feedback strategy maximising economic rent, which would also guarantee I-stability, once the safe set is reached.

Let us consider the following problem:
Given the system (13), (14), find constants a,b such that the equilibrium is economically feasible, and such that the nondimensional economic rent (6) accumulated over a period of time, [0,T] say, is maximised irrespective of adverse factors (e.g. fluctuations of demand). Denoting δ the nondimensional discounting rate, we can state the problem as

$$\max_{a,b} \int_0^T \frac{I_E}{c_o} e^{-\delta t} \, dt ,$$

subject to (13), (14), and (h_{eq}, p_{eq}) economically feasible.

The problem is a special type of game, where one player (the builder) manipulates the rate of construction by choosing the constants a,b, whereas the opponent (the rest of economy) changes the demand function y, which influences the position of the zero (equilibrium) solution. The equilibrium point moves with time, and it may or may not be economically feasible at all times. If the game could be played in such a way that the system can be brought into the economically feasible zone defined by $h \in [K_-^*; K_+^*]$, $p \in \theta(a,b)$, and kept there from a certain time t_* on, the system has been made I-stable. If this can be achieved at minimum cost (or maximum profit) to the builder, irrespective of what the rest of the economy does, we can say that the system is optimally managed, and I-stabilised.

To solve this problem, it is convenient to use some results obtained by Skowronski (1977).

Skowronski deals with a zero sum two player game with the objective functional

$$J = \int_{t_0}^{t_f} f_0(x,t,u_1,u_2)\, dt,$$

where the state vector $x \in \Delta$ R_n, $t \in R^+$, and strategies u_1, u_2 are measurable functions mapping $\Delta \times R^+$ into non-void compact sets $U_1(t)$, $U_2(t)$. The game is played on a dynamic system

$$\dot{x} = f(x,t,u_1,u_2),$$

whose solutions are $S(x_0,t_0,t)$.

The game is playable for capture with respect to a simply conected target set θ in Δ if one player can chose an admissible strategy u_1 such that the solution $S(x_0,t_0,t)$ enters θ at time $t=T$, and remains there. If such a strategy also maximises the objective functional, the game is optimally playable for capture. It has been shown (Proposition 2.1 in Skowronski 1977) that for a game to be optimally playable for capture, it is sufficient if there exists a Lyapunov function $V(x,t)$ satisfying the following conditions:

(i) V is a mapping $(\Delta-\theta) \times R^+ \to R$, which is bounded from below and from above by functions
a: $R^+ \to R^+$, which are continuous, and strictly increasing with $a(0)=0$.

(ii) if $J(x_0, t_0, u_1^*, u_2, x, t)$

$$\leq J(x_0, t_0, u_1^*, u_2^*, x,t) \leq J(x_0, t_0, u_1, u_2^*, x, t)$$

for (x_0,t_0) from a given emission zone, then

$$\frac{\partial V}{\partial t} + \Delta V(x,t)\, f(x,t, u_1^*, u_2) \leq - f_0(x, t, u_1^*, u_2), \quad (28)$$

and

$$\frac{\partial V}{\partial t} + \Delta V(x,t)\, f(x, t, u_1, u_2^*) \geq - f_0(x, t, u_1, u_2^*). \quad (29)$$

The strategies u_1^*, u_2^* are optimal strategies for all u_1, u_2.

We shall now apply these results to our problem.

As Lyapunov function we shall use the function defined by (25), which obviously satisfies (i).

The condition (ii) requires that

$$-\frac{I_E}{c_0}(a^*, b^*, y) e^{-\delta t} \leq -\kappa(h-y)^2, \quad (30)$$

and

$$-\frac{I_E}{c_0}(a, b, y^*) e^{-\delta t} \geq -\kappa(h-y^*)^2, \quad (31)$$

These inequalities can be written

$$-(a^* + b^*p)[p(1-b^*\beta) - a^*\beta - 1] + 1 \leq -\kappa(h-y)^2 e^{\delta t}$$

$$-(a + bp)[p(1-b\beta) - a\beta - 1] + 1 \leq -\kappa(h-y^*)^2 e^{\delta t}.$$

By adding we obtain:

$$p^2[A-A^*] + p[B-B^*] + A-A^* \leq \kappa(y^*-y)(y^*+y-2h) e^{\delta t},$$

where $A = b(1-\beta b)$, $B = a-b-2ab\beta$, $C = -(1+a+a^2\beta)$, (32)

and A^*, B^*, C^* are defined similarly in terms of a^*, b^*.

The right hand side is maximized by the strategy

$$y^* = \frac{K_-}{\kappa} \text{ if } h > \frac{K_-+K_+}{2}, \quad (33)$$

and $y^* = \frac{K_+}{\kappa}$ if $h \leq \frac{K_-+K_+}{2}$.

To find the optimum strategy (a^*, b^*), we must first determine the range of values (a,b) can acquire. In section 3.2, we have established the existence of two families of strategies, (21), (22) and (23), (24), which kept the industry profitable in the long run. We shall endeavour to determine the optimum strategies, which belong to the family (21), (22).

The following Lemma is useful:

Lemma 1
If (a,b) belong to the family (3.14), (3.15),

$$Z = Ap^2 + Bp + C \geq 0 \text{ for } p \geq p_1 > 0, p < p_2 < 0,$$

for all $b \in (0, \frac{1}{\beta})$, $K_- > 0$; $p_1 = \frac{1}{k_-}(K_-^2 \beta + K_- \beta) + K_-$.

The proof of this lemma is straightforward and is omitted here.

Let us consider the family of functions

$Z(a,b) = A(a,b) p^2 + B(a,b) p + C(a,b)$ with a,b satisfying (21), (22).

Stabilisation and Optimal Management in the Housing Industry

Using Lemma 1, it is easy to see that the function $Z(a,*,b*)$ defined by

$$a* = -(\frac{1}{\beta} + \frac{1}{\beta\kappa}),$$
$$b* = b_{max} = \frac{1}{\beta} \quad \text{if } 1 - K_-^2 \beta > 0 \ , \tag{34}$$

$$a* = K_-$$
$$b* = b_{min} = 0 \quad \text{if } 1 - K_-^2 \beta \leq 0$$

has the property $Z(a*,b*) > Z(a,b)$, for all (a,b) satisfying (21), (22), and $p > p_1$.

It follows that $Z(a,b) - Z(a*,b*) \leq 0$, $p \geq p_1$, and hence (34) are the optimal strategies required by (32), which are to be used if $p > p_1$, i.e. when the building activity is profitable.

To find the optimal strategies for the building industry operating with a loss we need the following Lemma.

Lemma 2
Consider the family of parabolas $Z(a,b) = A(a,b) p^2 + B(a,b) p + C(a,b)$, with $A(a,b)$, $B(a,b)$ $C(a,b)$ defined as before.

In the domain $b \in [0, \frac{1}{\beta}]$, $p \in [0,p_1]$,

for $a* = -\frac{1}{2\beta}$, and $\tag{35}$

$$b* = \frac{K_-(1+2K_-\beta)}{2\beta(K_-^2\beta+K_-+1)} \ , \ Z(a*,b*) \geq Z(a,b), \text{ for all } p < p_1.$$

The proof is not difficult and therefore it is omitted.

It is convenient to summarize the last results briefly: The optimum strategy for the building industry operated by a sole owner depends on the following factors:
a) price and its relation to economic feasibility
b) estimated bounds on demand, and their relation to the locus of economic feasibility.

The profit maximizing strategy for the builder is given by (35) if the operation is not profitable, and by (34) in the profitable region. Having found the optimizing strategies, we conclude that optimum management of building industry facing unknown but bounded fluctuations of demand is possible.

NOTES

1. To facilitate typing the hat denoting nondimensional quantities will be no longer used.

REFERENCES

AIRG-CSIRO (1980) Housing 2000, A joint pilot project on Technological Forecasting in the Australian Building Industry, AIRG-CSIRO Vol.1-3
Botman, J.J.(1981), Dynamics of housing and planning, Seminar on the forecasting and Programming of housing, UN economic commission of Europe, Martinus Nijhoff, Delft
Bromilow, B.J. (1979), 'Accessibility of housing', The Australian builder pp.26-33
Lujanen, M. (1981) Review paper on forecasting and programming of housing, UN economic commission for Europe
Lujanen, M. (1979) 'Financing of housing in the market-economy countries', UN economic commission for Europe
Needleman, L., (1965) The economics of housing, London
Skowronski, J.M. (1977) 'Lyapunov Type Design of Lumped Systems in Conflict with Environment'. Department of Mathematics, University of Queensland Control Theory Report, 77-1
Tucker, S. (1980) 'Economic decision making in the building development process', Proceedings CIB Symposium: Quality and Cost in Building, Vol.I, pp.93-105
Tucker, S. (1981) 'Quantitative comparisons of the costs of housing finance and subsidy schemes', DBR-CSIRO Report

Chapter Five

MODELLING THE SUPPLY-DEMAND DYNAMICS OF A SLOWLY RENEWABLE RESOURCE

David F. Batten and Paul F. Lesse

INTRODUCTION

During the last few decades, modellers exploring the growth of various economic and demographic systems have largely polarized into two distinct groups. On the one hand, there are those modellers who embrace the complexity of the system involved by developing large sets of differential equations which can only be solved using computer simulation. The system dynamics school (Forrester, 1969) is a well-known example. Dynamic models of this type have been developed for the forest sector by Randers et al. (1979) and Levack (1981). Unfortunately, such approaches are often intractable and generally require many unsubstantiated assumptions concerning causal relationships and feedback mechanisms. They can rarely provide useful insights into the basic dynamic processes underlying the system's behaviour.

On the other hand, there are those modellers who carefully evade complexity by constructing statistical equations which are based on simple regression analysis. Econometric models typify this group. Dynamic econometric models have been developed for the forest sector by Adams and Haynes (1980) and Nomura and Yukutake (1982). Rather than burying the basic processes within a large system of differential equations, these modellers prefer to overlook causality and fundamental interdependencies by resorting to simple econometric relationships. The potential shortcomings of this approach hardly require further clarification.

Rather fortunately, a third modelling camp has emerged recently. This compromise approach advocates models capable of generating complexity in the phenomena of interest, while retaining extreme simplicity in model structure (May, 1976). The resulting differential theory of dynamical systems emphasizes economy in the construction of models to predict a system's behaviour, in contrast to large scale simulation models. Reduced computational effort and improved model understanding are the main advantages of this pragmatic approach.

The present chapter conforms to this third modelling tradition, as do earlier ones in this volume (see Chapters 2 through 4). The aim here is to further demonstrate a simple application of the differential theory of dynamical systems by examining the supply and demand dynamics of a slowly renewable resource. The growth, control and management of a single species forest is the chosen resource application.

The next section discusses the dynamics of timber supply. A number of plausible models are considered, emanating from the largely deterministic nature of domestic availability forecasts. The pertinent components of the demand for forest products are then introduced. Although future levels of domestic demand are essentially deterministic, likely export demand is difficult to predict. Thus an element of uncertainty influences the dynamics of demand, compounded by the need to distinguish between different prices in the domestic and international markets. In a later section, the objectives and policies of the forest owner are considered, leading to the specification of the complete model as an optimal control problem. We finally examine various solutions and the concept of maximum sustainable yield.

THE DYNAMICS OF SUPPLY

We shall firstly explore the development of a simple differential equation to describe the aggregate availability of timber in a region or nation which is predominantly self-sufficient in timber. In such a model, the forest sector relies solely on domestic timber supplies and is not subject to the vagaries of foreign import dependency. This market structure will be termed 'supply-independent', and corresponds to a situation in which the data on forest resources are plentiful and reliable and the resulting forecasts of future timber availability are largely deterministic. The following approaches (amongst others) are plausible in this situation:

The Dynamics of a Simple Stand
At the micro level, it is possible to formulate a simulation model which can reproduce the development over a period of time of certain key supply parameters in a forest stand, such as volumetric density, tree density, natural regeneration, and natural thinning (Kalgraf, 1979). Such models have been conceived to test the dynamic effects on volumetric density and the mean tree dimension of activities such as thinning, fertilization, spraying and irrigation. The cause-and-effect relationships in a stand can be captured in a system dynamics model in which the forest is seen as a feedback-loop system.

For our present purpose, such a supply model is too complex and disaggregated. We wish to restrict our attention to the aggregate supply of timber over a whole region or nation, for which the behaviour of a single stand is an unnecessary complication.

Dynamic Modelling of Renewable Resources

Logistic Growth

One of the more popular models which has been adopted to study the behaviour of biological systems and single-species populations over time is based on the logistic growth assumption (Allen, 1976; Batten, 1982). A simple model of forest growth based on this assumption would take the following form:

$$\frac{dx}{dt} = \alpha\ x\ (N-x) - \beta\ x \qquad (1)$$

where x denotes the number of trees belonging to a given species or timber class, N delimits the carrying capacity of the forest or region, α is a parameter related to the natural rate of growth and regeneration, and β is related to the rate of natural thinning. The resulting model postulates exponential growth for small values of x, when the capacity of the forest is unlimited, followed by a slowdown of the tree growth rate as the forest's carrying capacity is reached. The term (N-x) introduces a saturation of the tree population to a stable stationary level, defining a level of sustainable yield (Figure 5.1).

Although the logistic model is a useful vehicle for simulating forest growth, it has two disadvantages for our present purpose. Firstly, the model is applicable to a specific forest or region (the meso level) which must be delimited by a predetermined tree-carrying capacity. In contrast, our aggregate approach to timber supply at the macro level should be able to encompass a number of different forests and regions. Secondly, the logistic model assumes that the tree-carrying capacity is constant over time. This capacity may change for various reasons.

The Dynamics of Timber Availability

In reality, the supply of timber from a forest embraces not only that timber which is produced but also that which is available in stock at a given time (Hösteland, 1979). Given that the number of trees belonging to a given species or timber class is x, we now postulate the dynamics of aggregate timber stock or inventories in the following simple form:

$$\frac{dx}{dt} = \alpha - \beta \qquad (2)$$

where α is the species' rate of growth (planting and regeneration) and β measures the rate of thinning. Equation (2) is general enough to apply to both natural forests and plantations, although different growth and harvesting rates would apply.

A distinguishing feature of this equation is the absence of any price variable. The traditional market equilibrium models postulate supply as a function of price. For the case of the timber market, however, the forest owners are not in a position to alter their rate of supply substantially in response to prices because of the lengthy period to maturity and the need to adhere to

Fig. 5.1

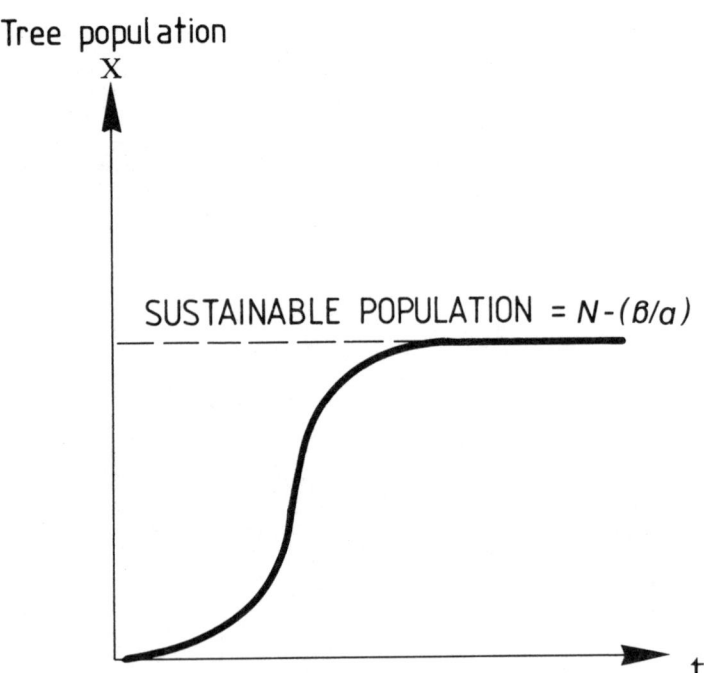

efficient rotation strategies and well-defined management policies. The stock equation (2) will therefore be adopted in our initial model to describe the dynamics of timber availability.

THE DYNAMICS OF DEMAND AND PRICE ADJUSTMENT

In contrast to the self-sufficiency assumption adopted on the supply side, we shall explore the development of a differential equation to describe the aggregate demand for a single species of timber which may arise from both domestic and international components. This hybrid market structure will be termed 'demand-dependent', and corresponds to an economy in which our understanding of market forces is limited and our ability to forecast future demand levels is therefore restricted. Although future levels of domestic demand may be largely deterministic, there is considerable uncertainty about levels of export demand. The nature of this demand problem is depicted in Figure 5.2.

In the following, we shall adopt the methodology described earlier by Lesse and Skowronski (see Chapter 4). The level of domestic demand, y_d, is relatively well-behaved, being principally derived in the advanced nations from the demand for dwellings. Although the dwelling construction industry is large and complex, reasonable demand predictions can usually be obtained by considering the future behaviour of the following factors: (i) population, (ii) average household size, (iii) prices, (iv) availability of substitutes, and (v) technical and taste changes in housing. For our present purpose, the following simplified model for domestic demand will be utilized:

$$y_d = a \frac{N}{h} \qquad (3)$$

where N denotes the population size, h defines the average household size, and a is a suitably chosen constant.

In contrast to y_d, the level of export demand, y_e, is largely determined by forces beyond the control of the domestic market. A key factor in determination of export potential is the relative price, π, namely the ratio of domestic price to average global price for each forest product. Thus we can postulate that

$$y_e = \Phi_e(\pi) \qquad (4)$$

where $\Phi_e(\pi)$ denotes an export potential function which is partly deterministic and partly stochastic.

Equation (3) contains two parameters which certainly follow their own development paths over time. Population growth is often assumed to be logistic, in which case it follows the pattern depicted in Figure 5.1 and specified in equation (1). Average household size depends largely on factors like household income and the price of housing. For any given population dynamics

Fig. 5.2

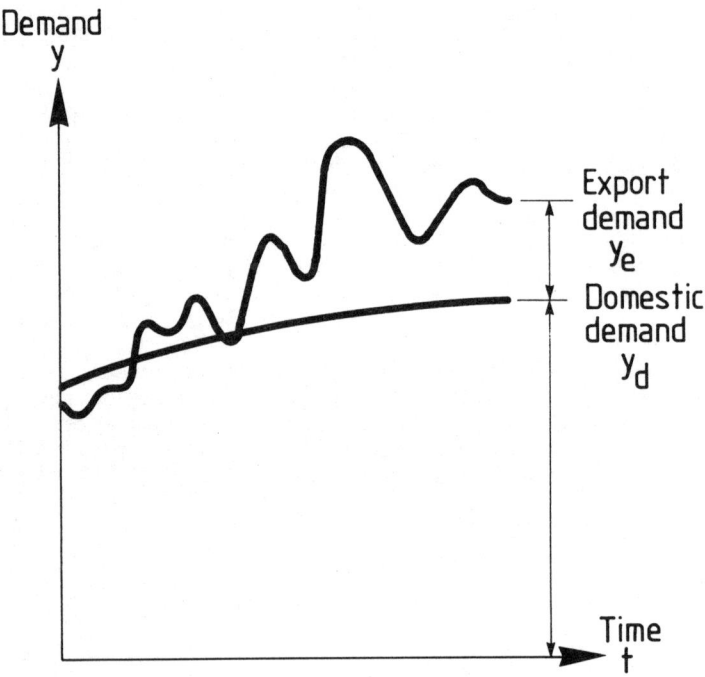

Dynamic Modelling of Renewable Resources

$$\frac{dN}{dt} = F(N,t)$$

we can construct the corresponding dynamic equation for domestic demand:

$$\frac{dy_d}{dt} = \frac{a}{h} \cdot F(hy_d) - \frac{d(\ln h)}{dt} \cdot y_d \qquad (5)$$

Nevertheless, the inclusion of the export demand component, y_e, necessitates consideration of the dynamics of price adjustments. Given that the relative price level is

$$\pi = \frac{p}{P_w}$$

where p and P_w are domestic and world market prices respectively, we can postulate the following form of domestic price adjustment:

$$\frac{dp}{dt} = k(y - \beta x) \qquad (6)$$

with the constant k denoting the speed of market adjustments, and $y=y_d+y_e$. Equation (6) implies that prices adjust upwards or downwards according to the imbalance between demand and supply.

OBJECTIVES AND CONSTRAINTS

For the plantation owner, his main objective is to maximize discounted economic return over the full period of thinning and rotation. To quantify this return, we introduce revenue and cost functions. Economic revenue, R, is a function of prices and the quantity of timber harvested and sold, namely

$$R = p\beta$$

whereas cost generally depends on the harvesting and rotation management schemes adopted, i.e.,

$$C = C(\beta).$$

The economic return or income, I, is then given by

$$I = R - C$$

and the objective of the forest owner is to maximize the discounted return over a specific period of time, T, namely

$$\max_{\beta} \int_0^T I\, e^{-\delta t}\, dt$$

where δ is the discount rate.

The timber buyers, however, are not likely to pay more than the average price on the world market, i.e.

$$p \leq P_w$$

The feasibility of any thinning or rotation strategy is then determined by the normal profitability criterion, namely $\beta : I \geq 0$. This criterion imposes a constraint on the relationship between domestic or relative price and the rate of thinning, which depends on the character of C. Assuming C is quadratic, a positive economic return emanates from the following domestic price level:

$$p \geq \frac{c_0}{\beta} + c_1 + c_2 \beta$$

where c_0, c_1 and c_2 are interpreted, respectively, as maintenance or overhead costs per unit of time, the cost of materials and labour per tree planted, and the extra costs associated with earlier plantings (per tree per unit rate of rotation). All these costs are regarded as real to the forest or plantation owner. The constants c_0, c_1 and c_2 must satisfy

$$c_1 < 2 \sqrt{c_0 c_2}$$

since $C > 0$ for all $\beta > 0$.

It is convenient to nondimensionalize the complete model. We therefore introduce the following nondimensional variables:

nondimensional price: $\quad p' = p \cdot c_1^{-1}$

nondimensional growth rate: $\quad \alpha' = \alpha \cdot c_0^{-1} c_1$

nondimensional thinning rate: $\quad \beta' = \beta \cdot c_0^{-1} c_1$

nondimensional time: $\quad t' = t \cdot k^{0.5} c_0 c_1^{-1.5}$

nondimensional stock: $\quad x' = x \cdot k^{0.5} c_1^{-0.5}$

nondimensional demand: $\quad y' = y \cdot k^{0.5} c_0^{-1} c_1^{0.5}$

cost parameter: $\quad \gamma = c_0 c_1^{-2} c_2$

In terms of the above nondimensional variables, the basic model becomes the following:

$$\underset{\beta'}{\text{Maximize}} \int_0^T \frac{I}{c_0} e^{-\delta t'} \, dt'$$

where nondimensional economic return is now

$$\frac{I}{c_0} = p'\beta' - [1 + \beta' + \gamma (\beta')^2] \qquad (7)$$

subject to the following constraints:

$$p' \geq \frac{1}{\beta'} + 1 + \gamma \beta' \qquad (8)$$

$$\frac{dx'}{dt'} = \alpha' - \beta' \qquad (9)$$

$$\frac{dp'}{dt'} = y' - \beta' x' . \qquad (10)$$

If the cost function $C(\beta)$ is linear then $\gamma=0$; if it is quadratic then $\gamma = 0.25$.

The absence of a separate differential equation for total demand y has two purposes. Firstly, it allows us to explore the underlying processes at work without computer simulations since a model containing two nondimensional differential equations is quite manageable by hand. Secondly, it permits us to examine the sensitivity of the model to large fluctuations in the level of demand. By specifying the shape of the demand function exogenously, we can concentrate on thinning rates or rotation strategies which are largely functions of prices. Such an approach seems justified in view of the observed behaviour of forest and plantation owners in terms of price sensitivity.

We could examine the problem of designing a feedback strategy which would keep the forest owners in business irrespective of what fluctuations in demand they encounter. However, this type of problem has already been addressed for the case of the construction industry earlier in this monograph (see Chapter 4). In that case, stabilization and optimal management are shown to be mathematically equivalent to the solution of a differential game played by the builder against the rest of the economy. Under certain assumptions, the industry can be stabilized and managed efficiently.

Rather than follow this gaming strategy, at this stage we prefer to address three fundamental questions pertaining to the above model for a single species forest: (1) What limits must be set for the intensity of thinning so that the species will not be in any danger of extinction and yet the owners can remain profitable? (2) What rotation strategy (constant, increasing or decreasing rates of thinning) yields the maximum return? (3) What range of fluctuations in demand can be withstood if we are to ensure a profitable operation? To answer these questions requires little more than a handful of solutions to the model, most of which can be conveniently ascertained.

In what follows, we shall delete the prime sign for denoting nondimensional variables since all the quantities under examination may now be assumed nondimensional.

MODEL SOLUTIONS

Equilibrium Solutions

Tentative harvesting limits are set by assuming a constant rate of thinning and then examining the resulting positive equilibrium solution (i.e. $(dx/dt) = 0$). At equilibrium, equations (9) and (10) reduce to

$$\beta = \alpha \qquad (11)$$

$$\beta x = y. \qquad (12)$$

For any single species, the rate of growth (planting and regeneration) α can be controlled. Equation (11) defines a simple equilibrium state of sustainable yield in which the rate of thinning is equal to α. Equation (12) defines a linear relationship between demand y and the tree population x.

In reality, there is a maximum harvesting rate, $\beta(max)$, beyond which an equivalent rate of growth cannot be sustained unless the planting rate is increased. We must therefore add an additional constraint to the model, namely

$$\beta \leq \beta(max) \qquad (13)$$

where $\beta(max)$ denotes an upper limit to the thinning rate which is consistent with our assumption of an equivalent growth rate. Beyond $\beta(max)$, the value of α may begin to decline unless the rate of planting is increased.

For a given value of α, all points on the straight line defined by

$$y = \alpha x \qquad (14)$$

define values of x and y for which the net growth of the tree population is zero and at which prices do not change. These points define the locus of equilibrium solutions to the model.

A tentative answer to the first of our questions is now straightforward. For any forest growing at a uniform rate α, the following tentative limits on the rate of thinning are required to avoid extinction yet maintain a profitable operation (assuming a linear cost function):

$$\alpha \geq \beta \geq \frac{1}{p-1}.$$

Partial Equilibrium Solutions

An interesting and pertinent set of solutions emerges from the case where the overall tree population remains stationary but prices can fluctuate. These conditions correspond to the partial equilibrium state of sustainable yield, and are largely demand-dependent. In this case, our model can be simplified to the

following linear approximation over a discrete number of time
periods T:

$$\text{Maximize} \sum_{t=0}^{T} p_t (1-\delta)^t \qquad (15)$$

subject to the following constraints:

$$p_t \geq \frac{1}{\alpha} + 1 + \gamma\alpha \qquad (16)$$

$$p_t - p_{t-1} = y_t - \alpha x_t . \qquad (17)$$

Since α and x_t are constant over the entire rotation period, demand levels y_t are the driving mechanism for this model. The discount rate δ will favour the earlier periods, but the maximum return is largely determined by the shape of the demand function. However, we shall postpone our discussion of fluctuations in demand until the next section.

Robust solutions
Perhaps the most pertinent case which warrants investigation involves a fluctuating rate of thinning which can be attributed to several factors such as (i) rapid changes in demand, (ii) changing prices on the world market, and (iii) unexpected changes in availability arising from natural hazards (e.g. fire, drought, etc.) Under these conditions, we must search for a rotation strategy which the forest owners can employ to remain profitable in the face of severe fluctuations in demand. Obviously such strategies should be simple to implement and based upon information which is readily available. In the following, we shall restrict our attention to rotation strategies which are functions of prices (see Chapter 4).

The third of our earlier questions is the one which shall now be addressed. Its solution involves the design of a rotation strategy which can keep the owners profitable despite severe fluctuations in demand. The chosen strategy can be viewed as a relation between β and p, since all pairs $\beta > 0$, $p \geq 1$ can be regarded as profitable if $I > 0$ or unprofitable if $I \leq 0$. The state $[\beta, p:I=0]$ defines the supply curve of zero return (see Figure 5.3), which is a boundary to the feasible region. For simplicity, we shall limit the following discussion to the case of a linear cost function ($\gamma=0$).

Since prices are relatively easy to monitor, the forest owners can attempt to remain economically feasible (i.e. profitable) by adopting a cutting strategy based on prices. For example, the strategy is always economically feasible since each point lies above the supply curve of zero return. A simpler approach is to use a linear feedback strategy. The question is how efficient such a strategy can be made when facing a severely fluctuating demand function.

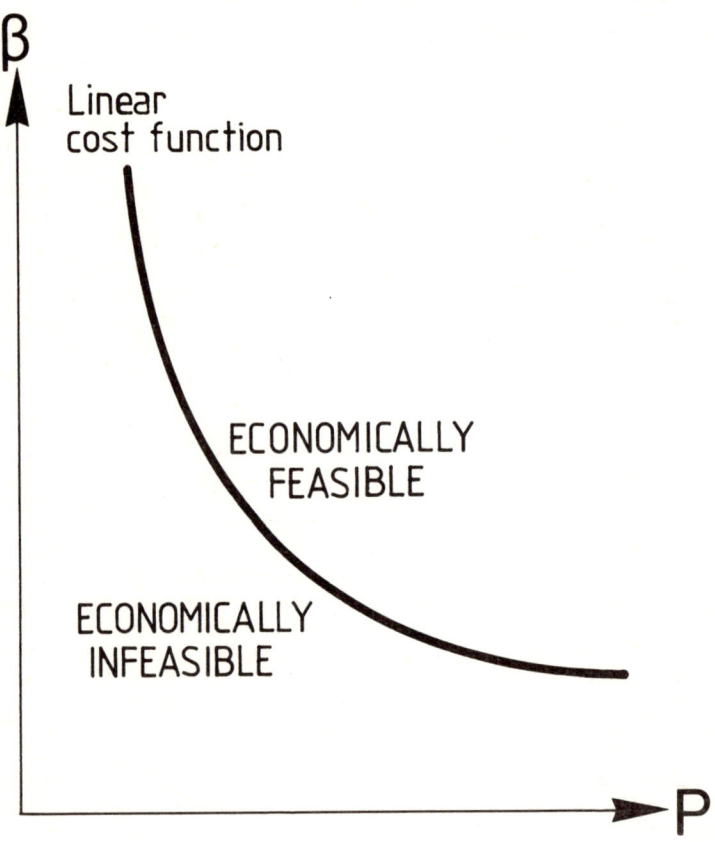

Fig. 5.3

Dynamic Modelling of Renewable Resources

$$\beta = \frac{1+\varepsilon^2}{p-1}$$

Let us reconsider equations (9) and (10) with the thinning rate β as a function of prices, i.e.

$$\beta = \beta(p).$$

Provided $\beta(p)$ is sufficiently smooth it can be expressed as a power series around an arbitrary price level. Equation (9) becomes

$$\frac{dx}{dt} = \alpha - a - bp - \ldots \qquad (18)$$

and equation (10) becomes

$$\frac{dp}{dt} = y - x(a + bp + \ldots \qquad (19)$$

The system of equations consisting of the linear parts of (18) and (19) has an equilibrium point at

$$x_{eq} = \frac{y}{\alpha}$$

$$p_{eq} = \frac{\alpha-a}{b}$$

In keeping with Skowronski (1977), we describe an arbitrary demand function $y(t) > 0$ as <u>admissible</u> in a subset of state space w if for each set of initial conditions, $[\beta_o, p_o]$ εw, the corresponding solutions of (18) and (19) are absolutely continuous. Any solution which corresponds to an admissible level of demand $y(t)$, a rotation strategy (a,b), and emanates from an initial point $[\beta_o, p_o]$ εw, will be denoted by $S_{ab}[\beta_o, p_o, y(t)]$. Let $\Psi_{ab}(w)$ denote the set of all such solutions emanating from w.

A solution $S_{ab}[\beta_o, p_o, y(t)]$ is economically feasible over the time period (T_1, T_2), $0 \leq T_1 \leq T_2$ if

$$\alpha > a + bp > \frac{1}{p-1} \text{ and } P_w > p$$

for $p(t) \varepsilon S_{ab}[\beta_o, p_o, y(t)]$, $t \varepsilon (T_1, T_2)$. Denote by $\Phi(T_1, T_2)$ the set of all economically feasible points satisfying

$$P_w > p(t) > \frac{1}{2b}[b - a + \sqrt{(a+b)^2 + 4b}] \qquad (20)$$

thus forming the desired set.

An equilibrium point $[\frac{y}{\alpha}, \frac{\alpha-a}{b}]$ corresponding to a linear construction strategy $\beta = a+bp$ is therefore economically feasible at all times $t>0$ if

$$a + bP_w > \alpha > \frac{1}{2}[a + b + \sqrt{(a+b)^2 + 4b}] \qquad (21)$$

The set of initial values $[\beta_0, p_0]$ ϵw with the property that the solutions emanating from them are economically feasible at all times t>0 will be defined as the set Ψ, i.e. $\Psi=\{(\beta_0, p_0) : S_{ab} [\beta_0, p_0, y] \epsilon \Phi (0, \infty)\}$. If this feasible set Ψ is nonempty then the growth rate α is bounded from above and below, but the admissible demand y is theoretically unbounded (limited only by the level of β at which α begins to decline).

It is certainly possible to select a linear rotation strategy (a, b) such that $\Psi \neq \Phi$ (meaning there is at least one feasible equilibrium point). The constants a and b are chosen by setting

$$a + b P_w = \alpha_+$$
$$a + b + \sqrt{(a+b)^2 + 4b} = 2\alpha_-.$$

where $\alpha_+ = \alpha + \Delta_1$, $\alpha_- + \alpha - \Delta_2$, and Δ_1, Δ_2 are arbitrary nonnegative constants. We obtain the following solutions:

$$a = \frac{P_w \alpha_-^2 - \alpha_+(\alpha_- + 1)}{\alpha_-(P_w - 1) - 1} \qquad (22)$$

and $b = \dfrac{\alpha_+ - a}{P_w}$.

Conclusion

Given an arbitrary but admissible demand function y(t), and an initial point $[\beta_0, p_0] \epsilon w$, the likelihood of finding a linear rotation strategy $\beta = a + bp$ which can keep the system economically feasible at all times depends largely on the intrinsic rate of growth (planting and regeneration) α. If values of a and b can be found which satisfy condition (21) for the corresponding values of α, then all fluctuations in demand can be withstood profitably provided that the rotation strategy β does not cause α to decline.

It is possible to construct a safety zone which has the property that any solution $S_{ab} [\beta_0, p_0, y]$ emanating from the point $[\beta_0, p_0] \epsilon w$ is always economically feasible. For a derivation of the useful range of a, b and the safety zone using a simple geometric argument, see Chapter 4.

REFERENCES

Adams, D.M. and Haynes, R.W. (1980) 'The 1980 Softwood Timber Assessment Market Model: Structure, Projections, and Policy Simulations', Forest Science, Monograph 22, 64p.

Allen, P.M. (1976) 'Evolution, Population Dynamics and Stability', Proceedings of the National Academy of Sciences 73, 665-668

Batten, D.F. (1982) 'On the Dynamics of Industrial Evolution', Regional Science and Urban Economics 12, 449-462

Batten, D.F. (1983) 'Towards an Integrated System of Models for

Australian Forest Sector Analysis', in R. Seppälä, C. Row and A. Morgan (eds.), Forest Sector Models, AB Academic Publishers, London, pp.119-130

Forrester, J.W. (1969) Urban Dynamics, MIT Press, Cambridge, Massachusetts

Hösteland, J.E. (1979) 'Stock Fluctuations in the Pulp Industry', in L. Lönnstedt and J. Randers (eds.), Wood Resource Dynamics in the Scandinavian Forest Sector, Swedish University of Agricultural Sciences, Uppsala, pp.46-54

Kalgraf, K. (1979) 'The Dynamics of a Simple Stand', in L. Lönnstedt and J. Randers (eds.), Wood Resource Dynamics in the Scandinavian Forestry Sector, Swedish University of Agricultural Sciences, Uppsala, pp.55-64

Lesse, P.F. and Skowronski, J.M. (1985) 'Stabilization and Optimal Management of the Housing Industry', Chapter 4, this volume

Levack, H.H. (1981) 'Towards a Systems Dynamics Model for the Development of the Forest Sector in New Zealand', Unpublished paper, New Zealand Forest Service

May, R.M. (1976) 'Simple Mathematical Models with Very Complicated Dynamics', Nature 261, 459-467

Nomura, I. and Yukutake, K. (1982) 'Forest Sector Model in Japan and its Simulation Analysis', Unpublished paper, Japanese Forestry and Forest Products Research Institute

Randers, J., Stenberg, L. and Kalgraf, K. (1979) The Forest Sector in Transition, U.S. Library of Congress Order No. LB 78-2339

Skowronski, J.M. (1977) 'A Note on Liapunov Design of Systems in Conflict with the Environment', Proceedings, IFAC Symposium on Environmental Systems Planning, Design and Control, Pergamon Press, London

PART II

DIFFERENTIAL GAMES

Chapter Six

COMPETITIVE DIFFERENTIAL GAME OF HARVESTING UNCERTAIN RESOURCES

Janislaw M. Skowronski

INTRODUCTION

STATEMENT OF THE PROBLEM

Let $x_i(t) > 0$, $i=1,\ldots,N$, $t \in J'_o = [t_o, t_f)$, $t_f \leq \infty$ be the instantaneous <u>uncertain</u> amount of the resource i <u>either</u> produced <u>or</u> consumed, (depending upon the interpretation explained below), and let $h_i(t) \geq$, $i=1,\ldots,N$, be the harvest rate of such production or consumption by a competing agent (<u>player</u>) $\sigma=1,\ldots,k$. Then we may form the <u>state</u> vector $x(t) = (x_1(t),\ldots, x_N(t)) \in \Delta_x$ in $\mathbb{R}^N$, where Δ_x is an open bounded <u>playing region</u>, and the <u>control vectors</u> $h^\sigma(t) = (h^\sigma_1(t),\ldots, h^\sigma_N(t)) \in U_\sigma$ in $\mathbb{R}^N$, $\sigma=1,\ldots,k$, with U_σ given compact sets of <u>admissible control</u> values. The control vectors $h^\sigma(t)$ are to be selected by the corresponding players, while $h(t) = (h^1(t),\ldots, h^k(t)) \in U_1 \times \ldots \times U_k$ in $\mathbb{R}^M$ represents the <u>composite control</u> acting upon the system. If convenient we may also use the i-th component of such composite control namely $h_i(t) = (h^1_i(t),\ldots, h^k_i(t))$ in $\mathbb{R}^k$. The dynamics of the harvested growth of the mentioned production or consumption is defined by the system

$$\dot{x}_i = f_i(x, t) - \sum_\sigma h^\sigma_i, \quad i=1,\ldots, N. \tag{1}$$

In particular $f_i(x,t) = f_{ii}(x_i) + \Sigma_j f_{ij}(x_i, x_j, t)$, $j=1,\ldots, N$, $j \neq i$, where f_{ii} is the rate of growth for the resource i and f_{ij} represents the interaction (diffusion) between the resources i and j, $j \neq i$. The functions $f_1,\ldots, f_N$, $(f_1,\ldots, f_N)^T = f$, must secure unique solution $x(x_o, t_o,.) : J'_o \to \Delta_x$ through each $(x^o, t_o) \in \Delta_x \times R$, $x^o = x(t_o)$.

The interpretation of (1) is two-fold: <u>either</u> the resource i grows (is produced) and then is harvested (used, sold) for the benefit of the players <u>or</u> the consumption of this resource grows and is 'harvested' by supplies produced by the players. The first case will be called <u>harvested production</u>, the second <u>supplied consumption</u>. Obviously in each case there are different applications of the system (1). As an example of the harvested production we may quote the bio-economic model of fishery (see Clark, 1976), with several types of fish growing in the ocean and a set of harvesting vessels which compete for the highest profit or at least to catch enough to stay in the market. More generally the same applies to management of any renewable resource (see Vincent-Skowronski, 1980) like forestry, agriculture, etc. Examples typical for the supplied consumption case are obtainable when modelling the market situation created by the demand of various population groups for water, electricity, coal, oil, housing, and medical service 'harvested' by supplies from the corresponding industries which compete in the market (see Chapter 4, this volume). The shape of the functions f_i (or f_{ii}, f_{ij}) depends upon the interpretation of (1). In harvested production they may represent logistic growth and be of the Lotka-Volterra type, etc. In the case of supplied consumption they will be represented by any form of population growth reduced by some dependence on prices and a level of income of such population.

In what follows we concentrate on harvested production. The adjustment of our discussion to supplied consumption is almost immediate. With this comment, let $p_i(t) > 0$, $t \in J_0^t$ be the price of the resource i, generating the price vector, $p(t) = (p_1(t), \ldots, p_N(t)) \in \mathbf{R}_+^N$. When the system studied is considered predictive, the prices may not be assumed known (monitored) but must come from the market dynamics. The market dynamics corresponding to (1) is determined by the demand equations

$$\dot{p} = D_i(p, t, h_i), \quad i=1, \ldots, N. \tag{2}$$

Given h, the functions D_i must secure unique solution $p(p^o, t_o, h, \cdot) : J_o 85/f \to \Delta_p$ to (2) through each $(p^o, t_o) \in \Delta_p \times \mathbf{R}$, $p^o = p(t_o)$, where Δ_p in $\mathbf{R}^N$ is the set that adjoins the playing region Δ_x in $\mathbf{R}^N$. The functions D_i represent the <u>excess demand</u> over a given supply on the market. In our harvested production case the demand for the resource i may be specified as a function of the prices and a time dependent income, monotone decreasing in p. Let us define it by $d_i(p, t)$, $t \in J_o^t$, $(d_1, \ldots, d_N)^T = d$. Consequently (2) becomes

$$\dot{p}_i = d_i(p, t,) - \sum_\sigma h_i^\sigma, \quad i=1, \ldots, N. \tag{2}'$$

In more particular terms than (1), the dynamic game approach has already been applied to the harvested growth problem (see Clark, 1976), taking the price as a known constant. Independently, the oligopolistic market dynamics generalized by (2), has been investigated with the use of differential games (see Simaan-Takayama, 1976). The full study of the resource harvesting game requires that the choice of h must be adjusted to both (1) and (2) together.

The net revenue of the player σ is

$$f_0^\sigma(h) = \sum_i h_i^\sigma p_i(h_i, t) - \sum_i c_i^\sigma(h_i^\sigma) \tag{3}$$

where $c_i^\sigma(h_i 85/\sigma) \geq 0$ is the cost of harvesting the resource i by the player σ. Here $\Sigma_i\, h_i^\sigma p_i(h_i, t) = h^\sigma p(h,t)$: with $p(h,t)$ representing the solution to (2) through any$(p^\circ t_\circ)\; \varepsilon\; \Delta_p \times \mathbf{R}$. Below, the arguments will be dropped from under $p_i(h_i, t)$.

Then, given the initial x°, p°, $t_\circ$, the <u>profit flow</u> for the player δ at some $t\; \varepsilon\; J_o^\delta$ is defined by

$$\pi_\sigma(x^0, p^0, t_0, h, t) = \int_{t_0}^{t} e^{-\rho\tau}\, [\Sigma\, h_i^\sigma p_i - \Sigma\, c_i^\sigma(h_i^\sigma)]\, d\tau \tag{4}$$

where ρ is a suitable discount rate, $\rho > 0$. The profit flow (4) is <u>accumulative</u> on $[t_\circ, t]$ if

$$\pi_\sigma(x^0, t_0, h^\sigma, t) \geq \pi_\sigma(x^0, t_0, h^\sigma, t_0) ; \tag{5}$$

otherwise it is <u>dissipative</u>. We call the total revenue $h^\sigma p$ the <u>harvesting power</u> for the player σ and recognize it as a profit accumulation factor.

Consequently the cost c^σ represents the profit dissipation. In particular $c_i^\sigma(h_i^\sigma)$ may be assumed linearly dependent upon the harvest

$$c_i^\sigma(h_i^\sigma) = \hat{c}_i^\sigma h_i^\sigma \; ; \; i=1,\ldots,N \tag{6}$$

where $\hat{c}_i^\sigma$ = constant is a given constant coefficient (\$/harvesting unit) for the cost of materials, machinery and labour associated with harvesting of the resource i by the player σ. In general $c_i^\sigma(h_i^\sigma)$ might also include such adjustable terms as a fixed overhead administration cost, additional cost connected with harvesting capacity depending upon $(h_i^\sigma)^2$, and other costs.

The choice of h^σ by the player σ is feedback programmed by the strategies

$$h_i^\sigma(t) = E_i^\sigma(x_i)\, x_i, \; i=1, \ldots, N \tag{7}$$

where $E_i^\sigma(x_i) > 0$ is the <u>harvesting effort</u> applied to the resource i to be chosen by the player σ. Note that this player does not know the efforts of his competitors. Consequently in (1) and (2)', for each σ we have $h_i^\sigma = E_i^\sigma(x_i)\, x_i$, $i=1, \ldots, N$, but $h_i^\nu(t)$ $\varepsilon\; U_\nu$, $\nu=1, \ldots, k$, $\nu \neq \sigma$, remain <u>open-loop</u> controls. This corresponds to the mode of play called the <u>game against nature</u>. Note moreover that substituting (7) into (2) makes the market dynamics dependent on x.

On the other hand the state information $x(t)$ is uncertain and is yet to be identified. The observation available to the player σ

is

$$y^\sigma(t) = g^\sigma(x, t) + w(t), \quad t \in J_o^f \qquad (8)$$

where $y^\sigma(t) \in \mathbf{R}^n$, $n \leq N$, is a <u>read-out</u> vector and $w(t) \in W$ in $\mathbf{R}^s$ is the <u>measurement noise</u>, with W being a <u>known compact set</u>. The functions g^σ are continuously differentiable and such that (8) cannot in general be solved for x. In particular $y^\sigma(t)$ may be represented by a triple of the observable components of $x(t)$. It is assumed that each player knows only his own read-out vector.

Now introduce (6) into (3), then substitute (7) and require that each i-component of the net revenue (3) be non-negative and bounded above by a given constant $\kappa_i^\sigma > 0$ estimating the physical ability of the player σ to harvest the resource i. We obtain

$$0 \leq E_i^\sigma (x_i) \, x_i \, (p_i - c_i^\sigma) \leq \kappa_i^\sigma, \quad i=1, \ldots, N \qquad (9)$$

which defines the <u>target set</u> $\theta_\sigma \subset \Delta$ in $\mathbf{R}^{2N}$, $\Delta := \Delta_x \times \Delta_p$, for the player σ.

The player σ knows the functions f_i, d_i, c_i^σ, the discount rate ρ, the constraint sets Δ, U_1, ..., U_k, and his noisy read-out $y^\sigma(t)$, $t \in J^f_o$. He tries to <u>identify</u> $x(t)$, $p(t)$ in order to gain information, at the same time choosing $E_1^\sigma, \ldots, E_N^\sigma$, ($E_1^\sigma, \ldots, E_N^\sigma$) = E^σ, to attain the following game objectives, no matter what the other players may do within their U_ν, $\nu \neq \sigma$.
<u>Qualitative objectives</u>: the solutions of (1), (2)' should reach θ_σ in suitable time and stay there permanently.
<u>Quantitative (optimal) objective</u>: the pay-off (4) should be maximized along these solutions.

To provide tools for the identification and the objectives, the theory of nonlinear dynamic observers will be used together with the Liapunov formalism (see Skowronski, 1981).

The subsets Δ_σ in Δ of the initial $x^o = x(t_o)$, $p^o = p(t_o)$, where the above objectives may be achieved are fundamental to the solution of the game and must be determined.

OBSERVABILITY AND PLAYABILITIES

The theory of dynamic adaptive observers (see Luenberger, 1964) would assume $x(t)$, $p(t)$ in the system (1), (2)' as given. Then the natural process of observation built in any living organism is followed. The problem is to design a certain <u>image</u> of (1), (2)' i.e. an auxiliary model called <u>observer</u> (predictor, estimator) with known states from Δ. Then we adjust this observer adaptively (on-line) to make sure that its solutions converge to those of the system (1), (2)' in suitable time with suitable accuracy. In the case of a game each player must build himself his own observer based upon independent observations $y^\sigma(t)$, $t \in J^f_o$. Luenberger (1969) used the observer theory for linear games. The adjustment of this theory to general nonlinear harvested system has been proposed by Skowronski (1981) and to a nonlinear zero-sum game by Galperin-Skowronski (1984). We adopt this approach here to the case of a Nash competitive game of resource harvesting and marketing.

We let the model designed by the player σ be

$$\dot{z}_i^\sigma = f_i^\sigma(z^\sigma, t, y^\sigma) - \sum_{\mu=1}^{k} h_i^\mu(t)$$

$$\dot{q}_i^\sigma = d_i^\sigma(q^\sigma,t) - \sum_{\mu=1}^{k} h_i^\mu(t), \; i=1, \ldots, N \quad (10)$$

where $z^\sigma(t) \; \varepsilon \; \Delta_x$, $q^\sigma(t) \; \varepsilon \; \Delta_p$, $t \; \varepsilon \; J'_o$ are <u>known</u> vectors, $f_1^\sigma, \ldots, f_N^\sigma, (f_1^\sigma, \ldots, f_N^\sigma)^T = f^\sigma$ and $d_1^\sigma, \ldots, d_N^\sigma$, $(d_1^\sigma, \ldots, d^\sigma 76/N)^T = d^\sigma$ are <u>known</u> functions, at least Lipshitz continuous and such as to satisfy the definitions introduced in this Section. Moreover $h_i^\sigma = E_i^\sigma (z_i^\sigma) z_i^\sigma$, $i=1, \ldots, N$, while $h_i^\nu(t) \; \varepsilon \; U_\nu$ for all $\nu \neq \sigma$.

We introduce the vectors $(x(t), p(t), z^\sigma(t), q^\sigma(t^\sigma))^T = z^\sigma(t) \; \varepsilon \; \Delta \times \Delta = \Delta^2$ in $\mathbb{R}^{4N}$, and designate

$$F^\sigma (z^\sigma, t, y^\sigma, h^1, \ldots, h^k) = \begin{Bmatrix} f(x,t) - \Sigma h^\sigma \\ \sigma \\ d(p,t) - \Sigma h^\sigma \\ \sigma \\ f^\sigma(z^\sigma,t,y^\sigma) - \Sigma h^\sigma \\ \sigma \\ d^\sigma(q^\sigma,t) - \Sigma h^\sigma \\ \sigma \end{Bmatrix} \quad (11)$$

Then we may form the <u>product system</u>

$$\dot{z}^\sigma = F^\sigma(z^\sigma, t, y^\sigma, h^1, \ldots, h^k), \quad (12)$$

for each player $\sigma = 1, \ldots, k$. The control $h^\sigma(t)$ is chosen by the strategies (7) with suitable E^σ <u>against all</u> $h^\nu(t) \; \varepsilon \; U_\nu$, $\nu = 1, \ldots, k, \; \nu \neq \sigma$, and the noise in (8). This transforms (12) into the generalized (<u>contingent</u>) equation

$$\dot{z}^\sigma \; \varepsilon \; \mathbf{F}^\sigma (z^\sigma, t) \quad (13)$$

where $\mathbf{F}^\sigma(z^\sigma,t) = \{F^\sigma(z^\sigma, t, y^\sigma, h^1, \ldots, h^k) \; | \; w \; \varepsilon \; W, \; h^\nu \; \varepsilon \; U_\nu, \; \nu \neq \sigma\}$. Denote $z^{\sigma o} = z^\sigma(t_o)$. For suitable functions f, f^σ, d, d^σ and $E_1^\sigma, \ldots, E_N^\sigma$ given $(z^{\sigma o}, t_o,.) \; \varepsilon \; \Delta^2 R$, there exist absolutely continuous solutions $k_o(z^{\sigma o}, t_o,.): \; J'_o \to \Delta^2$ satisfying (13) for almost all $t \; \varepsilon \; J'$, and conversely there are measurable $h^\sigma : J'_o \to U_\sigma, \; \sigma = 1, \ldots, k$, such that $k(t) = F^\sigma(k_o(t), t, y^\sigma, h^1, \ldots, h^k)$ for all $t \; \varepsilon \; J'_o$, (see Filippov, 1971). The corresponding functions $f, f^\sigma, d, d^\sigma, E^\sigma$ are called <u>admissible</u>. Consequently to the above, given $h^\sigma(\cdot)$ generated by an admissible E^σ we may identify the corresponding $k_\sigma(z^\infty, t_o, \cdot)$ with a solution of (12) through the same (z^∞, t_o). We designate the class of such solutions by $K_\sigma(z^\infty, t_o)$.

Now let us split $z^\sigma(t)$ into two vectors $z^\sigma(t) = (\xi(t), \zeta^\sigma(t))^T$, with $\xi(t) = (x(t), p(t))^T \varepsilon \Delta$ and $\zeta^\sigma(t) = (z^\sigma(t), q^\sigma(t))^T \varepsilon \Delta$, and then define the diagonal sets

$$M^\sigma = \{z^\sigma(t) \varepsilon \Delta^2 \mid \|\zeta^\sigma(t) - \xi(t)\| = 0, \forall t\}$$

where $\|\cdot\|$ designates any norm in R^{4n}. Moreover, given $\eta^\sigma > 0$, we define the η^σ-neighbourhood, of M^σ : $M^\sigma_\eta = \{z^\sigma(t)\varepsilon\Delta^2 \mid \|\zeta^\sigma(t) - \xi(t)\| < \eta^\sigma, \forall t\}$.

Suppose now that Δ_σ in Δ is a set selected a-priori (or to be determined a-posteriori) by some player σ. Denote $\Delta_\sigma \times \Delta_\sigma = \Delta^2_\sigma$ and let $M^\sigma = M^\sigma \cap \Delta^2_\sigma$, $M^\sigma_\eta = M^\sigma_\eta \cap \Delta^2_\sigma$.

Definition 2.1. A model (10) is an observer on Δ_σ for the player σ with accuracy η^σ (briefly, η^σ-observer on Δ_σ) if given $\eta^\sigma > 0$ there are admissible f^σ, d^σ, E^σ and a constant $T_\eta > 0$ such that for each $k_\sigma(\cdot) \varepsilon K_\sigma(z^\infty, t_o)$ we have

$$k(z^{\sigma o}, t_o, t) \varepsilon M^\sigma_\eta, \quad t \varepsilon [t_o + T_\eta, t_f] \qquad (14)$$

for all $(z^\infty, t_o) \varepsilon \Delta^2_\sigma \times R$.

Now denote $\theta^2_\sigma = \theta_\sigma \times \theta_\sigma$, $\theta^2_{\eta\sigma} = M^\sigma_\eta \theta^2_\sigma$.

Definition 2.2. An η^σ-observer is <u>playable</u> on Δ_σ <u>for capture</u> in θ_σ in Δ_σ, if the effort E^σ of Def. 2.1 is such that for some $T_c > T_\eta$, every $k_\sigma(\cdot) \varepsilon K_\sigma(z^\infty, t_o)$ yields

$$k(z^{\sigma o}, t_o, t) \varepsilon \theta^2_{\eta\sigma}, \quad t \varepsilon [t_o + T_c, t_f], \qquad (15)$$

for all $(z^\infty, t_o) \varepsilon \Delta^2_\sigma \times R$ (see Skowronski-Vincent, 1982).

As mentioned, the sets Δ_σ of the above definitions are fundamental to the solution of our game. Their union consisting of all (x^o, p^o) where from the objective concerned is available is called the <u>region</u> of η^σ-observability or playability, respectively. Such a region may be determined by an <u>a-posteriori</u> calculation, a task which is difficult. Alternatively, a far more practical method may be used. One may introduce <u>candidates</u> for Δ_σ either <u>required a-priori</u> by physical demand or calculated from, say, necessary conditions for the objective concerned. Then these candidates must be checked against sufficient conditions for this objective.

SUFFICIENT CONDITIONS

Consider a candidate set Δ_σ in Δ generating Δ^2_σ and let $N(\partial\Delta^2_\sigma)$ be a neighbourhood its boundary. Denote $N^\sigma_\varepsilon = N(\partial\Delta^2_\sigma)\Delta^2_\sigma$, $CM^\sigma_\eta = \Delta^2_\sigma - M^\sigma_\eta$ and let S^σ_η (open) enclose CM^σ_η. Moreover introduce two test C^1-functions $V_s : N^\sigma_\varepsilon \times R \to R$ and $V_\eta : S^\sigma_\eta \times R \to R$

Competitive Differential Game

and define

$$v_s = \inf V_s(z^\sigma, t) \mid (z^\sigma, t) \; \varepsilon \; \partial\Delta_\sigma^2 \times R \; ;$$

$$v_\eta^- = \inf V_\eta(z^\sigma, t) \mid (z^\sigma, t) \; \varepsilon \; (\partial M_\eta^\sigma \cap CM_\eta^\sigma) \times R \; ;$$

$$v_\eta^+ = \sup V_\eta(z^\sigma, t) \mid (z^\sigma, t) \; \varepsilon \; (\partial\Delta_\sigma^2 \cap \overline{CM_\eta^\sigma}) \times R \; .$$

Theorem 3.1. Given Δ_σ, η^σ, the model (10) is an η^σ-observer on Δ_σ if there are admissible f^σ, d^σ, E^σ and two functions V_s, V_η such that

(i) $\quad V_s(z^\sigma, t) \; v_s \; ;$ (16)

(ii) $\quad \dfrac{\partial V_s}{\partial t} + \nabla_{z^\sigma} V_s(z^\sigma, t) \cdot F^\sigma(z^\sigma, t, y^\sigma, h^\sigma, h^\nu) < 0 \; ,$

for all $h^\nu \; \varepsilon \; U_\nu$, $\nu \neq \sigma$ and all $w \; \varepsilon \; W \; ;$

(iii) $\quad v_\eta^- \leq V_\eta(z^\sigma, t) \leq v_\eta^+ \; ;$

(iv) there is a constant $c > 0$ such that (17)

$$\dfrac{\partial V_\eta}{\partial t} + \nabla_{z^\sigma} V_\eta(z^\sigma, t) \cdot F^\sigma(z^\sigma, t, y^\sigma, h^\sigma, h^\nu) \leq -c$$

for all $h^\nu \; \varepsilon \; U_\nu$, $\nu \neq \sigma$ and all $w \; \varepsilon \; W$.

Proof. The solutions may not leave Δ_σ^2 unless through N_ε^σ, so we consider $k_\sigma(\cdot) \; \varepsilon \; K_\sigma(z^\infty, t_0)$, $(z^\infty, t_0) \; \varepsilon \; N_\varepsilon^\sigma \times R$, and suppose it crosses $\partial\Delta_\sigma^2$. Then there is $t_1 \geq t_0$ such that $k_\sigma(t_1) \; \varepsilon \; \partial\Delta^2 \;_\sigma$ and by (i) we have $V_s(k_\sigma(t_1), t_1) \geq v_s \geq V_s(k_\sigma(t_0), t_0)$ contradicting (ii). Hence no solution of K_σ leaves Δ_σ^2.

We shall show now that solutions from $\overline{CM_\eta^\sigma}$ may not stay in this set permanently. Indeed, consider $k_\sigma(\cdot) \; \varepsilon \; K_\sigma(z^\infty, t_0)$, $(z^\infty, t_0) \; \varepsilon \; \overline{CM_\eta^\sigma} \times R$. By (iv), $V_\eta(k_\sigma(t), t) \leq -c$. Integrating along $[t_0, t]$ we obtain the estimate

$$t \leq t_0 + \dfrac{1}{c} [V_\eta(z^{\sigma 0}, t_0) - V_\eta(z^\sigma, t)]. \qquad (18)$$

Note that $v_\eta^+ - v_\eta^- > 0$ estimates the diameter of CM_η^σ. By (iii) such values exist and we have

$$V_\eta(z^\sigma, t) - v_\sigma^- \geq 0, \; V_\eta(z^{\sigma 0}, t_0) - v_\eta^+ \leq 0$$

whence $V_\eta(z^\infty, t_0) - V(z^\sigma, t) \leq v_\eta^+ - v_\eta^-$ which allows us to rewrite (18) as $t \leq t_0 + \dfrac{1}{c}(v_\eta^+ - v_\eta^-)$. Hence there is

$$T_\eta = (v_\eta^+ - v_\eta^-)/c. \qquad (19)$$

93

depending upon the diameter of $\overline{CM_q^\sigma}$ and c but nothing else, such that for $t \geq t_o + T_\eta$, the solution must be out of $\overline{CM_q^\sigma}$. It may not leave Δ_σ^2, whence it must enter M_q^σ. There is no return to $\overline{CM_q^\sigma}$. Indeed, if there were $t_2 > t = t_o + T_\eta$ such that $k_\sigma(t_2) \in \overline{CM_q^\sigma}$, then by (iii) $V_\eta(k_\sigma(t_2), t_2) \geq \bar{v}_\eta \geq V_\eta(k_\sigma(t_\eta), t_\eta)$ contradicting (iv). Since the above applies to all solutions from K_σ the Definition 2.1 holds, QED. Note that T_η may be calculated from (19). Suppose now that T_η is given a-priori. We then have

Corollary 3.1: Given Δ_σ and η^σ, $T_\eta > 0$, the model (10) is an η^σ-observer on Δ_σ <u>compatible after</u> T_η, if the conditions of Theorem 4.1 hold with

$$c = (v_\eta^+ - v_\eta^-)/T_\eta.$$

Now let $C\theta_\sigma^2 = \Delta_\sigma^2 - \theta_\sigma^2$, S_σ^σ (open) $\supset \overline{C\theta_\sigma^2}$ and consider the test C^1-function V_θ : $S_\sigma^\sigma \times \mathbb{R} \to \mathbb{R}$ with

$$v_\theta^- = \inf V_\theta(z^\sigma, t) \mid (z^\sigma, t) \in \partial\theta_\sigma^2 \times \mathbb{R} ;$$

$$v_\theta^+ = \inf V_\theta(z^\sigma, t) \mid (z^\sigma, t) \in \partial\theta_\sigma^2 \times \mathbb{R} .$$

Theorem 3.2. Given Δ_σ, η^σ and θ_σ in Δ_σ, the model (10) is an η^σ-observer playable on Δ_σ for capture in θ_σ if there are admissible f^σ, d^σ, E^σ and two functions V_θ, V_η (V_η as in Theorem 3.1) such that

(i) $v_\theta^- \leq V_\theta(z^\sigma, t) \leq v_\theta^+$

(ii) there is a constant $c_1 > 0$ such that

$$\frac{\partial V_\theta}{\partial t} + {}_{z\sigma}V_\theta(z^\sigma,t).F^\sigma(z^\sigma,t,y^\sigma,h^\sigma,h^\nu) \leq -c_1 \quad (20)$$

for all $h^\nu \in U_\nu$, $\nu \neq \sigma$ and all $w \in W$;

(iii) $v_\eta^- \leq V_\eta(z^\sigma,t) \leq v_\eta^+$;

(iv) there is a constant $c_2 > 0$ such that

$$\frac{\partial V_\eta}{\partial t} + {}_{z\sigma}V_\eta(z^\sigma,t).F^\sigma(z^\sigma,t,y^\sigma,h^\sigma,h^\nu) \leq -c_2 \quad (21)$$

for all $h^\nu \in U_\nu$, $\nu \neq \sigma$ and all $w \in W$.

<u>Proof.</u> Supppose some $k_\sigma(\cdot) \in K_\sigma(z^{\sigma o}, t_o)$, $(z^{\sigma o}, t_o) \in C\theta_\sigma^2 \times \mathbb{R}$ leaves this set i.e. crosses $\partial\Delta_\sigma^2$. Then there is $t_1 \geq t_o$ such that $k_\sigma(t_1) \in \partial\Delta_\sigma^2$ and by (i) we have $V_\theta(k_\sigma(t_1),t_1) \geq V_\theta^+ \geq V_\theta(k(t_0),t_0)$ contradicting (ii). Hence no solution leaves Δ_σ^2.

Competitive Differential Game

We will show now that no $k_\sigma(\cdot) \in K_\sigma(z^{\sigma 0}, t_0)$, $(z^{\sigma 0}, t_0) \in \overline{C\bar\theta}_\sigma^2$ x R can stay permanently in $\overline{C\bar\theta}_\sigma^2$. Indeed consider such solution. By (ii), $\dot V_\theta(z^\sigma, t) \leq -c_1$. Integrating along $[t_0, t]$ we obtain

$$t \leq t_0 + \frac{1}{c_1} V_\theta(z^{\sigma 0}, t_0) - V_\theta(z^\sigma, t). \tag{22}$$

By (i), $V_\theta(z^\sigma, t_1) \geq V_\theta^-$, $V_\theta(z^{\sigma 0}, t_0) \leq v_\theta^+$ whence $V_\theta(z^{\sigma 0}, t_0) - V_\theta(z^\sigma, t) \leq v_\theta^+ - v_\theta^-$ implying

$$t \leq t_0 + \frac{1}{c_1}(v_\theta^+ - v_\theta^-).$$

Hence there is $T_\theta = (V_\theta^+ - V_\theta^-)/c_1$ such that for $t \geq t_0 + T_\theta$ the solution must be outside $\overline{C\theta_\sigma^2}$. As it must not leave Δ_σ^2, it must enter θ_σ^2.

There is no return to $\overline{C\theta_\sigma^2}$. Indeed, if there were $t_2 \geq t_\theta = t_0 + T_\theta$ such that $k_\sigma(t_2) \in C\theta_\sigma^2$ then by (i), $V_\theta(k(t_2) t_2) \geq v_\theta^- \geq V_\theta(k(t_\theta), t_\theta)$ which contradicts (ii). The above holds for any $k_\sigma(\cdot)$ in K_σ, hence all solutions enter θ_σ^2 after t_θ and stay there permanently.

On the other hand comparing (i)-(iv) with the corresponding conditions of Theorem 3.1, from the proof of Theorem 3.1, we conclude that all solutions of $K_\sigma(z^\infty, t_0)$, $(z^\infty, t_0) \in \Delta^2_\sigma$ x R, enter M^σ_η after $t_0 + T_\eta$ and stay there. Hence, there is $T_c = \max(T_\theta, T_\eta)$ such that for $t \geq t_0 + T_c$ all $k_\sigma(\cdot) \in K_\sigma(z^\infty, t_0)$, $(z^\infty, t_0) \in \Delta^2_\sigma$ x R, stay in $\theta^2_\sigma = M^\sigma_\eta \theta^2_\sigma$, QED.

Note that we may calculate

$$T_c = \max(T_\theta, T_\eta), \quad T_\theta = \frac{1}{c_1}(v_\theta^+ - v_\theta^-), \quad T_\eta = \frac{1}{c_2}(v_\eta^+ - v_\eta^-) \tag{23}$$

Suppose now that T_θ, T_η are given a-priori. We have
<u>Corollary 3.2</u>: Given Δ_σ, η^σ, θ_σ, T_θ, T_η, the model (10) is an η^σ-observer playable on Δ_σ for capture in θ_σ after the time $T_c = \max(T_\theta, T_\eta)$, if Theorem 4.2 holds with

$$c_1 = \frac{v_\theta^+ - v_\theta^-}{T_\theta}, \quad c_2 = \frac{v_\eta^+ - v_\eta^-}{T_\eta}. \tag{24}$$

IMPLEMENTATION OF THE CONDITIONS

Let us now discuss the implementation of the sufficient conditions, in particular Theorem 3.2. We write (1), (2)' again

Competitive Differential Game

$$\begin{aligned}\dot{x} &= f_i(x,t) - \sum_\sigma h_i^\sigma, \\ \dot{p}_i &= d_i(p,t) - \sum_\sigma h_i^\sigma, \quad i=1,\ldots,N.\end{aligned} \tag{25}$$

Suppose that the case study considered allows us to subtract from $f_i(x,t)$ and $d_i(p,t)$ the <u>storage interactions</u> between the resources (stock) and prices concerned i.e. the functions $\Psi_i^R(x)$, $\Psi_i^P(p)$ respectively (this in general is always possible), such that the system

$$\begin{aligned}\dot{x}_i &= \Psi_i^R(x), \\ \dot{p}_i &= \Psi_i^P(p), \quad i=1,\ldots,N\end{aligned} \tag{26}$$

has a first integral $H(x,p) = $ constant, i.e.

$$\nabla_\xi H(\xi)\cdot\Psi(\xi) = 0 \tag{27}$$

where $\Psi(\xi) = (\Psi_1^R(x),\ldots,\Psi_N^R(x),\Psi_1^P(p),\ldots,\Psi_N^P(p))^T$ and (25) obtains the Hamiltonian form

$$\begin{aligned}\dot{x}_i &= \frac{\partial H}{\partial p_i} + \phi_i^R(x,t) - \sum_\sigma h_i^\sigma, \\ \dot{p}_i &= -\frac{\partial H}{\partial x_i} + \phi_i^P(p,t) - \sum_\sigma h_i^\sigma, \\ & \quad i=1,\ldots,N\end{aligned} \tag{28}$$

where

$$\phi_i^R(x,t) = f_i(x,t) - \Psi_i^R(x),$$

$$\phi_i^P(p,t) = d_i(p,t) - \Psi_i^P(p),$$

represent the <u>net-growth</u> (non-storage) influences upon the growth rate of the resource i, while $\sum_\sigma h_i^\sigma$ represents the <u>resultant harvest</u> of this resource.

The function H is a <u>storage function</u>. Conservation of its values, i.e. (27), produces the <u>balanced growth</u> (26) i.e. steady-state growth-harvest relation preserving $H(x,p)$ at the initial conditions level $H(x^0,p^0)$. The continuous family of such levels $H(\xi) = $ constant $= H_c \in [0, H_\Delta] \subset \mathbf{R}$, $H_\Delta = \sup H(\xi)$, $\xi \in \Delta$, forms a smooth surface above Δ. The extrema of such a surface coincide by definition with the equilibria of (26) and it is reasonable to take the H-levels as a reference frame for the unbalanced growth (28). We consider successively the minima of $H(x,p)$, possibly shifting the origin of $\mathbf{R}^N$ there, and assume Ψ^R_i, Ψ^P_i such that H is monotone increasing in the neighbourhood of each minimum. Taking the time derivative of H along a solution, in view of (27) we obtain

Competitive Differential Game

$$\dot{H}(\xi(t)) = \sum_i \frac{\partial H}{\partial x_i} \phi_i^R(x,t) + \sum_i \frac{\partial H}{\partial p_i} \phi_i^p(p,t)$$
$$- \sum_i \left[\sum_\sigma h_i \left(\frac{\partial H}{\partial x_i} + \frac{\partial H}{\partial p_i}\right)\right] ,$$
(29)

with all the components of gradient $H(\xi)$ positive in view of the monotonicity of H about the origin. Choosing the same function H for the observers, we write again

$$\dot{H}(\zeta^\sigma(t)) = \sum_i \frac{\partial H}{\partial z_i^\sigma} \phi_i^R(z_i^\sigma,t) + \sum_i \frac{\partial H}{\partial q_i^\sigma} \phi^p(q^\sigma,t)$$
$$- \sum_i \left[\sum_\sigma h_i^\sigma \left(\frac{\partial H}{\partial z_i^\sigma} + \frac{\partial H}{\partial q^\sigma}\right)\right] ,$$
(30)

The natural candidate for V_s is

$$V_s(z^\sigma,t) = H(\xi) + H(\zeta^\sigma) \tag{31}$$

yielding

$$\dot{V}(z^\sigma, t) = \dot{H}(\xi(t)) + \dot{H}(\xi^\sigma) ,$$

with (30), (31) substituted. As the partial derivatives of H are positive for the system and the observers, the sign of $\dot{V}_s(t)$ obviously depends upon the balance between the net growth and the resultant harvest for each resource. The latter makes a clear physical sense. Requiring (16) i.e. $\dot{V}(t) < 0$, we may obtain from (28), (29) and (30) conditions specifying $\Sigma_\sigma h_i^\sigma$, $i=1,\ldots,N$. Further conclusions must obviously be left to case studies. In quite the same fashion we may design and discuss the function V_θ and its $\dot{V}_\theta(z^\sigma(t),t)$.

Similarly, the natural candidate for V_η is

$$V_\eta(z^\sigma,t) = |H(\xi) - H(\zeta^\sigma)| = |\delta H(z^\sigma)| , \tag{31}'$$

yielding

$$\dot{V}_\eta(z^\sigma(t),t) = \frac{d}{dt} |\delta H(z^\sigma(t))|.$$

Since M^σ in M^σ_η, for any $z^\sigma(t) \in CM_\eta$ we must have $\delta H(z^\sigma(t)) \neq 0$ for all $t \in J_0^t$, i.e. this difference never crosses zero. Thus, choosing $z^{\sigma 0} \in CM_\eta$ we decide upon the sign of $\delta H(z^\sigma(t))$. Let us focus attention on $\delta H(z^\sigma(t)) > 0$, $t \in J_0^t$. Then

$$\dot{V}_\eta(z^\sigma(t),t) = \dot{H}(\xi^\sigma(t)) - \dot{H}(\xi(t)) ,$$

and substituting (30), (31) we have

97

Competitive Differential Game

$$\dot{V}_\eta(z^\sigma(t),t) = \sum_i \left[\frac{\partial H}{\partial z_i^\sigma} \phi_i^R(z_i^\sigma,t) - \frac{\partial H}{\partial x_i^\sigma} \phi_i^R(x,t)\right]$$
$$+ \sum_i \left[\frac{\partial H}{\partial q_i^\sigma} \phi_i^p(q^\sigma,t) - \frac{\partial H}{\partial p_i} \phi_p^\sigma(p,t)\right]$$

in view of

$\frac{\partial H}{\partial z_i^\sigma} = \frac{\partial H}{\partial x_i}$, $\frac{\partial H}{\partial q_i^\sigma} = \frac{\partial H}{\partial p_i}$, by design of H.

This clearly makes the derivative dependent upon the net-growth balance between the system and its observer. Again any further conclusions must be left to the case studies.

Most of the time, function H will be obvious. This refers particularly to the cases where the direct (without uncertainty) stability problems have been already solved via the Lyapunov Method and we know the Lyapunov function for such solutions. Then we do not need to seek the first integral H at all. The functions $H(\xi)$, $H(\zeta^\sigma)$ of (31), (31)' are the Liapnunov function in question taken successively in terms of the system (1), (2)' and the model (10). The observability problem is solved immediately by applying (31), (31)' as specified. For instance this is the case with f_{ii}, f_{ij} of (1), (2)' formed in terms of the known Lotka-Volterra growth functions. Here the test function is the well established Volterra function (see Kerner, 1957), which is the Lyapunov function for the case.

COMPARISON WITH LUENBERGER OBSERVER

It seems interesting to compare our method with those for linear observability. We choose Luenberger observers (see Luenberger, 1964). Let (1), (2) be given as

$$\dot{\xi} = A\xi + \sum_\sigma h^\sigma \qquad (32)$$

with A as a given N x N matrix, and let the observations be obtained as

$$y^\sigma = G^\sigma \xi \qquad (33)$$

where G^σ is a n x N constant matrix. Suppose each player σ chooses the Luenberger model

$$\dot{\zeta}^\sigma = (A-K^\sigma G^\sigma)\zeta^\sigma + K^\sigma y^\sigma + \sum_\sigma h^\sigma, \qquad (34)$$

where K^σ is some constant N x n matrix to be designed by the player σ. We want to concentrate on comparing observers rather than on achieving the objectives, hence we shall use Theorem 3.1 only, and assume the strategies already chosen and h^ν given. Substituting (33) into (34) and subtracting (32) we obtain

$$\dot{\zeta}^\sigma - \dot{\xi} = (A - K^\sigma G^\sigma)(\zeta^\sigma - \xi) .\qquad(35)$$

If the eigenvalues of $(A - K^\sigma G^\sigma)$ have negative real parts, then $(\zeta^\sigma - \xi) \to 0$ at a certain exponential rate as $t \to \infty$. The 'more negative' these real parts are the faster the rate becomes. To obtain the desired accuracy of the approximation it remains to propose a suitable K^σ.

In order to compare the above with our method we let (10) be specified by (34) and use Theorem 4.1. Suppose $||\cdot||$ is a norm in R^m and let Δ_σ^2 be defined in terms of such norm: $\Delta_\sigma^2 = \{z^\sigma \varepsilon \Delta^2 | \ ||z^\sigma|| < \alpha\}$ for some $\alpha > 0$. Then choosing $V_*(z^\sigma, t) = ||z^\sigma||$, we have the condition (i) satisfied automatically. The fact that the solutions are bounded (stabilized) in Δ_σ^2 is part of the objectives - considered assumed. Then with the chosen V_* the condition (ii) holds as well. Now we want to check upon (iii), (iv) yielding the observability. We let $V_\eta = (\zeta^\sigma - \xi)^T(\zeta^\sigma - \xi)$, satisfying (iii). Then also

$$\dot{V}_\eta = (\dot{\zeta}^\sigma - \dot{\xi})^T(\zeta^\sigma - \xi) + (\zeta^\sigma - \xi)^T(\dot{\zeta}^\sigma - \dot{\xi}) \qquad(36)$$

Substituting into (35) we obtain

$$\dot{V}_\eta(k_\sigma(z^{\sigma 0}, t_0, t), t) = -(\zeta^\sigma - \xi)^T Q^\sigma (\zeta^\sigma - \xi) \qquad(37)$$

where $-Q^\sigma = (A - K^\sigma G^\sigma)^T + (A - K^\sigma G^\sigma)$. With the Luenberger K^σ's the matrices Q^σ become positive definite and thus (iv) is satisfied. This makes the Luenberger-type linear models our dynamic observers.

OPTIMAL PLAYABILITY

In the optimal game (i.e. the quantitative Nash equilibrium situation) feedback strategies of all the players are involved. Thus the state information must be correlated between players. This can be achieved by identifying the observers. To do this we need to consider the product system consisting of (1) and the models (10) for all $\sigma = 1, \ldots, k$. Letting $(\xi(t), \zeta^1(t), \ldots, \zeta^k(t))^T = z(t) \varepsilon \Delta^{k+1}$ in $R^{(k+1)N}$, $(y^1(t), \ldots, y^k(t)) = y(t) \varepsilon R^{km}$, $t \varepsilon J_0$ and

$$F(z,t,y,h) = \begin{bmatrix} f(x,t) - \sum_\sigma h^\sigma \\ d(p,t) - \sum_\sigma h^\sigma \\ f^1(z^1,t) - \sum_\sigma h^\sigma \\ d^1(q^1,t) - \sum_\sigma h^\sigma \\ \cdot \quad \cdot \quad \cdot \quad \cdot \quad \cdot \\ f^k(z^k,t) - \sum_\sigma h^\sigma \\ d^k(q^k,t) - \sum_\sigma h^\sigma \end{bmatrix} \quad (38)$$

we obtain

$$\dot{z} = F(z,t,y,h), \quad (39)$$

instead of (12) for all $\sigma=1,\ldots,k$. Subject to the strategies and noisy read-outs the system (39) becomes

$$\dot{z} \in \{F(z,t,y,E^1,\ldots,E^k) \mid w \in W\}, \quad (40)$$

with the Filippov solutions $k(z^0, t_0, \cdot) : J_0^f \to \Delta^{k+1}$, where $z^0 = z(t_0)$. We designate their family by $K(z_0, t_0, E^1, \ldots, E^k)$. The corresponding classes of admissible f, f^σ, d, d^σ, E coincide with such of (13). We introduce now the diagonal set $M = M^1 \times \ldots \times M^k$ and its η-neighbourhood $M_\eta = M^1_\eta \times \ldots \times M^k_\eta$, for $\eta = \eta^1 = \ldots = \eta_k$. Then also $M = \bar{M} \cap \Delta_\sigma^{k+1}$ and $M_\eta = \bar{M}_\eta \cap \Delta_\sigma^{k+1}$, where $\Delta_\sigma^{k+1} = \Delta_\sigma \times \ldots \times \Delta_\sigma$ in favour of the player σ.

<u>Definition 6.1</u>: The σ-family of models (10) is a set of k <u>optimal η-observers on</u> Δ_σ <u>during</u> $T_f > 0$, iff there are admissible f^σ, d^σ, E^σ, $\sigma=1,\ldots, k$, and a constant $T_\eta > 0$ such that

(i) for each $k(z^0, t_0, \cdot) \in K(z^0, t_0, E^1_*, \ldots, E^k_*)$,

$$k(z^0, t_0, t) \in M_\eta, \quad t \in [t_0 + T_\eta, t_0 + _\eta + T_f] \quad (41)$$

for all $(z^0, t_0) \in \Delta_\sigma^{k+1} \times R$;

(ii) for each $\sigma=1,\ldots, k$,

Competitive Differential Game

$$\left.\begin{array}{c}\sup_{k(\cdot)} \Pi_\sigma(\xi^o, t_o, E_*^1, \ldots, E_*^{\sigma-1}, E^\sigma, E_*^{\sigma+1}, \ldots, E_*^k) \\ \leq \sup_{k(\cdot)} \Pi(\xi^o, t_o, E_*^1, \ldots, E_*^k)\end{array}\right\} \quad (42)$$

for all admissible E^σ, and all $(z^o, t_o) \in \Delta_\sigma^{k+1} \times R$.
Denote $N_\epsilon = N(\partial \Delta_\sigma^{k+1}) \cap \Delta_\sigma^M$ and $CM_\eta = \Delta_\sigma^{k+1} - M_\sigma$. Then let $S_\eta(\text{open}) \supset \overline{CM_\eta}$, and introduce two C^1-functions $V_s : N_\epsilon \times R \to R$, $V_\eta : S_\eta \times R \to R$ with

$$v_s = \inf V_s(z, t) \mid (z, t) \in \partial \Delta_\sigma^{k+1} \times R ;$$

$$v^- = \inf V(z, t) \mid (z, t) \in (\partial M_\eta \cap CM_\eta) \times R ;$$

$$v^+ = \sup V(z, t) \mid (z, t) \in (\partial \Delta_\sigma^{k+1} \cap \overline{CM_\eta}) \times R .$$

<u>Theorem 6.1:</u> Given Δ_σ, η the σ-family of models (10) is the set of optimal η-observers on Δ_σ during $T_f > 0$ if there are admissible f^σ, d^σ, E_*, $\sigma=1,\ldots,k$ and two functions V_*, V_η such that

(i) $V_s(z, t) \leq v_s$;

(ii) $\dfrac{\partial V_s}{\partial t} + \nabla V_s(z, t) \cdot F(z, t, y, E_*^1, \ldots, E_*^k) < 0 $, (43)

(iii) $\bar{v}_\eta \leq V_\eta(z, t) \leq v_\eta^+$;

(iv) $\left.\begin{array}{c}\dfrac{\partial V_\eta}{\partial t} + \nabla_z V_\eta(z,t) \cdot F(z,t,y,E^1,\ldots,E^{\sigma-1},E^\sigma,E^{\sigma+1},\ldots,E^k) \\ \leq - f_o^\sigma(E^1, \ldots, E^{\sigma-1}, E_*^\sigma, E^{\sigma+1}, \ldots, E^k)\end{array}\right\}$ (44)

for all E^ν, $\nu \neq \sigma$ and all $w \in W$;

(v) $\dfrac{\partial V_\eta}{\partial t} + \nabla_z V_\eta(z, t) \cdot F(z, t, y, E_*^1, \ldots, E_*^k) = 0$ (45)

for all $w \in W$.

<u>Proof:</u> By similar argument as in the proof of Theorem 3.1 the conditions (i), (ii) imply that no solution $k(z^o, t_o, \cdot) \in K(z^o, t_o, E^1, \ldots, E^k)$ from $(z^o, t_o) \in \Delta_i^{k+1} \times R$ may leave Δ_i^{k+1}. Note that f_o^σ are positive values. Replacing c by $f_o(E^1, \ldots, E^{\sigma-1}, E_*, E^{\sigma+1}, \ldots, E^k)$ in (17), by the same argument as in the proof of Theorem 3.1 the conditions (iii), (iv) imply the existence of

$$T_\eta = \frac{v_\eta^+ - v_\eta^-}{f_o} > 0$$

such that for $t \geq t_o + T_\eta$ the solutions $k(\cdot) \in K(z^o, t_o, E^1, \ldots, E^k)$ from CM_η must be permanently out of this set, and hence in M_η. This makes the models of (10) a collection of observers. We must now show that they are Nash optimal i.e. satisfy (42). Indeed, from (44) and (45) one obtains successively

$$\left. \begin{array}{l} f_o(E^1, \ldots, E^{\sigma-1}, E_*^\sigma, E^{\sigma+1}, \ldots, E^k) + \dfrac{\partial V_\eta}{\partial t} + \\ + \nabla_z V_\eta(z, t) F(z, t, y, E^1, \ldots, E^{\sigma-1}, E_*^\sigma, E^{\sigma+1}, \ldots, E^k) \\ = -p(t) \end{array} \right\} \quad (46)$$

for some $p(t) > 0$, $t \in [t_o, t_f]$ and

$$f_o(E_*^1, \ldots, E_*^k) + \frac{\partial V}{\partial t} + \nabla_z V_\eta(z,t) F(z,t,y,E_*^1, \ldots, E_*^k) = 0. \quad (47)$$

Integrating,

$$\int_{t_0}^{t_f} f_o(E^1, \ldots, E^{\sigma-1}, E_*^\sigma, E^{\sigma+1}, \ldots, E^k)\, dt +$$
$$V_\eta(z^o, t_o) - V\eta(z^f, t_f) + \int_{t_0}^{t_f} p(t)\, dt, \quad (48)$$

and

$$\int_{t_0}^{t_f} f_o(E_*^1, \ldots, E_*^k)\, dt = V_\eta(z^o, t_o) - V\eta(z^f, t_f), \quad (49)$$

where $z^f = z(t_f)$. The conditions (iv), (v) yield (44), (45) for all $k(\cdot)$ concerned, whence (42) follows directly from (48) and (49), QED.

Designate $\theta_\sigma^{k+1} = \theta_\sigma \times \ldots \times \theta_\sigma$ in Δ_σ^{k+1}, $\theta_{\eta\sigma}^{k+1} = M_\eta \cap \theta_\sigma^{k+1}$. Then comparing Definition 2.2 and Definition 6.1 it is seen immediately that the optimal η-observer is playable on Δ_σ for capture in θ_σ in Δ_σ provided the condition (41) is replaced by

$$k(z^o, t_o, t) \in \theta_{\eta\sigma}^{k+1}, \quad t \in [t_o + T_c, t_o + T_c + T_f] \quad (41)'$$

for all $(z^o, t_o) \in \Delta_\sigma^{k+1} \times R$. Since both M_η and $\theta_{\eta\sigma}^{k+1}$ are given a-priori the adjustment from M_η to $\theta_{\eta\sigma}^{k+1}$ is immediate and, accordingly modified, Definition 2.2 may be used. Similarly, by referring to $\theta_{\eta\sigma}^{k+1}$ in Theorem 6.1 instead of M_η we obtain conditions for playability for capture in θ_σ. Neither the form of this theorem nor its proof change.

REFERENCES

Clark, C.W. (1976) *Mathematical Bioeconomics*, Wiley, New York

Filippov, A.F. (1971) 'The Existence of Solutions of Generalised Differential Equations', *Mathematical Notes* (Matematicheskye Zametki), 10, 608-611

Galperin, E.A. and Skowronski, J.M. (1984) 'Playable Asymptotic Observers of Differential Games with Incomplete Information', Proceedings, Optimization Days, 23rd IEEE conf. on Decision-control, Las Vegas, 1984

Kerner, E.H. (1957) 'On Statistical Mechanics of Biological Associations', *Bulletin of Mathematical Biophysics* 19, 121

Lesse, P.F. and Skowronski, J.M. - Chapter 4, this volume

Luenberger, D.G. (1964) 'Observing the State of a Linear System', *IEEE Transactions on Military Electronics*, MIL-8, 74-80

Luenberger, D.G. and Rhodes, I.B. (1969) 'Differential Games with imperfect state information', *IEEE Transactions on Automatic Control*, AC-14, 29-38

Narendra, K.S. and Valavani, I.S. (1976) 'Stable Adaptive Observers and Controllers', *Proceedings of the IEEE*

Simaan, M.A. and Takayama, T (1976) 'Optimum Monopolist Control in Dynamic Market', *IEEE Transactions* SMC-6, 799-807

Skowronski, J.M. (1981) 'Adaptive identification of models stabilizing under uncertainty'. *Lecture Notes in Bio-mathematics*, Vol.40, Springer, Berlin, 64-78

Skowronski, J.M. and Vincent, T.L. (1982) 'Playability With and Without Capture', *Journal of Optimization Theory and Applications*, 36, 1

Vincent, T.L. and Skowronski, J.M. (eds.) (1980) *Renewable Resource Management*, Lecture Notes in Bio-mathematics, Vol.40, Springer, Berlin

Chapter Seven

IDENTIFICATION OF STOCK AND SYSTEM PARAMETERS IN A PARETO HARVESTING GAME OF TWO PLAYERS

Glen J. Crouch and Janislaw M. Skowronski

INTRODUCTION

We attempt stabilisation and Pareto optimisation (maximising the sum of profits) for the dynamic game of harvesting renewable resources (such as forestry, agriculture, fishery, water), with particular reference to fishery. The available amounts of the resources (or particular species of fish in the sea) are uncertain, and the carrying capacities of their growth are not known, but assumed bounded. The information on stock is available to the harvesters (players) in the form of noisy measurements. This information must be obtained together with values of the carrying capacities and diffusion coefficients before attempting the objectives. We propose to do the identification on-line using nonlinear (adaptive) dynamic identifiers (see Skowronski, 1981). The game is formalized in terms of two players but the extension to higher dimensions and more players is immediate.

STATEMENT OF THE PROBLEM

The dynamics of the harvested growth is given by the equations

$$\dot{x}_i = r_i x_i (1 - \frac{x_i}{K}) - s(x_i - x_j) - h_i^1(t) - h_i^2(t) \qquad (1)$$

$$i, j = 1, 2 \ , \ i \neq j,$$

where $x_i(t) > 0$, $t \in J'_o = [t_o, t_f]$ $\mathbb{R}$, $t_f < \infty$ is the <u>uncertain</u> stock of the <u>resource</u> i; r_i is the known intrinsic growth rate of i; $K = k_1 + k_2 = \text{const} \in [0, K_{max}]$ is the <u>uncertain carrying capacity</u> of both resources, $s = [0,1]$ is an <u>uncertain</u> diffusion coefficient between resources and $h_i^\sigma(t)$ is the rate of harvest of the resource i by the player $\sigma = 1, 2$. We shall also use the vectors $x(t) \triangleq (x_1(t), x_2(t)) \in \Delta$ in $\mathbb{R}_2$, $h^\sigma(t) = (h_1^\sigma(t), h_2^\sigma(t)) \in U_\sigma$ in $\mathbb{R}^2$ with Δ being a <u>known</u> bounded <u>playing region</u> and U_σ, $\sigma = 1, 2$ being a <u>known</u> compact control-constraint sets.

Each player $\sigma = 1,2$ will use the set valued feedback <u>strategy</u> defined by

$$h_i^\sigma(t) = e_i^\sigma E_i^\sigma(t) [(1 - s) x_i' + sx_j] \qquad (2)$$

<u>for all</u> $s \in [0,1]$, $x(t) \in \Delta$, $t \in J_o^f$, where e_i^σ = constant, $E_i^\sigma(t)$, $t \in J_o^f$, are respectively the given <u>efficiency coefficient</u> and the controlling <u>effort</u> of the player σ in harvesting the resource i. We let $E_i^\sigma(t) \in [0,1]$ and denote $E^\sigma(t) \triangleq (E_1^\sigma(t), E_2^\sigma(t))$. Moreover, we let $E(t) = (E^1(t), E^2(t))$ be the composite (cooperative) control and $p_i(t)$, $t \in J_o^f$, $(p_1(t), p_2(t)) = p(t)$, be the current market <u>price</u> for the resource i and $c_i^\sigma(h_i^\sigma)$ is the current cost to the player σ for harvesting i. We may also use the vector $c^\sigma(h^\sigma) = (c_1^\sigma(h_1^\sigma), c_2^\sigma(h_2))$. Substituting (2); the net revenue of the player $\sigma = 1, 2$ is

$$\left. \begin{array}{l} f_o^\sigma(x,E_1^\sigma,E_2^\sigma) = \sum_i e_i^\sigma E_i^\sigma(t) p_i (1-s) x_i + \sum_i e_i^\sigma E_i^\sigma p_j s x_j \\ \qquad - \sum_i c_i^\sigma(x_i, E_i^\sigma) \quad , \quad i \neq j. \end{array} \right\} \qquad (3)$$

The player σ aims at $f_o^\sigma(x,p,1,1) > 0$ <u>for all</u> $s \in [0,1]$, i.e. for $\Sigma_i e_i^\sigma p_i x_i > \Sigma_i c_i^\sigma(x,1)$. Accordingly the <u>anti-target</u> set $\mathbf{A}_\sigma$ in Δ to be avoided as profit dissipative is defined by

$$\mathbf{A}_\sigma = \{x \in \Delta \mid \sum_i e_i^\sigma p_i x_i \leq \sum_i c_i^\sigma(1), i = 1,2\} . \qquad (4)$$

Given a solution $x = x(x^o, t)$, $t \in J_o^{t_f}$ of (1) through $x^o = x(t_o) \in \Delta$, the <u>profit</u> of the player σ is

$$\pi_\sigma(x^o, E^\sigma) = \int_{t_o}^{t_f} \exp(-\rho t) f_o^\sigma(x, E^\sigma) dt \qquad (5)$$

with $\rho > 0$ some discount rate. Thus the <u>performance index</u> to be <u>maximised by both players</u> is

$$\pi(x^o, E) = \int_{t_o}^{t_f} \exp(-\rho t)[f_o^1(x, E^1) + f_o^2(x, E^2)]dt . \qquad (6)$$

The information on $x(t)$ available to the cooperating players is given in terms of the rate of diffusion which can be approximated by experimental measurements and is assumed determined as a noisy <u>read-out</u> function

$$y_i(t) = s(x_i - x_j) , \quad i, j=1, 2 , \quad i \neq j, \qquad (7)$$

with $s \in [0,1]$ to be identified. We let $y(t) = (y^1(t), y^2(t)) \in Y$

R^2 with Y known noise band. Consequently each player σ knows the growth rates r_1, r_2 directly from experiment, and the sets Δ, U_1, U_2, Y as estimates. He is also advised about both efficiencies e_1^ν, e_2^ν, $i = 1, 2$ and his cooperant's $E^\nu(t)$, $t \varepsilon J$ $76o'$, $\nu \neq \sigma$. The player σ chooses his own effort $E^\sigma(t)$, $t \varepsilon J_o'$. With this he attempts the following objectives

(A) <u>Identify</u> adaptively (on-line) $x(t)$, $t \varepsilon J_o^*$; and the parameters K, s, with accuracy to a prescribed constant $\eta > 0$.
(B) From some Δ_o in Δ <u>stabilise</u> $x(x^o, t)$, $t \varepsilon J'_o$, $x^o \varepsilon \Delta_\sigma$, in $\Delta - \mathbf{A}_\sigma$ after suitable time interval.
(C) <u>Maximise</u> $\pi(x_1^\sigma, E)$ of (6) on $(x_1^\sigma, t_o) \varepsilon \Delta_1 \cup \Delta_2$ in Δ.

IDENTIFICATION AND PLAYABILITIES

According to the theory of (dynamic) adaptive identifiers (see Luenberger, 1964; Narendra and Valavani, 1976), the system (1) is considered as if $x(t)$, K, s were known. Then an <u>auxiliary model</u> called <u>identifier</u> (predictor) is constructed with known states from Δ and known parameters from [0,2], [0,1] repectively, and with solutions that converge to these of (1) in suitable time and with suitable accuracy. The theory has been adjusted to nonlinear harvested systems by Skowronski (1981 and Chapter 6, this volume). Each player constructs his own identifier based upon independent observations. Luenberger (1964) applied the identifier theory to linear games. Galperin-Skowronski (1983) applied it to nonlinear zero-sum games, and Skowronski (1984) used it in the Nash-type competitive game. We adopt a similar approach here to our case of Pareto-cooperative fishing. We let the model of (1) designed by the player σ be

$$\dot{z}_i^\sigma = r_i \, z_i^\sigma (1 - \frac{z_i^\sigma}{K_\sigma}) - y_i^\sigma - \sum_\sigma e_i^\sigma E_i^\sigma (z_i^\sigma - y_i^\sigma) \qquad (8)$$

where

$$y_i^\sigma(t) = s_\sigma(z_i^\sigma - z_j^\sigma), \quad i, j = 1, 2, \ i \neq j,$$

with $(z_1^\sigma(t), z_2^\sigma(t)) = z^\sigma(t) \varepsilon \Delta$, $t \varepsilon J'_o$ a <u>known</u> vector and $K_\sigma(t)$, $s_\sigma(t)$, $t \varepsilon J'_o$ <u>known</u> time dependent variables satisfying some <u>adaptive laws</u>

$$\dot{K}_\sigma = g_K^\sigma(x, z^\sigma, K_\sigma) \qquad (9)$$

$$\dot{s}_\sigma = g_s^\sigma(x, z^\sigma, s_\sigma) \qquad (10)$$

to be designed by the player σ together with (8). We let $K_\sigma^o = K_\sigma(t_o) \varepsilon [0, k_{max}]$, $s_\sigma^o = s_\sigma(t_o) \varepsilon [0,1]$ and form the parameter 'errors':

$$\lambda_\sigma(t) \triangleq K_\sigma(t) - K, \qquad (11)$$

Stock and System Parameters in a Pareto Harvesting Game

$$\mu_\sigma(t) \overset{\Delta}{=} s_\sigma(t) - s , \qquad (12)$$

with $\dot{\lambda}_\sigma(t) = K_\sigma(t)$, $\dot{\mu}_\sigma(t) = \dot{s}_\sigma(t)$, $t \varepsilon J_0^t$. Then introduce the vector $(x(t), z^\sigma(t), \lambda_\sigma(t), \mu_\sigma(t))^T = \mathbf{z}^\sigma(t) \varepsilon \Delta \times \Delta \times [0, K_{max}] \times [0,2] = \Delta^2 \times [0, K_{max}] \times [0,2] = \Delta^3$ in the product space $\mathbb{R}^6$, and designate

$$F_i^\sigma(\mathbf{Z}^\sigma, E_i^1, E_i^2) =$$

$$\begin{bmatrix}
r_1 x_1 (1 - \frac{x_1}{K}) - s(x_1 - x_2) - \sum_\sigma e_1^\sigma E_1^\sigma [x_1 - s(x_1 - x_2)] \\[6pt]
r_2 x_2 (1 - \frac{x_2}{K}) - s(x_2 - x_1) - \sum_\sigma e_2^\sigma E_2^\sigma [x_2 - s(x_2 - x_1)] \\[6pt]
r_1 z_1^\sigma (1 - \frac{z_1^\sigma}{K_\sigma}) - s_\sigma(z_1^\sigma - z_2^\sigma) - \sum_\sigma e_1^\sigma E_1^\sigma [z_1^\sigma - s^\sigma(z_1^\sigma - z_2^\sigma)] \\[6pt]
r_2 z_2^\sigma (1 - \frac{z_2^\sigma}{K_\sigma}) - s_\sigma(z_2^\sigma - z_1) - \sum_\sigma e_2^\sigma E_2^\sigma (z_2^\sigma - s_\sigma(z_2^\sigma - z_1^\sigma)] \\[6pt]
g_K^\sigma(x, z^\sigma, K_\sigma) \\[6pt]
g_s^\sigma(x, z^\sigma, s_\sigma)
\end{bmatrix}$$

(13)

forming the <u>product system</u>

$$\dot{\mathbf{z}}^\sigma = F^\sigma(\mathbf{z}^\sigma, E^1, E^2) , \qquad (14)$$

with solutions $k_\sigma(\mathbf{z}^\infty, E^1(\cdot), E^2(\cdot), \cdot) : J_0^t \to \Delta^3$,
$\mathbf{z}^\infty = \mathbf{z}^\sigma(t_0) \varepsilon \Delta^3$, for each chosen pair of functions $E^1(\cdot)$, $E^2(\cdot)$. Functions $K_\sigma(\cdot)$, $s_\sigma(\cdot)$, $E^\sigma(\cdot)$ allowing the above are called <u>admissible</u>.

Now let us define the diagonal set

$$M^\sigma \underset{\Delta}{=} \{z^\sigma(t) \varepsilon \Delta^3 | z^\sigma(t) = x(t) , \lambda_\sigma(t) = 0 , \mu_\sigma(t) = 0 , \forall t\} ,$$

and given $\eta^\sigma > 0$ define its neighbourhood

$$M_\eta^\sigma \underset{\Delta}{=} \{z^\sigma(t) \varepsilon \Delta^3 | \, ||z^\sigma(t) - x(t)|| < \eta^\sigma , \, |\lambda_\sigma(t)| < \eta^\sigma , \, |\eta_\sigma(t)| < \eta^\sigma, \forall t\},$$

where $||\cdot||$ designates any norm in $\mathbb{R}^6$.

Suppose Δ_σ in Δ is a <u>set desired by the player σ to host his objectives</u> (see objective (B) in §1) and let

Stock and System Parameters in a Pareto Harvesting Game

$\Delta_\sigma^3 = \Delta_\sigma \times \Delta_\sigma \times [0, K_{max}] \times [0,2]$. Moreover define $M^\sigma \triangleq M^\sigma \cap \Delta_\sigma^3$, $M^\sigma_\eta \triangleq M^\sigma_\eta \cap \Delta_\sigma^3$.

Definition 2.1: A model (8)-(10) is an identifier on Δ_σ for the player σ with accuracy η^σ (briefly, η^σ-<u>identifier on</u> Δ_σ) iff there are admissible functions g_k^σ, g_s^σ; E^σ and a constant $T_\eta > 0$ such that

$$k_\sigma(z^{\sigma 0}, E^1(\cdot), E^2(\cdot), t) \in M^\sigma_\eta, \ t \in [t_0 + T_0, t_f] \quad (15)$$

for all $z^\infty \in \Delta_\sigma^3$ and all $E^\nu(t) \in [0,1]$, $\nu \neq \sigma$.

Let $CA_\sigma^3 \triangleq \Delta_\sigma^3 - A_\sigma^3$, $A_\sigma^3 = A_\sigma \times A_\sigma \times [0,K_{max}] \times [0,2]$.

Definition 2.2: An η^σ- identifier is <u>playable on</u> Δ_σ <u>for ultimate avoidance</u> of A_σ iff the effort E^σ of Definition 2.1 is such that for some $T_A > T_\eta$,

$$k_\sigma(z^{\sigma 0}, E^1(\cdot), E^2(\cdot), t) \in M^\sigma \cap CA_\sigma^3, \ t \in [t_0 + T_A, t_f] \quad (16)$$

for all $z^\infty \in \Delta_\sigma^3$, $E^\nu(t) \in [0,1]$, $\nu \neq \sigma$.

Definition 2.2': The ultimate avoidance of Definition 2.2 becomes '<u>avoidance after</u>' $T_A > 0$' if the constant T_A is specified a-priori.

In optimisation (see the objective (C) in §1) the players cooperate, hence they may design a common identifier - exchanging information:
$z^1(t) = z^2(t) = z(t)$,
$K_1(t) = K_2(t) = K_{12}(t)$,
$s_1(t) = s_2(t) = s_{12}(t), t \in J'_0$,
$g_k^1(x,z^1,k_1) = g_k^2(x,z^2,K_2) = g_K(x,z,K_{12})$,
$g_s^1(x,z^1,s_1) = g_s^2(x,z^2,s_2) = g_s(x,z,s_{12})$,
$\eta^1 = \eta^2 = \eta$, playing on $\Delta_1 \cup \Delta_2 = \Delta_{12}$ and avoiding $A = A_1 \cup A_2$. Denote also $z^1(t) = z^2(t) = z(t)$, $k_1(\cdot) = k_2(\cdot) = k(\cdot)$, $M^1_\eta = M^2_\eta \triangleq M_\eta$, $CA^3 \triangleq \Delta_{12}^3 - A^3$, where $A^3 = A \times A \times [0,K_{max}] \times [0,2]$.

Definition 2.3: A model (8)-(10) is an η-identifier (for both players) <u>optimally playable on</u> Δ_{12} for avoidance of A after $T_A^* > 0$, iff there are admissible functions g_K, g_s and a pair of efforts $E_*^1(t)$, $E_*^2(t)$ such that

(i) $k(z^0, E_*^1, E_*^2, t) \in M_\eta \cap CA^3, \ t \in [t_A, t_f]$, (17)

for all $z^0 \in CA^3$, where $t_A = t_0 + T_A^*$;

(ii) given $x^A = x(t_A)$ all the values $\pi(x^A, E_*^1, E_*^2)$ are equal;

(iii) $\pi(x^A, E_*^1, E_*^2) \geq \pi(x^A, E^1, E^2)$ (18)

for all $E^1(t)$, $E^2(t) \in [0,1]$ and all $x \in C_A$.

109

The set of all z^σ where from a particular property defined in Definitions 2.1 - 2.3 is proved achievable will be called the region of that property. Defining the regions is a difficult task and more often than not an academic problem. In case studies we are interested in achieving our goal from specified subsets Δ_σ of the region and the practical way about it is to propose candidates for Δ_σ's and check them against some sufficient conditions.

SUFFICIENT CONDITIONS

Let $N(\partial \Delta_\sigma^3)$ be a neighbourhood of the boundary of Δ_σ^3 in $\mathbb{R}^6$ and denote $N_\xi^\sigma = N(\partial \Delta_\sigma^3) \cap \overline{\Delta_\sigma^3}$, $CM_\eta^\sigma = \Delta_\sigma^3 - M_\eta^\sigma$, and let an open $S_\eta^\sigma \supset \overline{CM_\eta^\sigma}$. We introduce two test functions $V_s(\cdot) : N_\xi^\sigma \to \mathbb{R}$, $V_\eta(\cdot) : S_\eta^\sigma \to \mathbb{R}$ of class C^1, and define

$$v_s = \inf V_s(z^\sigma) | z^\sigma \in \partial \Delta_\sigma^3,$$
$$v_\eta^- = \inf V_\eta(z^\sigma) | z^\sigma \in \partial M_\eta^\sigma \cap CM_\eta^\sigma$$
$$v_\eta^+ = \sup V_\eta(z^\sigma) | z^\sigma \in \partial \Delta_\sigma \cap \overline{CM_\eta^\sigma}.$$

Theorem 3.1: Given Δ_σ, η^σ the model (8)-(10) is an η^σ-identifier on Δ_σ, if there are admissible functions $g^\sigma{}_K$, g_s^σ, E^σ and two functions V_s, V_η such that

(i) $V_s(z^\sigma) < v_s$;

(ii) $V_s(z^\sigma) \cdot F(z^\sigma, E^\sigma, E^\nu) < 0$ (19)

for all $E^\nu \in [0,1]$, $\nu \neq \sigma$ and all $s \in [0,1]$.

(iii) $v_\eta^- \leq V_\eta(z^\sigma) \leq v_\eta^+$;

(iv) there is a constant $c > 0$ such that

$$\nabla V_\eta(z^\sigma) \cdot F^\sigma(z^\sigma, E^\sigma, E^\nu) \leq -c,$$ (20)

for all $E^\nu \in [0,1]$, $\nu \neq \sigma$ and all $s \in [0,1]$; and

(v) $v_\eta^+ - v_\eta^- < c(t_f - t_o)$. (21)

Proof: The solutions may not leave Δ_σ^3 but through N_ξ^σ and then there is $t_1 \geq t_0$ such that $k_\sigma(t_1) \in \partial \Delta_\sigma^3$ and by (i) we have $V_s(k_\sigma(t_1)) \geq v_s \geq V_s(z^\infty)$ contradicting (ii). Hence no solution of (14) leaves the set Δ_σ^3. On the other hand no solution of (14) may stay permanently in CM_η^σ. Indeed in this set we have $\dot{V}_\eta(k_\sigma(t)) \leq -c$ and integrating

$$t \leq t_o + \frac{1}{c}[V_\eta(z^{\sigma 0}) - V_\eta(z^\sigma)] .$$ (22)

Stock and System Parameters in a Pareto Harvesting Game

By (iii), $V_\eta(z^\sigma) - v_\eta^- \geq 0$, $V_\eta(z^\infty) - v_\eta^+ \leq 0$ whence $V_\eta(z^\infty) - V(z^\sigma) \leq v_\eta^+ - v_\eta^-$ and (22) becomes $t \leq t_0 + \frac{1}{c}(v_\eta^+ - v_\eta^-)$. Hence by (v) there is

$$T_\eta = (v_\eta^+ + v_\eta^-)/c < t_f - t_0 \tag{23}$$

which depends upon the diameter of $\overline{CM_\eta^\sigma}$ and c but on nothing else. The T_η is such that for $t \geq t_0 + T_\eta$ the solutions must be out of $\overline{CM_\eta^\sigma}$. There is no return to this set, as then (iii) and (iv) contradict. We conclude that all solutions are in M_η^σ after $t = t_0 + T_\eta$, Q.E.D.

Note that T_η may be calculated from (23), and if T_η is given a-priori (desired) we may set up

$$c = (v_\eta^+ - v_\eta^-)/T_\eta \tag{24}$$

in (20), (21), making the identifier compatible after a specific time interval.

<u>Theorem 3.2</u>: Given Δ_σ, η^σ the model (8)-(10) is an η^σ-identifier playable on Δ_σ for ultimate avoidance of $\mathbf{A}_\sigma$ if the conditions of Theorem 3.1. hold and there is a C^1-function $V_A(\cdot): \mathbf{A}_\sigma \to \mathbf{R}$ such that

(vi) $0 \leq V_A(z^\sigma) \leq v_A$, $z^\sigma \varepsilon \mathbf{A}_\sigma$,

where $v_A = \sup V_A(z^\sigma) | z^\sigma \varepsilon \partial \mathbf{A}_\sigma^3$, $V_A > 0$;

(vii) there is a constant $c_A > 0$ such that

$$V_A(z^\sigma) \cdot F^\sigma(z^\sigma, E^\sigma, E^\nu) \geq c_\alpha \tag{25}$$

for all $E^\nu \varepsilon [0,1]$, $\nu \neq \sigma$ and all $s \varepsilon [0,1]$.

<u>Proof</u>: Under the conditions of Theorem 3.1 we have all $k_\sigma(z^\infty, t)$ in M_η^σ after some $t = t_0 + T_\eta$. We have to show now that for $t \geq t_0 + T_A$, $T_A > T_\eta$ they are outside $\mathbf{A}_\sigma$. Consider an arbitrary $k_\sigma(z^\infty, \cdot)$, $z^\infty \varepsilon \mathbf{A}_\sigma$. By (vii), $V_A(z^\sigma(t)) > V_A(z^\infty)$ for all $t > t_0$. Hence by (vi) there is $t_1 > t_0$ such that $z^\sigma(t_1) \varepsilon C\mathbf{A}_\sigma^3$. There is no return as upon crossing $\partial \mathbf{A}_\sigma^3$, (vi) and (vii) contradict. By the same argument $k_\sigma(z^\infty, .,.)$, $z^\infty \varepsilon C\mathbf{A}_\sigma^3$ may not enter $\mathbf{A}_\sigma^3$, Q.E.D.

The proof uses the same argument as in Leitmann-Skowronski (1983).

Note that if $T_A > 0$ is prescribed a-priori, we use Theorem 3.2 with $c_A = \frac{v_A}{T_A}$.

Now recall that for the sake of optimisation both players design the same identifier and play on $\Delta_{12} = \Delta_1 \cup \Delta_2$ to avoid $\mathbf{A} = \mathbf{A}_1 \cup \mathbf{A}_2$ and maximise (6). Then we may combine Theorem 3.2

$A_1 \cup A_2$ and maximise (6). Then we may combine Theorem 3.2 defined on Δ_{12}, A with Leitmann's sufficient conditions for optimisation (see Leitman, 1981) to obtain

Theorem 3.3: Given Δ_{12}, A, $\eta > 0$, the model (8)-(10) is an η-identifier optimally playable on Δ_{12} for avoidance of A after some $T_A^* > 0$, if the conditions of Theorem 3.2 hold on the above sets and time, and moreover if among the applicable E^1, E^2 there is a pair E_*^1, E_*^2 and a C^1-function $V_K(\cdot) : CA^3 \to R$ such that

(i) $\lim\limits_{t \to t_f} V_K(z(t)) \leq \lim\limits_{t \to t_f} V_K(z^*(t)) = 0$, (26)

where $z(t) = k(z^A, t_A, t)$, $z^A = z(t_A)$, $t_A = t_0 + T_A^*$, generated by E^1, E^2 and in particular $z^*(t) = k^*(z^A, t_A, t)$ generated by E_*^1, E_*^2;

(ii) $\nabla V_K(z) F(z, E_*^1, E_*^2) = -[f_0^1(x, E_*^1) + f_0^2(x, E_*^2)]$,

$s \in [0,1]$; (27)

(iii) $\nabla V_K(z) F(z, E^1, E^2) \leq -[f_0^1(x, E^1) + f_0^2(x, E^2)]$, (28)

for all $E^1, E^2, s \in [0,1]$. Proof follows from Leitmann (1981).

Example

To illustrate the implementation of §3 we proceed to the example below, assuming $r_1 = r_2 = 0.4$, $e_1^s = e_2^s = 2 \times 10^{-4}$, $s = 0.3$, $K = 4 \times 10^5$, $\rho = 0$ (steady state), $p_1 = p_2 = 0.5$, $c_i{}''(x, E) = 10(E_{1i}^1 + E_{1i}^2)$, $i = 1, 2$. Substituting the above into (1)-(6) gives

$$\left.\begin{aligned}\dot{x}_1 &= 0.4x_1(1 - x_1/4 \times 10^{+5}) - 0.3(x_1 - x_2) \\ &\quad - 2 \times 10^{-4}(E_1^1 + E_1^2)(0.7x_1 + 0.3x_2) \\ \dot{x}_2 &= 0.4x_2(1 - x_2/4 \times 10^{+5}) - 0.3(x_2 - x_1) \\ &\quad - 2 \times 10^{-4}(E_2^1 + E_2^2)(0.3x_1 + 0.7x_2)\end{aligned}\right\} \quad (29)$$

$$\left.\begin{aligned}f_0^1 &= 0.5 \times 2 \times 10^{-4}(0.7E_1^1 x_1 + 0.3E_2^1 x_2) \\ &\quad + 0.5 \times 2 \times 10^{-4}(0.3E_1^1 x_2 + 0.7E_2^1 x_2) - 10(E_1^1 + E_2^1) \\ f_0^2 &= 0.5 \times 2 \times 10^{-4}(0.7E_1^2 x_1 + 0.3E_2^2 x_2) \\ &\quad + 0.5 \times 2 \times 10^{-4}(0.3E_1^2 x_1 + 0.7E_2^2 x_2) - 10(E_1^1 + E_2^1)\end{aligned}\right\} \quad (30)$$

and

$$\pi = \int_0^{t_f} (f_0^1 + f_0^2) dt . \quad (31)$$

Stock and System Parameters in a Pareto Harvesting Game

It seems that the general rule of implementing the sufficient conditions of §3 is to solve the corresponding straight (without identification) playability problem by finding some Lyapunov-type test functions $V(x)$. Then the sum of $V(x)$ and $V(z)$ generates V_s, V_A, and $|V(x) - V(z)|$ generates V_η (see Skowronski, 1984). Obviously we must check the above candidates against the conditions of §3. Applying this idea, we attempt the most demanding of the straight problems (i.e. optimal playability) by maximizing

$$\int_0^{t_f} \{1 \times 10^{-4}[(0.7x_1 + 0.3x_2)u_1 + (0.3x_1 + 0.7x_2)u_2] - 10(u_1 + u_2)\}dt \qquad (32)$$

with respect to $u_i = E^1_i + E^2_i$, $i = 1,2$, subject to the state equations obtained from (29):

$$\left.\begin{array}{l}\dot{x}_1 = 0.1x_1 + 0.3x_2 - 10^{-6}x_1^2 - 2 \times 10^{-4}(0.7x_1 + 0.3x_2)u_1 \\ \dot{x}_2 = 0.3x_1 + 0.1x_2 - 10^{-6}x_2^2 - 2 \times 10^{-4}(0.3x_1 + 0.7x_2)u_2\end{array}\right\} \quad (33)$$

Since our task is to illustrate the results of this paper, namely Theorems 3.1, 3.2, we use the necessary conditions for optimizations. They suffice in providing candidates for the test functions concerned. The corresponding Pontryagin function is

$$H = \lambda_0 f_0 + \lambda_1 f_1 + \lambda_2 f_2, \quad \lambda_0 = -1.$$

Substituting (32), (33) we obtain $H = H_1 + H_2$ with

$$H_1 = 10(u_1 + u_2) - (1 \times 10^{-4} + 2 \times 10^{-4}\lambda_1)(0.7x_1 + 0.3x_2)u_1$$
$$- (1 \times 10^{-4}\lambda_2)(0.3x_1 + 0.7x_2)u_2$$

$$H_2 = (0.1\lambda_1 + 0.3\lambda_2)x_1 + (0.3\lambda_1 + 0.1\lambda_2)x_2$$
$$- 1 \times 10^{-6}(\lambda_1 x_1^2 + \lambda_2 x_2^2).$$

H_2 does not depend upon u_1, u_2, so it is only H_1 which is to be maximized. The switching function is

$$W(t) = \begin{bmatrix} 10 - (1 \times 10^{-4} + 2 \times 10^{-4}\lambda_1)(0.7x_1 + 0.3x_2) \\ 10 - (1 \times 10^{-4} + 2 \times 10^{-4}\lambda_2)(0.3x_1 + 0.7x_2) \end{bmatrix} \quad (34)$$

so that $H_1 = W(t)u(t)$. For the singular control case applicable here we have

$$W(t) = 0, \qquad (35)$$

whence also

$$\begin{aligned}\dot{W}(t) = {} & 10 - (1\times10^{-4}+2\times10^{-4}\lambda_1)(0.7\dot{x}_1+0.3\dot{x}_2) \\ & -(1\times10^{-4}+2\times10^{-4}\dot{\lambda}_1)(0.7x_1+0.3x_2) \\ & 10 - (1\times10^{-4}+2\times10^{-4}\lambda_2)(0.3\dot{x}_1+0.7\dot{x}_2) \\ & -(1\times10^{-4}+2\times10^{-4}\dot{\lambda}_2)(0.3x_1+0.7x_2) = 0\end{aligned} \qquad (36)$$

The corresponding co-state equations are

$$\begin{aligned}\dot{\lambda}_1 &= -0.7(1\times10^{-4}+2\times10^{-4}\lambda_1)u_1 - 0.3(1\times10^{-4}+2\times10^{-4}\lambda_2)u_2, \\ \dot{\lambda}_2 &= -0.3(1\times10^{-4}+2\times10^{-4}\lambda_1)u_1 - 0.4(1\times10^{-4}+2\times10^{-4}\lambda_2)u_2 \;.\end{aligned} \qquad (37)$$

Substituting (33), (37) into (36) and solving with (35) we have

$$\lambda_1^* = \lambda_2^* \cong -0.103 \;. \qquad (38)$$

Let us now consider some function $V(x) : \Delta \to \mathbb{R}$ such that

$$\lambda_i^* = -\frac{\partial V}{\partial x_i} \;,\; i = 1,2.$$

Integration and (38) gives

$$V(x) = 0.103(x_1 + x_2) \;, \qquad (39)$$

positive definite, as $x_1, x_2 > 0$. Then let us introduce the functions

$$\begin{aligned}V_S &= V(x) + V(z^\sigma) + \lambda_\sigma^2 + \mu_\sigma^2, \\ V_A &= V(x) + V(z^\sigma) - \lambda_\sigma^2 - \mu_\sigma^2, \\ V_\eta &= |V(z^\sigma) - V(x)| + \lambda_\sigma^2 + \eta_\sigma^2;\end{aligned}$$

the adaptive laws

$$\begin{aligned}\dot{K}_\sigma &= \alpha(t)K_\sigma \;,\; \alpha(t) > 0 \;,\; K_\sigma^o > 0; \\ \dot{s}_\sigma &= \beta(t)s_\sigma \;,\; \beta(t) > 0 \;,\; s_\sigma^o > 0;\end{aligned}$$

and define the sets

$$\begin{aligned}\Delta_\sigma &= \{x \in \Delta \mid V(x) \leq a\}, \\ \mathbf{A}_\sigma &= \{x,z \in \Delta^2 \mid V(x) + V(z) \leq b\}\end{aligned}$$

where a, b are given positive numbers. Now we can check the conditions of Theorems 3.1, 3.2.

Consider Theorem 3.1 first. The conditions (i), (iii), (v) follow directly from our definition of Δ_σ and our shape of the function V_η. Regarding condition (ii) we require

$$V_S(z^\sigma) \cdot F^\sigma(z^\sigma, E^\sigma, E^\nu) = 0.103\dot{x}_1$$
$$+ 0.103\dot{x}_2 + 0.103\dot{z}_1^\sigma + 0.103\dot{z}_2^\sigma + 2\lambda_\sigma \dot{K}_\sigma + 2\mu_\sigma \dot{s}_\sigma < 0.$$

For suitable $\alpha(t)$, $\beta(t)$, $\dot{K}_\sigma^o < 0$, $\dot{s}_\sigma^o < 0$

$$\lambda_\sigma \alpha(t) \dot{K}_\sigma + \mu_\sigma \beta(t) \dot{s}_\sigma \leq - 0.0515 \, M_1$$

where $M_1 \geq \sup\{\dot{x}_1 + \dot{x}_2 + \dot{z}_1^\sigma + \dot{z}_2^\sigma\} \mid z \in \Delta_\sigma^3$.

Regarding condition (iv) observe that $V_\eta(z^\sigma) = 0$ only when $z^\sigma = x$. Since we have the choice of z^∞, we can take $x > z$ giving

$$V_\eta = 0.108(x_1 - z_1^\sigma + x_2 - z_2^\sigma) + \lambda_\sigma^2 + s_\sigma^2 > 0.$$

We require

$$0.103(\dot{x}_1 - \dot{z}_1^\sigma + \dot{x}_2 - \dot{z}_2^\sigma) + 2(\lambda_\sigma \alpha(t) \dot{K}_\sigma + \mu_\sigma \beta(t) \dot{s}_\sigma) \leq -c.$$

For suitable $\alpha(t)$, $\beta(t)$, $\dot{K}_\sigma^o < 0$, $\dot{s}_\sigma^o < 0$

$$\lambda_\sigma \alpha(t) \dot{K}_\sigma + \mu_\sigma \beta(t) \dot{s}_\sigma \leq - 0.0515 \, M_1$$

where $M_1 \geq \sup\{\dot{x}_1 - \dot{z}_1^\sigma + \dot{x}_2 - \dot{z}_2^\sigma + \varepsilon\} \mid z \in \Delta_\sigma^3$, $\varepsilon > 0$. It holds as there exist

$$M_1 \geq \max\{\sup(\dot{x}_1 - \dot{z}_1^\sigma + \dot{x}_2 - \dot{z}_2^\sigma + \varepsilon), \sup(\dot{x}_1 + \dot{x}_2 + \dot{z}_1^\sigma + \dot{z}_2^\sigma)\}$$

such that for suitable $\alpha(t)$, $\beta(t)$, $\dot{K}_\sigma^o < 0$, $\dot{s}_\sigma^o < 0$,

$$\lambda_\sigma \alpha(t) \dot{K}_\alpha + \mu_\sigma \beta(t) \dot{s}_\sigma \leq - 0.0515 \, M_1$$

for all t.

Consider now Theorem 3.2. The condition (vi) holds by definition of Δ_σ. Regarding (vii), we need

$$V_A(z^\sigma) \cdot F(z^\sigma, E^\sigma, E^\nu) = 0.103(\dot{x}_1 + \dot{x}_2 + \dot{z}_1^\sigma + \dot{z}_2^\sigma)$$
$$- 2\lambda_\sigma \alpha(t) \dot{K}_\sigma - 2\mu_\sigma \beta(t) \dot{s}_\sigma \geq 0.103(\dot{x}_1 + \dot{x}_2 + \dot{z}_1^\sigma + \dot{z}_2^\sigma)$$
$$+ 0.103 \, M_1$$

for all t, which holds for suitable α, β, $\dot{K}_\sigma^o$, $\dot{s}_\sigma^o$.

REFERENCES

Clark, C.W. (1976) *Mathematical Bioeconomics*, Wiley, New York
Galperin, E.A. and Skowronski, J.M. (1983) 'Playable asymptotic observers for differential games with incomplete information'. *Proc. Optimization Days* - Montreal
Leitmann, G. (1981) *Calculus of Variations and Optimal Control*, Plenum Press, New York
Leitmann, G. and Skowronski, J.M. (1983) A note on avoidance control, *Optimal Control - Applications and Methods* (OCAM), 4, 335-342
Luenberger, D.G. (1964) 'Observing the state of a linear system', *IEEE Transactions on Military Electronics*, MIL-8, 74-80
Luenberger, D.G. and Rhodes, I.B. (1969) 'Differential Games with imperfect state information'. *IEEE Transactions*. AC-14, 29-38
Narendra, D.S. and Valavani, I.S. (1976) 'Stable adaptive observers and controllers', *Proceedings of the IEEE* AC-64, 1198-1208
Skowronski, J.M. (1981) 'Adaptive identification of models stabilizing under uncertainty', *Lecture Notes in Biomathematics*, 40, Springer, Berlin, 64-78
Skowronski, J.M. (1984) Chapter 6, this volume

PART III

DYNAMIC MACROECONOMIC MODELS

Chapter Eight

THE SOLUTION PROCEDURE FOR THE ORANI MODEL EXPLAINED BY A SIMPLE EXAMPLE

Peter B. Dixon

INTRODUCTION

ORANI is a large multisectoral model of the Australian economy.[1] In standard applications it identifies 113 industries, 230 commodities (115 domestically produced and 115 imported), 9 types of labour, 7 types of agricultural land and 113 types of capital (one for each industry). It contains explicit modelling, at this disaggregated level, of many types of commodity and factor flows, e.g., inputs to current production, inputs to capital creation, household consumption, exports and margin services (retail, wholesale and transport). The multi-product characteristics of production in Australian agricultural industries are also explicitly modelled, and a facility is included for disaggregating economy-wide results to the regional level.

The reason for including so much detail in ORANI is to facilitate its use by a variety of Government agencies with interests in different spheres of economic policy. Among the agencies which have used the model are the Industries Assistance Commission, the Bureau of Agricultural Economics, the Bureau of Industry Economics and the Premier's Department of South Australia. Applications of ORANI made by these agencies and other groups include simulations of the effects on industries, occupations and regions of changes in tariffs, the exploitation of mineral resources, changes in world commodity prices, changes in the exchange rate, the adoption of import parity pricing for oil products, subsidies to ailing industries, the move towards equal pay for women, changes in real wages and the adoption of Keynesian demand stimulation policies. Each of these applications draws upon different aspects of the model's detail.

To solve such a large model, we followed initially the method pioneered by Johansen (1960). This method, which relies on linear approximations, enables us to obtain solutions at modest cost. It has the additional advantages of allowing flexibility in the selection of exogenous variables and of facilitating changes to the structure of the model. Recently we have extended the

119

Johansen method in a way which retains its principal advantages but which allows elimination or errors introduced by linear approximation.

In the second section of this chapter we describe our extended Johansen method by means of an elementary example. Complete descriptions of the mathematical theory underlying the method and the application of the method to the ORANI model are in DPSV (1982, Chapter 5).[2] Our aim in this chapter is to provide a quick introduction to the method for readers whose time constraints and interests would make more detailed reading impractical. The third section contains concluding remarks.

THE EXTENDED JOHANSEN METHOD FOR COMPUTING SOLUTIONS FOR A GENERAL EQUILIBRIUM MODEL: AN ILLUSTRATIVE EXAMPLE

The ORANI model can be thought of as a system of m equations in n variables of the form

$$F(V) = 0 \tag{1}$$

where F is a vector function of length m and V is a vector of length n. The number of variables n exceeds the number of equations m.

System (1) imposes conditions such as: demands equal supplies for goods and factors of production, prices reflect costs, demands reflect prices and incomes, and supplies reflect profit maximizing decisions. For the purposes of illustrating the computational approach adopted in ORANI, it is not necessary to describe further the economics underlying system (1). Sufficient motivation can be provided by a simple example devoid of economic content. Let us assume that system (1) consists of 2 equations in 3 variables and has the form

$$V_1^2 V_3 - 1 = 0 , \tag{2.1}$$

$$V_1 + V_2 - 2 = 0 . \tag{2.2}$$

Because system (1) contains more variables than equations, we assign exogenously-given values to (n-m) variables and solve for the remaining m, the endogenous variables. In applications of ORANI, many different allocations of the variables between the exogenous and endogenous categories have been made. For example, if we are using ORANI in an analysis of the effects of changing the tariff on footwear, then this variable is exogenous. On the other hand, if we are using ORANI to calculate the change in the tariff which would be required to ensure a given level of footwear employment, then the footwear tariff is an endogenous variable and footwear employment is exogenous. For our illustrative system (2.1)-(2.2), we will assume in this chapter that the exogenous variable is V_3 and the endogenous variables are V_1 and V_2.

With this assignment of the variables to the exogenous and

endogenous categories, we can easily derive solution equations for the system (2.1)-(2.2). That is, we can express the endogenous variables as functions of the exogenous variable as follows:

$$V_1 = V_3^{-1/2} \tag{3.1}$$

and

$$V_2 = 2 - V_3^{-1/2}, \tag{3.2}$$

where we assume (as is often the case in economic models) that only positive values for the variables are of interest.[3] With a solution system such as (3.1)-(3.2), we have no difficulty in evaluating the effects on the endogenous variables of shifts in the exogenous variable. For example, assume that we are initially in a situation where

$$V^I = (V_1^I, V_2^I, V_3^I) = (1,1,1) . \tag{4}$$

Notice that V^I satisfies (2.1)-(2.2). Then we want to evaluate the effects on V_1 and V_2 (employment and prices, say) of a shift in V_3 (the level of protection) from 1. to 1.1. by substituting into (3.1) and (3.2), we find that the new values for V_1 and V_2 are 0.9535 and 1.0465. We conclude that a 10 per cent increase in V_3 induces a 4.65 per cent reduction in V_1 and a 4.65 per cent increase in V_2.

The ORANI computations are similar to the approach just described in one respect: they make use of an initial solution such as (4) with results being reported as percentage deviations from this initial solution. The initial solution (i.e. the initial values for prices, quantities, tariffs, etc.) is known from the data used in setting the parameters of system (1).[4] In another respect, the ORANI computations differ from the simple approach using (3.1) and (3.2). This is because the complexity and size of the actual ORANI system rule out the possibility of deriving explicit solution equations. In other words, in the context of ORANI we cannot make the step from (2.1)-(2.2) to (3.1)-(3.2).

Instead, we follow the approach of Johansen (1960) and linearize system (1). That is, we derive from (1) a system of the form

$$A(V^I)v = 0 \tag{5}$$

where $A(V^I)$ is a m x n matrix whose components are functions of V evaluated at V^I, the initial values of the variables. The n x 1 vector v shows the percentage changes in the variables V.

The derivation of (5) can be illustrated by returning to (2.1)-(2.2). We totally differentiate the left hand sides of (2.1) and (2.2). Then we set these total differentials to zero recognizing that if (2.1) and (2.2) are to continue to be satisfied after a disturbance in the exogenous variables, then the changes in their left hand sides must be zero. Thus, we write

Solving the ORANI Model

$$2V_1 V_3(dV_1) + V_1^2(dV_3) = 0 \tag{6.1}$$

and

$$dV_1 + dV_2 = 0, \tag{6.2}$$

or equivalently, in linear-percentage-change form, we write

$$2v_1 + v_3 = 0 \tag{7.1}[5]$$

and

$$\left[\frac{V_1}{2}\right]v_1 + \left[\frac{V_2}{2}\right]v_2 = 0, \tag{7.2}[6]$$

where $v_i = 100(dV_i/V_i)$, $i=1,2,3$. In matrix notation, (7.1) and (7.2) are

$$\begin{bmatrix} 2 & 0 & 1 \\ V_1/2 & V_2/2 & 0 \end{bmatrix} \begin{bmatrix} v_1 \\ v_2 \\ v_3 \end{bmatrix} = 0. \tag{8}$$

With V set at its initial value given in (4), equation (8) becomes

$$\begin{bmatrix} 2 & 0 & 1 \\ .5 & .5 & 0 \end{bmatrix} \begin{bmatrix} v_1 \\ v_2 \\ v_3 \end{bmatrix} = 0. \tag{9}$$

This is a system of the form (5) for the model (2.1)-(2.2) with the initial solution (4).

In a Johansen-style computation, system (5) effectively replaces system (1) as the basic model. In evaluations of how far the endogenous variables will move from their initial values in response to given movements in the exogenous variables, system (5) is rewritten as

$$A_\alpha(V^I)v_\alpha + A_\beta(V^I)v_\beta = 0 \tag{10}$$

where v_α is the m x 1 vector of percentage changes in the endogenous variables, v_β is the (n - m) vector of percentage changes in the exogenous variables and $A_\alpha(V^I)$ and $A_\beta(V^I)$ are appropriate submatrices of $A(V^I)$, i.e. $A_\alpha(V^I)$ is the m x m matrix formed by the columns of $A(V^I)$ corresponding to the endogenous variables and $A_\beta(V^I)$ is th m x (n-m) matrix formed by the columns corresponding to the exogenous variables. Then (10) is solved for v_α in terms of v_β by matrix inversion,[7] giving

$$v_\alpha = -A_\alpha^{-1}(V^I) A_\beta(V^I)v_\beta \tag{11}$$

or more compactly

$$v_\alpha = B(V^I)v_\beta. \tag{12}$$

The typical element, $B_{ij}(V^I)$, of $B(V^I)$ is the elasticity in the region of V^I of the ith endogenous variable with respect to changes in the jth exogenous variable. That is, $B_{ij}(V^I)$ can be interpreted as the percentage change in $(V_\alpha)_i$ which would result from a one per cent increase in $(V_\beta)_j$, where the initial values for all variables are given by V^I.

The computations (10)-(12) can be illustrated via system (9). Where variable 3 is exogenous, we rewrite (9) as

$$\begin{bmatrix} 2 & 0 \\ .5 & .5 \end{bmatrix} \begin{bmatrix} v_1 \\ v_2 \end{bmatrix} + \begin{bmatrix} 1 \\ 0 \end{bmatrix} v_3 = 0 \; . \tag{13}$$

Then

$$\begin{bmatrix} v_1 \\ v_2 \end{bmatrix} = - \begin{bmatrix} 2 & 0 \\ .5 & .5 \end{bmatrix}^{-1} \begin{bmatrix} 1 \\ 0 \end{bmatrix} v_3 \; . \tag{14}$$

That is,

$$\begin{bmatrix} v_1 \\ v_2 \end{bmatrix} = \begin{bmatrix} -.5 \\ .5 \end{bmatrix} v_3 \; . \tag{15}$$

Equation (15) indicates that in the region of $V^I = (1,1,1)$ the elasticity of variable 1 with respect to variable 3 is $-.5$ and the elasticity of variable 2 with respect to variable 3 is .5. By using (15) we would say that a 10 per cent increase in V_3 would induce a 5 per cent reduction in V_1 and a 5 per cent increase in V_2. This is close to the answers (-4.65 and 4.65) which we found earlier by substituting into (3.1) and (3.2).

A little experimentation with (15) indicates that the Johansen approach is satisfactory for computing the effects on the endogenous variables of small changes in exogenous variables. However, when we make large changes in V_3, (15) may not give a satisfactory approximation to the effects on V_1 and V_2. For example, assume that we increase V_3 by 100 per cent (i.e. from 1 to 2). Then (15) implies that V_1 will fall by 50 per cent and V_2 will increase by 50 per cent. The correct values derived from (3.1) and (3.2) are that V_1 will fall by 29.3 per cent while V_2 will increase by 29.3 per cent.

The weakness of the Johansen method is that it fixes the elasticities of the endogenous variables with respect to the exogenous variables at their initial values, $B_{ij}(V^I)$. As we move away from V^I we should, ideally, allow the elasticities to move. Thus, when faced with a large change in the exogenous variables, our approach in ORANI is to make a sequence of Johansen-style computations. For example, if we want to evaluate the effects of a 100 per cent tariff increase, we can first use (12) to generate the effects of a 50 per cent increase. This would take us from the initial situation ($V = V^I$) to one where $V = V^I + \Delta V_{50}$, with ΔV_{50} denoting our estimate of the change in V arising from the first half

Solving the ORANI Model

of the tariff increase. then we can re-evaluate the elasticity matrix B at $V = V^I + \Delta V_\infty$ and use the re-evaluated matrix in computing the effects of the second half of the tariff increase.

To illustrate our extended Johansen method, we reconsider the problem of calculating the effects on V_1 and V_2 of an increase in V_3 from 1 to 2 in the model (2.1)-(2.2) with the starting condition (4). We tackle the problem in two steps. First we increase V_3 by 50 per cent from 1 to 1.5. According to (15), this will reduce V_1 by 25 per cent (i.e. from 1 to .75) and increase V_2 by 25 per cent (i.e. from 1 to 1.25). Next we revaluate the B matrix at $(V_1, V_2, V_3) = (.75, 1.25, 1.50)$. This requires re-evaluating the A(V) matrix on the left hand side of (8). We obtain

$$A(.75, 1.25, 1.50) = \begin{bmatrix} 2 & 0 & 1 \\ .375 & .625 & 0 \end{bmatrix}$$

which leads to

$$B(.75, 1.25, 1.50) = \begin{bmatrix} 2 & 0 \\ .375 & .635 \end{bmatrix}^{-1} \begin{bmatrix} 1 \\ 0 \end{bmatrix} = \begin{bmatrix} -.5 \\ .3 \end{bmatrix} . \quad (16)$$

In the second stage of the computation we use (16) in calculating the effects of moving V_3 from 1.5 to 2. For this 33 per cent increase in V_3, the responses indicated by equation (16) are a 16.66 per cent reduction in V_1 (i.e. from .75 to .625) and a 10 per cent increase in V_2 (i.e. from 1.25 to 1.375). Thus, our conclusion from the two-step computation is that a 100 per cent increase in V_3 (from 1 to 2) induces a 37.5 per cent decrease in V_1 (from 1 to .625) and a 37.5 per cent increase in V_2 (from 1 to 1.375).

Although our 2 step procedure has taken us closer to the correct answer than the one-step Johansen computation, we still have uncomfortably large errors. (Recall that the correct answer is that V_1 decreases by 29.3 per cent and V_2 increases by 29.3 per cent). On carrying out a 4 step computation (i.e. by increasing V_3 from 1 to 1.25, then from 1.25 to 1.5, etc.) we found that our extended Johansen method put the decrease in V_1 at 32.97 per cent (i.e. from 1 to 0.6703) and the increase in V_2 at 32.97 per cent (i.e. from 1 to 1.3297). Additional gains in accuracy can be achieved by further increasing the number of steps in our computations.

Fortunately, however, effective extrapolation techniques can be applied to give a high degree of accuracy even when our extended Johansen method is applied with only a small number of steps. Consider, for example, Table 8.1 where we have set out the results of our various computations of the effects on V_1 and V_2 in the system (2.1)-(2.2) of an increase in V_3 from 1 to 2. Notice that when we double the number of steps in our extended Johansen computations, we approximately halve our errors. With a 1 step

Solving the ORANI Model

Table 8.1: Various Solutions for V_1 and V_2 in the System (2.1)-(2.2) when V_3 increases from 1 to 2

Endogenous variables	Initial values	Estimated values after an increase in V_3 from 1 to 2				
		1 step computation	2 step computation	4 step computation	1, 2 step extrapolation (a)	2, 4 step extrapolation (b)	Correct Value (c)
V_1	1	.5	.625	.6703	.75	.716	.707
V_2	1	1.5	1.375	1.3297	1.25	1.284	1.293

(a) Computed according to (17).
(b) Computed according to (18).
(c) Computed using (3.1) and (3.2).

Solving the ORANI Model

Table 2: Industry-Output Effects of a 100 per cent Across-the-Board Tariff Cut Computed in the ORANI Model via the Extended Johansen Method (main gaining and losing industries only)

Industry Indentifi-cation number	(1) 1-step	(2) 2-step	(3) Computed Projections(a) 4-step	(4) 8-step	(5) 16-step	(6) Extrapolations(b) 1-2 steps	(7) 8-16 steps	(8) Percentage Errors Johansen [$\frac{(1)}{(7)}$]-1|100	(9) 1-2 step extrapolation [$\frac{(6)}{(7)}$]-1|100
14	14.41633	14.78293	14.96247	15.05172	15.09640	15.14953	15.14108	-4.79	0.06
25	13.34001	13.98722	14.34011	14.52664	14.62299	14.63443	14.71933	-9.37	-0.58
11	10.02261	10.10874	10.16028	10.19008	10.20635	10.19487	10.22263	-1.96	-0.27
64	8.88825	9.08601	9.19812	9.25948	9.29187	9.28377	9.32426	-4.68	-0.43
63	8.59218	9.38494	9.82725	10.06176	10.18273	10.17769	10.30370	-16.61	-1.22
13	7.30533	7.37633	7.42870	7.46112	7.47926	7.44733	7.49741	-2.56	-0.67
76	7.28429	6.70584	6.43846	6.31306	6.25293	6.12740	6.19280	17.63	-1.06
6	5.61351	5.87919	6.02332	6.09933	6.13856	6.14487	6.17780	-9.13	-0.53
3	5.56409	5.65745	5.71728	5.7197	5.77079	5.75081	5.78960	-3.90	-0.67
18	4.92539	5.03666	5.10865	5.15050	5.17321	5.14794	5.19592	-5.21	-0.92
41	-3.90072	-4.13497	-4.26576	-4.33476	-4.37051	-4.36921	-4.40553	-11.46	-0.82
50	-4.03336	-4.28160	-4.40859	-4.47327	-4.50596	-4.52984	-4.53865	-11.13	-0.19
67	-6.18812	-6.75976	-7.08976	-7.26824	-7.36118	-7.33141	-7.45412	-16.98	-1.65
28	-7.07837	-7.68314	-8.01120	-8.18385	-8.27268	-8.28791	-8.36152	-15.35	-0.88
79	-7.24562	-8.47378	-9.36506	-9.91805	-10.22755	-9.70193	-10.53704	-31.24	-7.93
31	-9.25475	-9.92945	-10.27842	-10.45820	-10.54992	-10.60415	-10.64163	-13.03	-0.35
73	-9.63989	-10.25516	-10.61353	-10.80751	-10.90845	-10.87043	-11.00939	-12.44	-1.26
68	-10.37971	-11.15557	-11.54041	-11.73343	-11.8303	-11.93143	-11.92733	-12.98	0.03
39	-10.52144	-13.35426	-15.54377	-16.94308	-17.73697	-16.18709	-18.53086	-43.22	-12.65
32	-12.68090	-13.49826	-13.91897	-14.13490	-14.24474	-14.31561	-14.3459	-11.66	-0.77

Solving the ORANI Model

(a) All projections are percentage changes from the initial values of the variables. Column (1) contains results from a Johansen-style solution. Columns (2)-(5) were computed via the n-step extended Johansen method for n=2,4,8 and 16 respectively.

(b) Column (6) was calculated from columns (1) and (2) via extrapolations similar to those described in equations (17) and (18). Column (7) was calculated in an analogous way from columns (4) and (5). The results in column (7) are assumed to be free from linearization errors and are used as the exact solution to the model in calculating the percentage errors given in columns (8) and (9).

computation, our errors are $-.207$ for V_1 (i.e. $.5 - .707$) and $.207$ for V_2 (i.e. $1.5 - 1.293$). With a 2 step computation, our errors are $-.082$ and $.082$. With 4 steps, the errors are $-.037$ and $.037$. This suggests that we can estimate V_1 and V_2 by

$$V_i(1,2) = V_i(2) + [V_i(2) - V_i(1)], \quad i=1,2 \qquad (17)$$
or
$$V_i(2,4) = V_i(4) + [V_i(4) - V_i(2)], \quad i=1,2 \qquad (18)$$

where $V_i(n)$ is the estimate for V_i from an n step computation and $V_i(n,2n)$ is an improved estimate based on extrapolation using results from n step and 2n step computations. The values for $V_i(1,2)$ and $V_i(2,4)$ are set out in Table 8.1 under the headings "1, 2 step extrapolation" and "2, 4 step extrapolation". It is clear that the extrapolations have sharply reduced the errors associated with the extended Johansen method.

CONCLUSION

Table 8.2 is reproduced from DPSV (1982, p.332). It shows computations from the ORANI model of the effects on industry outputs of an elimination of tariffs. The computations have been performed with a 1-step procedure (the Johansen method) and with 2, 4, 8 and 16 step procedures (the extended Johansen method). Extrapolations similar to those described in equations (17) and (18) are shown in columns (6) and (7). We accept the 8-16 extrapolation as being the correct solution (i.e., free from linearization error).[8] Column (8) shows the percentage errors in the Johansen-style computation. Column (9) shows that these errors are sharply reduced by a 1-2 step extrapolation.

The policy shock being simulated in Table 8.2 is a large one, much larger than those routinely examined in applications of the ORANI model. Consequently, the Johansen-style errors shown in column (8) of Table 8.2 are larger than those normally encountered. Our experience with the model has been that Johansen-type computations are usually adequate. Certainly we have found that 1-2 step extrapolations reduce linearization errors well beyond the point where they could have any practical significance. Thus, our extended Johansen method enables us to eliminate uncertainties concerning linearization errors for the computational cost of one extra evaluation of the $A(V)$ matrix [the matrix on the left hand side of (8) in our example in the second section], one extra computation of the elasticities matrix $B(V)$, and one application of a simple extrapolation procedure such as (17).[9]

Compared with various non-linear procedures often used in solving general equilibrium models, the Johansen method has several important advantages.[10] First, because only simple matrix operations are required, model size presents no computational problem. Data limitations constrain the size of system (5) long before computational considerations play a role.

Second, maximum flexibility is retained by the user of the model in his choice of exogenous and endogenous variables. Changes in this choice are easily handled by a re-partitioning of the $A(V^I)$ matrix [see equation (10)]. Finally, model development can be accommodated without requiring the reassessment of algorithms or extensive reprogramming. Often all that is required is a re-dimensioning of the $A(V)$ matrix. The advantages of the Johansen method are retained by our extended Johansen method.

NOTES

1. ORANI is fully documented in Dixon, Parmenter, Sutton and Vincent (1982), cited hereafter as DPSV (1982).
2. The relevant mathematics is that of Euler's method for the numerical solution of systems of differential equations, supplemented by Richardson's extrapolation.
3. Thus in deriving (3.1) from (2.1) we can ignore the possibility of negative or complex roots.
4. See DPSV (1982, pp.201-202).
5. (7.1) is derived from (6.1) by dividing through by $V_1^? V_3$. We assume that $V_i > 0$ for all i.
6. We divide through by 2. This is not necessary. It is customary, however, to use share coefficients in the linear-percentage-change system. Notice that $V_1/2$ and $V_2/2$ are the shares of V_1 and V_2 in the sum of V_1 and V_2.
7. We assume that the relevant inverse exists. Otherwise, the Johansen method will fail. However, it is likely that if $A_\alpha(V\ 85/I)$ is singular, then our classification of endogenous and exogenous variables is illegitimate. That is, it is likely that system (1) cannot be solved for V_α in terms of V_β in the region of V^I. See DPSV (1982, Section 35).
8. That this is a highly accurate solution has been confirmed by substitution back into the original ORANI system (1).
9. Computational costs are discussed in DPSV (1982, Section 34).
10. Alternatives to the Johansen method are examined in DPSV (1982, Section 8).

REFERENCES

Dixon, P.B., Parmenter, B.R., Sutton, J. and Vincent, D.P. (1982) <u>ORANI: A Multisectoral Model of the Australian Economy</u>, North Holland, Amsterdam

Johansen, L. (1960) <u>A Multi-Sectoral Study of Economic Growth</u>, North Holland, Amsterdam (2nd edition, 1974)

Chapter Nine

ANALYSIS OF THE EFFECTS OF TIME LAGS AND NONLINEARITIES IN A MACROECONOMIC MODEL INCORPORATING THE GOVERNMENT BUDGET CONSTRAINT

Carl Chiarella

INTRODUCTION

It has become traditional in macroeconomic theory to analyse a dynamic macroeconomic model by linearising around an equilibrium point the system of nonlinear differential equations governing the dynamics of the macroeconomic model in question. Attention is then usually focussed on the necessary and sufficient conditions guaranteeing stability of the resulting system of linear differential equations. Quite often the system of linear differential equations is reached directly by assuming linear macroeconomic relationships from the outset. In either event, the system of linear differential equations governing the dynamics of the macroeconomic model is usually a local approximation to a far more complex system of non-linear differential equations.

Some interesting examples of this type of analysis include (i) the generalised Tobin monetary growth model by Hadjimichalakis (1971) and Hadjimichalakis and Okuguchi (1979); (ii) models of exchange rate dynamics by Dornbush (1976), and Gray and Turnovsky (1979), and (iii) macroeconomic models which include the government financing constraint, e.g. by Blinder and Solow (1973), Christ (1979) and Infante and Stein (1980). A common feature of most of these models is that for certain critical combinations of the structural parameters of the model the equilibrium switches from being locally stable to locally unstable. Since economic quantities are never observed to tend to either plus or minus infinity, the values of the structural parameters implying local instability are assumed not to hold. Furthermore, the linear model cannot serve as a basis for a theory of the persistent economic fluctuations observed in the business cycle. This is because linear differential equations can exhibit periodic solutions only for very precise combinations of the structural parameters. Since it is unlikely that such precise combinations of the structural parameters would hold, the linear model is not capable of yielding a theory of the business cycle.

Reliance upon local linearisation is to some extent imposed upon the economic theorist by the extreme difficulty in analysing non-linear differential equations, especially those whose right-hand sides are only specified qualitatively. Nevertheless, there is a continuing tradition of nonlinear dynamic macroeconomics starting with the work of Kalecki (1943), Kaldor (1940), and Hicks (1950), continuing with the important contributions of Goodwin (1950), (1951) and (1967) and Allais (1956), and culminating recently in the work of Medio (1979) and others. In this strand of research, the nonlinearities and time lags inherent in the models considered generate persistent economic fluctuations which are seen to be an inherent feature of the macroeconomic system.

Despite this long tradition the theory of nonlinear dynamic macroeconomics remains in the wings, with the centrestage of dynamic macroeconomic analysis being occupied by models of the linearization type as indicated in the first paragraph. The relationship between these two strands of research is unclear. On the one hand a system of linear differential equations expressing the dynamics of the models discussed in the first paragraph is unsuitable mathematically to generate _persistent_ oscillations. On the other hand, because the non-linear models generally involve a special structure in order to make their analysis tractable,[1] they seem largely unrelated to what are considered the mainstream models of dynamic macroeconomics.[2]

If one accepts the view that the business cycle is due to a series of random shocks,[3] then the use of the linear model in macroeconomic analysis could be justified. However, Blatt (1980) has argued that Frisch type models cannot provide a satisfactory explanation of business cycle fluctuations to a high level of statistical confidence. Blatt (1978) has also argued that the econometric evidence levelled against nonlinear models is invalid.

Our aim in this paper is to begin a systematic approach to the analysis of nonlinear dynamic macroeconomic models. The adopted approach reduces the study of the model's dynamic behaviour to the study of a differential equation containing two elements. The first of these elements captures the standard linear theory whilst the second addresses the nonlinear effects. For the particular model which we shall analyse here, the inclusion of the nonlinear term alters the resulting picture substantially from that obtained using standard linear theory. The situation which (according to standard linear theory) might otherwise have the economic quantities moving with explosive oscillations, turns out to be one in which the economic quantities exhibit oscillatory behaviour which converges to a periodic path. This periodic path is known as a _limit cycle_. In order to discuss the stability properties and qualitative features of this limit cycle, we shall apply the Krylov-Bogoliubov method of averaging.[4]

The setting in which we illustrate our approach is a version of the Blinder-Solow (1973) model which includes the government budget constraint. In the model discussed here, the government's deficit is financed by a combination of a constantly growing money supply and bond issues. A particular feature of our model is a nonlinear investment function similar to the one in Kaldor's (1940) model. Following Kaldor, we assume that the marginal rate of investment with respect to output is relatively high near the equilibrium value of output and relatively low far from equilibrium.

We find that the interaction of this nonlinearity with the time lag in the adjustment of the output market can lead to limit cycle motion of output and the stock of bonds. We go on to discuss the effect on the amplitude (of the limit cycle) of the rate of growth of the money supply and the rate of government spending, both of which are traditional instruments of government stabilisation policy.

SPECIFICATION OF THE MODEL

Consider a model in which there is a market for a homogeneous good whose level of output is denoted by Y. The model also contains a money market where the demand for money depends upon output Y, the nominal rate of interest r and total wealth W. If B represents the number of outstanding government bonds paying $1 per year in perpetuity, then wealth is measured by $W = M + B/r$. Using the three variable function L to denote the money demand function and M the supply of money at any given moment, the condition for equilibrium of the money market is

$$M = L(Y, r, M + B/r). \qquad (1)$$

We make the standard assumptions: $L_1 > 0$, $L_2 < 0$, $0 < L_3 < 1$ where the subscripts denote the partial derivatives with respect to the numbered argument. Equation (1) implicitly defines the nominal interest rate r as a function of Y, B and M, which we write as

$$r = r(Y, B, M). \qquad (2)$$

Setting $p = L_3 B/r^2 - L_2 > 0$, we find that

$$r_1 = L_1/p > 0,$$
$$r_2 = L_3/rp > 0,$$
$$r_3 = -(1-L_3)/p < 0. \qquad (3)$$

Turning now to the output market, <u>consumption demand</u> may be written as

$$C = c_1(1-\tau)(Y+B) + c_2(M+B/r), \qquad (4)$$

where c_1 is the propensity to consume from disposable income, c_2 is the propensity to consume from wealth, and τ is the tax rate.

Here disposable income is the sum of output Y and the interest payments on the stock of outstanding government bonds held by consumers. <u>Investment demand</u> may be written as

$$I = I_1 Y + I_2 r \tag{5}$$

where we make the standard assumptions: $I_1 > 0$, $I_2 < 0$. Following our discussion in the introduction, we assume that I_1 is relatively high around the equilibrium value of output (to be determined below) and relatively low far from this equilibrium value.

We assume that the demands of the government sector are of the form

$$G = \bar{G} + \omega \dot{Y} . \tag{6}$$

where $\bar{G}$ is some base level of government spending and ω is a constant. For $\omega > 0$, Equation (6) states that government spending rises above the base level when output is increasing (i.e. during a boom) and falls below the base level when output is declining (i.e. during a recession). When $\omega < 0$, the government spending is reversed, namely output falls below the base level during a boom and rises above this level during a recession.

Aggregate demand for output is given by

$$Z = C + I + G,$$
or
$$Z = F(Y, B, M) + \omega \dot{Y} , \tag{7'}$$

which we write in the form

$$Z = (1-\phi)Y + \beta B + \delta M + \bar{G} + \omega \dot{Y} \tag{7}$$

where
$$\phi = 1 - c_1(1-\tau) - I_1 - I_2 r_1 + c_2(L_1 + L_2 r_1)/L_3 , \tag{8a}$$

$$\beta = c_1(1-\tau) + I_2 r_2 - c_2 L_2 r_2 / L_3 \tag{8b}$$
and
$$\delta = I_2 r_3 + c_2(1-L_2 r_3)/L_3 . \tag{8c}$$

We shall assume that the supply of output adjusts sluggishly to excess demand, so that the evolution of output Y conforms to the differential equation

$$\dot{Y} = \gamma(Z - Y) , \tag{9}$$

where γ is a positive constant. After substituting (7) into (9), we find that the differential equation for Y reduces to

$$\dot{Y} = \gamma^*[-\phi Y + \beta B + \delta M + \bar{G}], \tag{10}$$

where $\gamma^* = \gamma/(1 - \gamma\omega)$.

The government increases the money stock and issues or retires bonds at a rate sufficient to finance its budget deficit. Thus we have the government finance or budget constraint

$$\dot{M} + \frac{\dot{B}}{r} = \bar{G} + \omega Y - \tau Y + (1-\tau)B , \qquad (11)$$

where the right hand side defines the government's budget deficit consisting of the difference between government outlays, $\bar{G} + \omega Y + B$, and government receipts, $\tau(Y + B)$, from taxation of disposable income. The pair of differential equations (10) and (11) determines the evolution of Y, B and M once the 'mix' of money and bond financing is set.

In the particular financing regime which we consider, we assume that the authorities allow the money supply to grow at a constant rate μ so that $\dot{M} = \mu M$. It seems reasonable to assume that the base level of government spending $\bar{G}$ would also grow at the same rate. The growth rate of the money supply imposes an underlying exponential trend on the differential system (10-11). This underlying exponential trend may be eliminated by setting

$$Y(t) = Y'(t)e^{\mu t}, \ B(t) = B'(t)e^{\mu t}, \ \bar{G}(t) = \bar{G}'e^{\mu t} \qquad (12)$$

The pair of differential equations (10-11) then reduce to

$$\dot{Y}' = -(\gamma^*\phi + \mu)Y' + \gamma^*\beta B' + \gamma^*(\delta\bar{M} + \bar{G}'), \qquad (13)$$

and

$$\frac{\dot{B}'}{r} = \omega\dot{Y}' - (\tau - \mu\omega)Y' + (1 - \tau - \mu/r)B' + \mu\bar{M} + \bar{G}' , \qquad (14)$$

where $\bar{M}$ and $\bar{G}'$ are the initial levels of the money stock and rate of government spending respectively, and the interest rate r is evaluated at the equilibrium levels ($\bar{Y}'$, $\bar{B}'$, $\bar{M}$).

The equilibrium values ($\bar{Y}'$, $\bar{B}'$) are obtained by setting $\dot{Y}' = \dot{B}' = 0$ in (13-14) and solving the resulting pair of algebraic equations. Setting $y = Y' - \bar{Y}'$ and $b = B' - \bar{B}'$, we are led to consider the homogeneous differential system

$$\dot{y} = -(\gamma^*\phi + \mu)y + \gamma^*\beta b , \qquad (15)$$

and

$$\frac{\dot{b}}{r} = \omega\dot{y} - (\tau - \mu\omega)y + (1 - \tau - \mu/r)b. \qquad (16)$$

The purpose of the change of variables (Y, B) to (Y',B') is to make the differential system governing the evolution of the model economy autonomous, by removing the exponential trend term. Figure 9.1 shows the relationship between the untransformed output Y (Figure 9.1a) and the transformed output Y' (Figure 9.1b). In Figure 9.1.a, motion is around the dashed equilibrium path, $\bar{Y}'e^{\mu t}$; in Figure 9.1b, motion is around the static equilibrium value, $\bar{Y}'$. The variable y measures deviations about this static equilibrium.

We now specify more precisely the nonlinearity (or jump) in I_1, the marginal rate of investment out of income. In particular, we define

$$I_1 = \begin{cases} \bar{I}_1, & |y| < |y_0| \\ \hat{I}_1, & |y| > |y_0| \end{cases} \tag{17}$$

where y_0 is some fixed value and $0 < \hat{I}_1 < \bar{I}_1 < 1$. This particular form for the marginal rate of investment out of income is drawn from Kaldor's (1940) nonlinear investment function. The reasons put forward by Kaldor for this type of investment behaviour are as follows:

(i) given the amount of real capital, 'low levels of activity can be carried out by existing capital so that they will not induce net investment. At the same time, gross investment will not be zero, for there is always some investment undertaken for long run development purposes which is independent of current activity.',

(ii) gross investment is small for unusually high levels of activity, owing to the increasing costs of borrowing and construction, and also to the increasing difficulty of both.

For the purposes of our analysis, the important impact of the nonlinear marginal rate of investment is on the coefficient ϕ, which assumes the form shown in Figure 9.2, where

$$\hat{\phi} = 1 - c_1(1-\tau) - \hat{I}_1 - I_2 r_1 + c_2(L_1 + L_2 r_1)/L_3, \tag{18a}$$

and

$$\bar{\phi} = 1 - c_1(1-\tau) - \bar{I}_1 - I_2 r_1 + c_2(L_1 + L_2 r_1)/L_3 \tag{18b}$$

Letting $\bar{\varepsilon} = \hat{\phi} - \bar{\phi}$ and defining the following function:

$$\varepsilon(y) = \begin{cases} 0, & |y| < |y_0| \\ -\bar{\varepsilon}, & |y| > |y_0|, \end{cases} \tag{19}$$

the differential equation (15) for y may be written as

$$\dot{y} = -(\gamma^*\bar{\phi} + \mu)y + \gamma^*\beta b + \gamma^* y \varepsilon(y). \tag{20}$$

Time Lags and Nonlinearities in Macroeconomic Models

The dynamics of our income-expenditure model, with the government deficit financed by a combination of steady growth of the money supply and bond issues, is given by the pair of differential equations (20) and (16). The possibility of limit cycle motion in this model arises through the nonlinear form of the coefficient $\bar{\phi}$. As we shall see below, the relationship of $\bar{\phi}$ to $\hat{\phi}$ may cause the system to move away from the origin if (y, b) are small, but to move towards the origin for (y, b) large. For further clarification, we now turn to a dynamic analysis of the differential equation in y and b.

THE DYNAMIC BEHAVIOUR OF THE MODEL

After some rearrangement, the pair of differential equations (20) and (16) may be written in matrix form as

$$\begin{bmatrix} \dot{y} \\ \dot{b} \end{bmatrix} = A \begin{bmatrix} \dot{y} \\ \dot{b} \end{bmatrix} + \gamma^* y \varepsilon(y) \begin{bmatrix} 1 \\ \omega \end{bmatrix} \tag{21}$$

where the matrix A has components a_{ij} given by

$$\begin{cases} a_{11} = -(\gamma^*\bar{\phi} + \mu), \\ a_{12} = \gamma^*\beta, \\ a_{21} = -r(\tau + \omega\gamma^*\bar{\phi}), \\ a_{22} = r(\omega\gamma^*\beta + 1 - \tau - \mu/r). \end{cases} \tag{22}$$

Straighforward calculations yield

$$\det(A) = r(\gamma^*\bar{\phi}+\mu).(\tau-\mu\omega). \left[\frac{\gamma^*\beta}{\gamma^*\bar{\phi}+\mu} - \frac{(1-\tau-\mu/r)}{\tau-\mu\omega} \right] \tag{23}$$

and

$$\text{tr}(A) = -(\gamma^*\bar{\phi} + \mu) + r(\omega\gamma^*\beta + 1 - \tau - \mu/r)$$

$$= -\gamma^*(\bar{\phi} - r\omega\beta) + r(1 - \tau) - 2\mu. \tag{24}$$

We assume that the values of γ and ω are such that $\gamma^* > 0$, and that the values of μ and ω are such that $\tau - \mu\omega > 0$. Hence, $\det(A) > 0$ when

$$\frac{\gamma^*\beta}{\gamma^*\bar{\phi} + \mu} > \frac{1 - \tau - \mu/r}{\tau - \mu\omega} \tag{25}$$

in which case the origin of the (y, b) axes is either a source or a sink, thereby excluding saddle point behaviour. Henceforth, we shall assume that (25) holds and note that it is a generalisation to

137

Fig. 9.1a

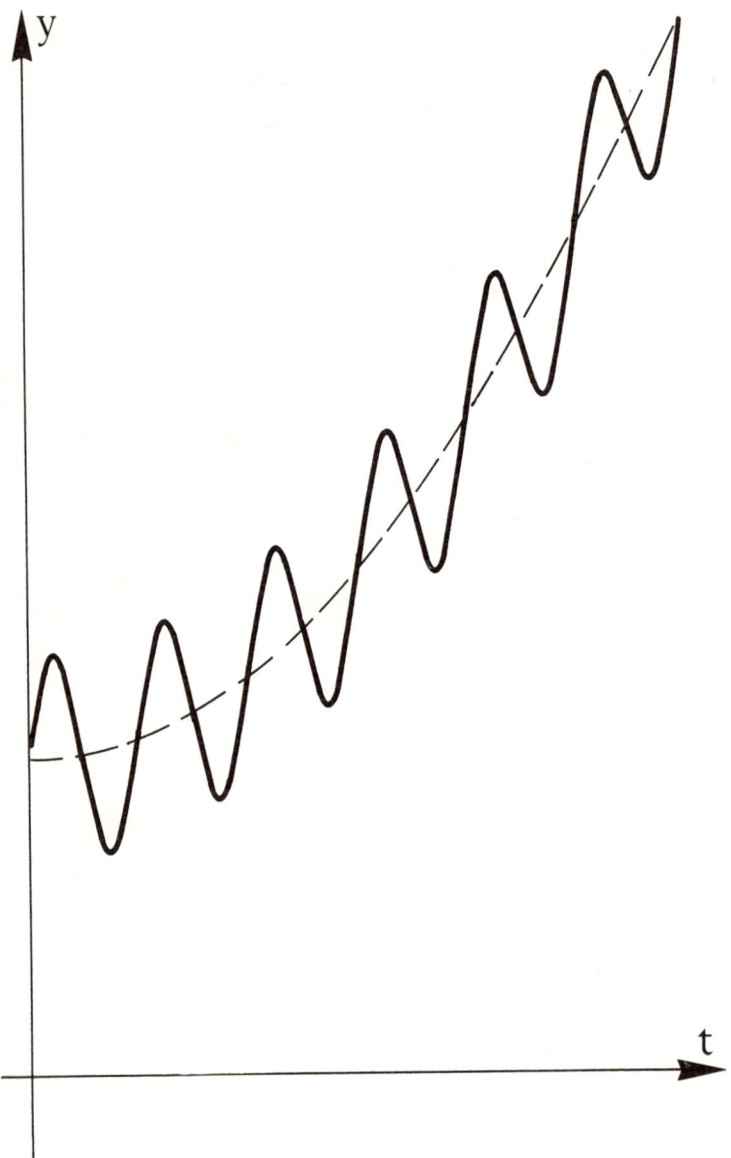

Fig. 9.1b

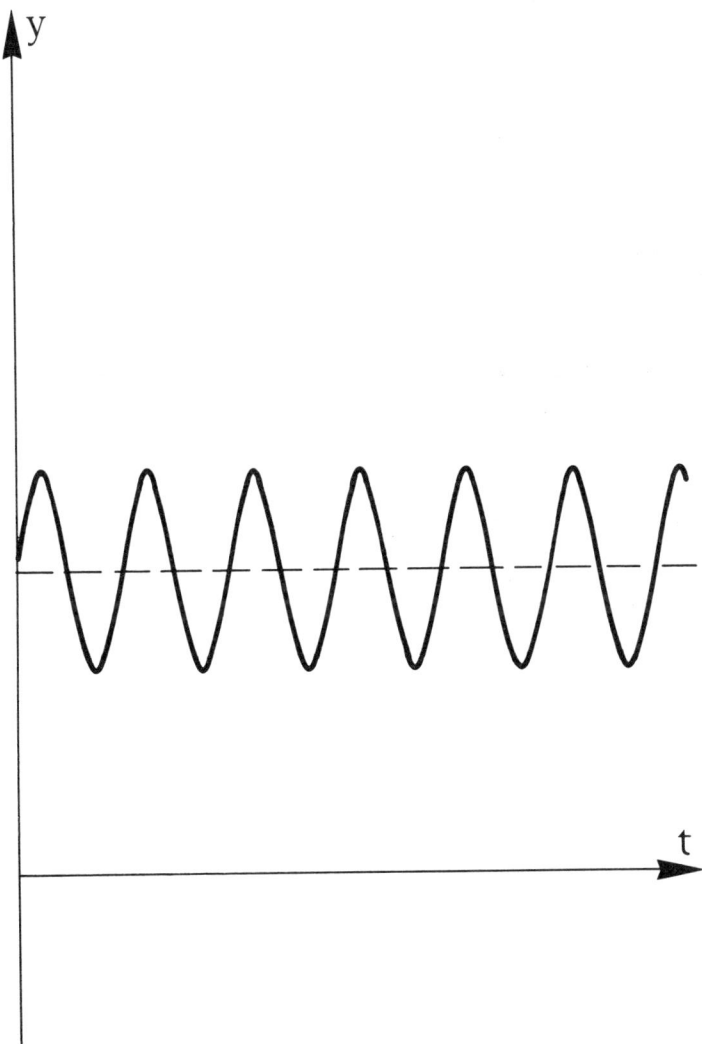

Fig. 9.2

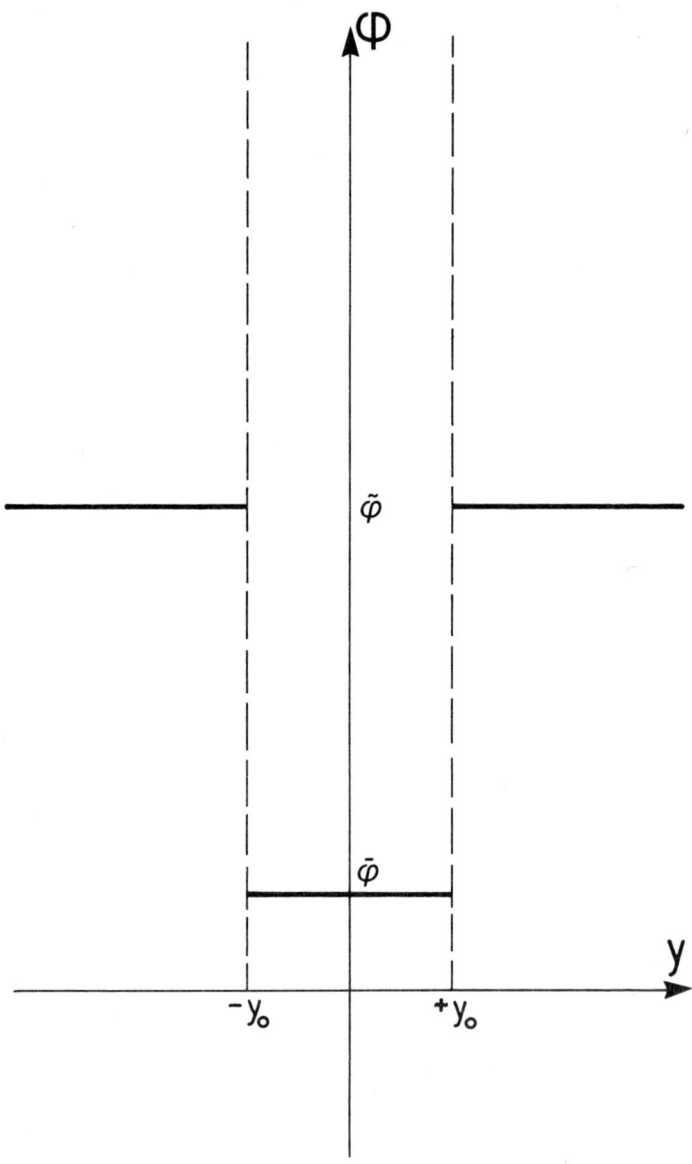

the case of a growing money supply and variable government expenditure of the Blinder - Solow (1973) condition for the stability of bond financing when the output clears instantaneously. In our notation, the Blinder - Solow condition is $\beta/\bar{\phi} > (1 - \tau)/\tau$, to which (25) reduces when $\mu = 0$.

The interesting dynamic features of our model arise from consideration of the trace, tr(A). Assuming $r(1 - \tau) - 2\mu > 0$ and $\bar{\phi} > r\,\omega\beta$, we see that tr(A) is a monotonically decreasing function of γ^* (which in turn is an increasing function of γ), with tr(A) > 0 at $\gamma^* = 0$. Thus there is a critical value of γ^*, which we denote by γ_c^*, at which tr(A) = 0. If we assume that the speed of adjustment in the output market is such that $\gamma^* < \gamma_c^*$, then tr(A) > 0 and the equilibrium point y = b = 0 is locally unstable. However, as y and b move away from the equilibrium the nonlinear investment mechanism comes into play, and $\bar{\phi}$ is replaced by $\hat{\phi}$ in tr(A). This jump in the coefficient ϕ leads to a decline in the value of tr(A).

If the parameters of the model are such that tr(A) changes from positive to negative as a result of the change in the coefficient ϕ, then far from equilibrium the motion of y and b is governed by a linear differential equation whose coefficient matrix has negative eigenvalues. Hence, far from equilibrium the motion of y and b is back towards the origin. The balancing of these two tendencies leads to stable limit cycle motion of y and b. The sign switching of tr(A) is illustrated in Figure 9.3.

We recall that the eigenvalues of the matrix A are given by

$$\lambda = tr(A) \pm \sqrt{tr(A)^2 - 4\det(A)} = u \pm iv. \qquad (26)$$

Now at $\gamma^* = \gamma_c^*$, tr(A)=0 and hence the eigenvalues are pure complex. Since we are assuming γ^* is close to γ_c^*, the eigenvalues will be complex with a small real part. Thus the motion away from the origin will be cyclical.

The dynamic motion of the nonlinear differential equation (21) is most easily analysed by transformation to a new set of coordinates, (x, a), given by

$$\begin{bmatrix} x \\ a \end{bmatrix} = P \begin{bmatrix} y \\ b \end{bmatrix} \qquad (27)$$

where the matrix P is formed from the eigenvectors of the matrix A. The change of coordinates is essentially a rotation and rescaling of the (y, b) axes. The details of this transformation to (x, a) coordinates are given in the Appendix (see also Figure 9.4). There we show that if the differential equation in (x, a) coordinates is further transformed to polar coordinates (ρ, θ), then (to a first approximation) the radius vector ρ satisfies the

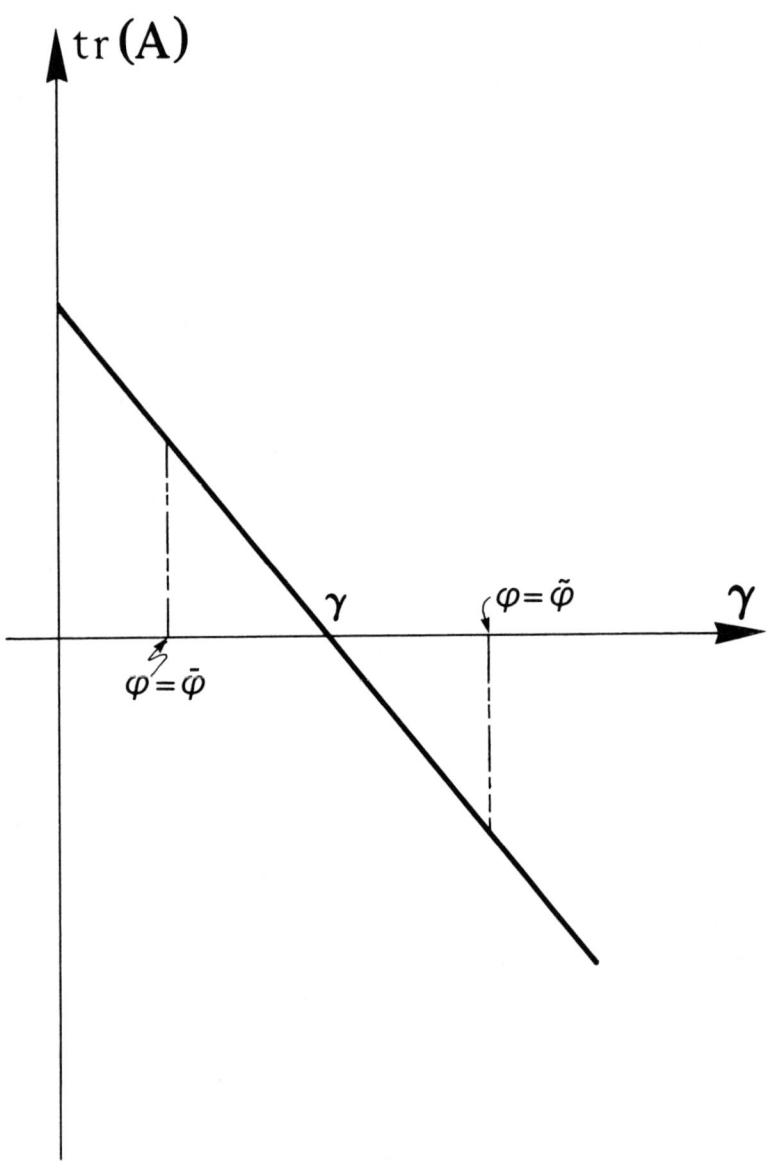

Fig. 9.3

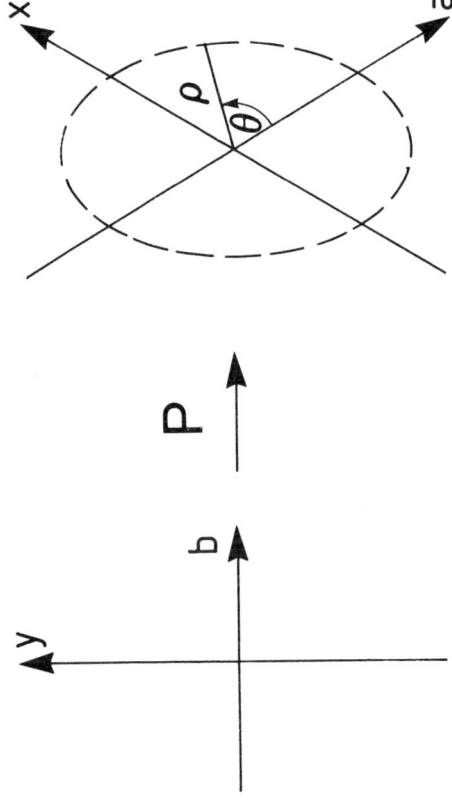

Fig. 9.4

differential equation

$$\dot{\rho} = u\rho + \bar{f}(\rho), \qquad (28)$$

where u=tr(A) and $\bar{f}(\rho)$ depend upon the second nonlinear term on the right-hand side of (21), whose expression is given in the Appendix. Equation (28) is obtained by an application of the Krylov-Bogoliubov method of averaging.

If, as in standard macroeconomic theory, we ignore the nonlinear term, then (28) reduces to

$$\dot{\rho} = u\rho \qquad (29)$$

which implies growth away from or steady decline towards the origin in the (x, a) plane [and therefore in the (y, b) plane], depending on whether u is positive or negative. Consideration of the nonlinear effects which, to a first approximation, are embodied in the $\bar{f}(\rho)$ term in (28) changes the picture obtained from the standard macroeconomic theory. It is more convenient to write (28) in the form

$$\dot{\rho} = \rho(u + \bar{f}(\rho)/\rho). \qquad (30)$$

From the expression given for $\bar{f}(\rho)/\rho$ in the Appendix, we can deduce that its general shape is as displayed in Figure 9.5. [See equation (A.16) for the definition of h.] The nonlinear differential equation (30) has two equilibrium points: one at $\rho=0$, the equilibrium point of the standard linear analysis which as we have seen is unstable under the present assumptions; the other at the point $\bar{\rho}$ given by

$$\bar{f}(\rho)/\rho = -u, \qquad (30)$$

the graphical determination of which is displayed in Figure 9.5. It turns out that $\bar{\rho}$ is a stable equilibrium point which means that in the (x, a) plane all motions are onto a circle of radius $\bar{\rho}$. This circle is the stable limit cycle. Transforming back to the (y, b) plane, the limit cycle turns out to be a rotated ellipse as shown in Figure 9.6. For initial values close to the origin, the motion of y and b spirals outwards towards the periodic limit cycle solution. For initial values far from the origin, the motion of y and b spirals inwards onto the limit cycle. We turn now to a consideration of the effect of the government policy parameters μ (the rate of growth of the money supply) and ω (the factor of proportionality by which the government changes its rate of spending as output changes). Using an approximation to $\bar{f}(\rho)/\rho$, we find that both the major and minor axes of the limit cycle ellipse increase as μ increases, indicating that increases in the rate of growth of the money supply tend to increase the amplitude of

Fig. 9.5

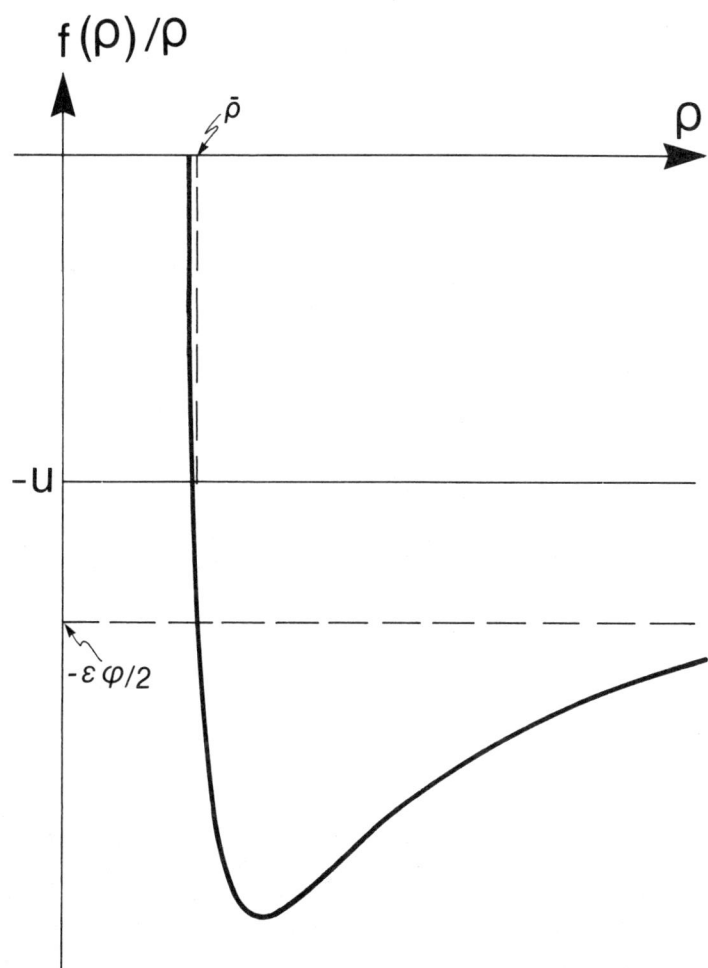

Fig. 9.6

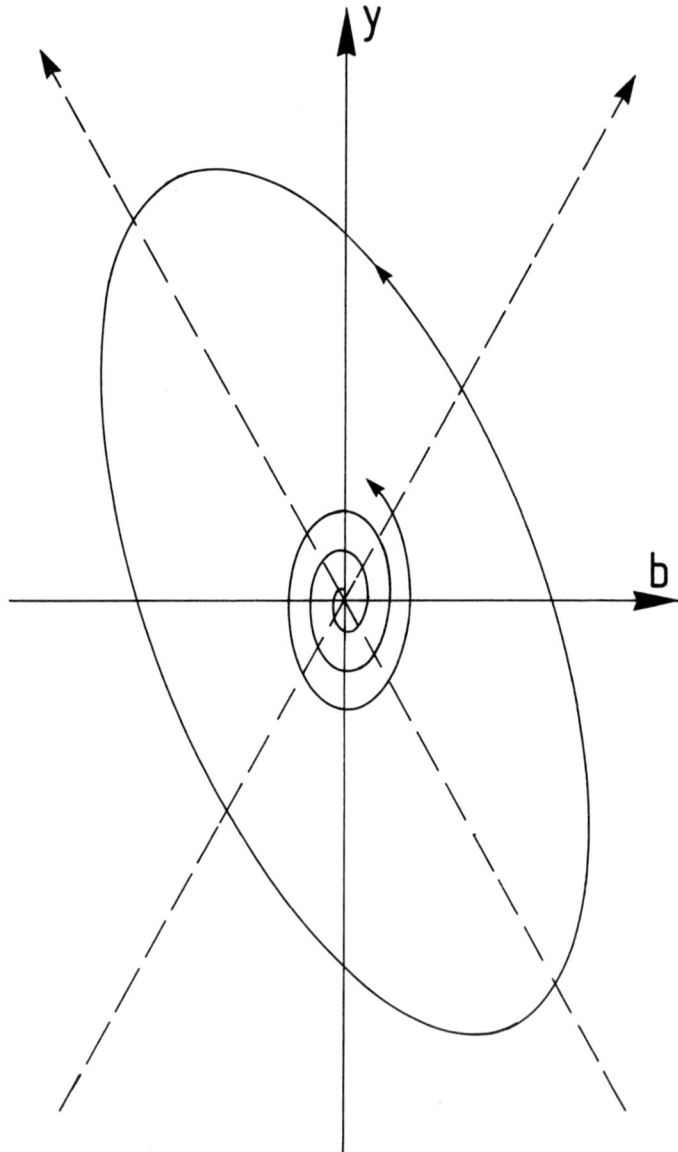

economic fluctuations. At the same time the speed of approach towards the limit cycle is increased.

The effect of changes in ω on the amplitude of economic fluctuations is not obvious. It is possible to reach either situation depicted in Figure 9.7. In the one case (a) the amplitude of economic fluctuations increases as ω increases through zero; in the other case (b) the amplitude decreases as ω increases through zero. The mathematical conditions separating these two cases are a complicated expression of all the parameters of the model and do not seem to admit any simple interpretation; nor is it possible to decide whether one particular case will prevail under the assumptions we have made. The main point of this analysis is that the use of government spending policy as a means of dampening the economic cycle may be a subtler matter than is suggested by standard linear theory which indicates that $\omega < v$ (i.e. a contracyclical policy) always dampens economic fluctuations. If case (b) prevails, then the reverse policy would be stabilising.

CONCLUSIONS

The model we have considered is essentially the Blinder-Solow (1973) model of the government budget constraint, but with a nonlinear investment mechanism and lagged adjustment in the output market. Allowance is also made for a variable rate of government spending. We consider a financing regime in which the money supply is allowed to grow at a constant rate and bonds are issued to cover the remaining deficit.

We find that situations arise in which the interaction of a time lag in the clearing of the output market with the nonlinear investment function leads to stable limit cycle motion around the equilibrium, so that all paths of output and stock of bonds tend to periodic paths. In such a limit cycle situation, the traditional comparative static analysis of the effect of government policies on equilibrium is inconclusive. Of more interest is the effect of government policies on the amplitude of the limit cycle. In this respect, our main result is that an increase in the growth rate of the money supply increases the amplitude of the economic fluctuations whilst at the same time shortening the period of these fluctuations. It has not been possible to obtain such a convincing result with respect to changes in the rate of government spending, but our results suggest that the use of government spending (countercyclical) policies as a stabilisation instrument may be a more subtle matter than is suggested by standard linear theory.

The general nonlinear approach which we have adopted here is not restricted to income expenditure models of the type analysed. These techniques have also been applied to a model of monetary dynamics and it was found that this class of macroeconomic model can also generate limit cycles.[5] Medio (1979) has investigated a number of income-expenditure models of the multiplier-

Fig. 9.7

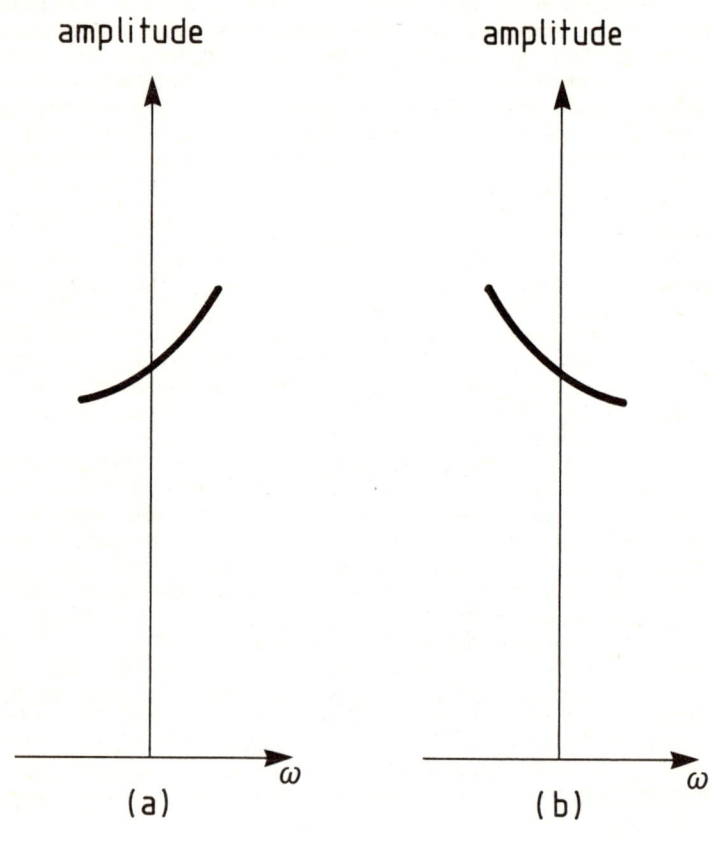

accelerator type and found that many of these display limit cycle behaviour. We have treated (in a very elementary manner) the problem of removing the underlying growth trend of the economy in order to concentrate on the fluctuations about the trend. This process is not valid in a nonlinear model relying, as it does, on the principle of superposition which is only applicable to linear systems. The ultimate aim of the current line of research is the development of a nonlinear model which can incorporate both growth and cycles. One probe in this direction has been completed by Medio (1979).

The idea that time lags and nonlinearities in dynamic macroeconomic models can lead to persistent economic fluctuations is certainly not new; indeed these were precisely the factors giving rise to such fluctuations in the Kalecki-Kaldor-Hicks-Goodwin line of research. The contribution of this study is to present a systematic approach to nonlinear dynamic macroeconomics, and to demonstrate that persistent economic fluctuations are possible in many standard macroeconomic models.

The existence of persistent fluctuations in macroeconomic models, which are the theoretical underpinning of many policy prescriptions, renders more difficult the task of economic control and stabilisation. The search for appropriate control and stabilisation policies in nonlinear models may hopefully lead macroeconomic theory in new directions.

NOTES

1. See, for example, the nonlinear accelerator principle of Goodwin (1951), or the floors and ceilings in Hicks (1950) model.
2. However, we should stress that the work of Medio (1979) probes in the direction of a more systematic approach.
3. An idea proposed initially by Frisch (1933).
4. For which Andronov, Vitt and Khaikin (1966) is the standard reference.
5. See Chiarella (1982).

REFERENCES

Allais, M. (1956) 'Explication des Cycles Economiques par un Modele Non Lineaire a Regulation Retardee', Metroeconomica 8, 4-83

Andronov, A.M., Vitt, A.A. and Khaikin, S.E. (1966) Theory of Oscillators, Pergamon Press, London

Blatt, J.M. (1978) 'On the Econometric Approach to Business Cycle Analysis', Oxford Economic Papers 30, 292-300

Blatt, J.M. (1980) 'On the Frisch Model of Business Cycles', Oxford Economic Papers, 32, 467-479

Blinder, A.S. and Solow, R.M. (1973) 'Does Fiscal Policy Matter?' Journal of Public Economics 2, 319-337

Chiarella, C. (1982) 'Analysis of a Nonlinear Model of Monetary Dynamics', Working Paper 8207, IRES, Universite Catholique de Louvain

Christ, C.F. (1979) 'On Fiscal and Monetary Policies and the Government Budget Constraint', American Economic Review, 69, 526-538

Dornbusch, R. (1976) 'Exchange Rate Expectations and Monetary Policy', Journal of Political Economy, 84, 1161-1176

Frisch, R. (1933) Propagation Problems and Impulse Problems in Dynamic Economics: Essays in Honour of Gustav Cassell, Allen and Unwin, London

Goodwin, R.M. (1950) 'A Nonlinear Theory of the Cycle', Review of Economic Statistics, 32, 316-320

Goodwin, R.M. (1951) 'The Nonlinear Accelerator and the Persistence of Business Cycles', Econometrica, 19, 1-17

Goodwin, R.M. (1967) A Growth Cycle, (Ed.) C.H. Feinstein, Cambridge University Press

Gray, M.R. and Turnovsky, S.J. (1979) 'The Stability of Exchange Rate Dynamics under Perfect Myopic Foresight', International Economic Review, 20, 643-660

Hadjimichalakis, M.G. (1971) 'Equilibrium and Disequilibrium Growth with Money: The Tobin Models', Review of Economic Studies, 38, 457-470

Hadjimichalakis, M.G. and Okuguchi, K. (1979) 'The Stability of a Generalised Tobin Model', Review of Economic Studies, 46, 175-178

Hicks, J.R. (1950) A Contribution to the Theory of the Trade Cycle, Clarendon Press, Oxford

Infante, E.F. and Stein, J.L. (1980) 'Money-Financed Fiscal Policy in a Growing Economy', Journal of Political Economy, 88, 259-287

Kaldor, N. (1940) 'A Model of the Trade Cycle', Economic Journal, 197, 78-92

Kalecki, M. (1943) Studies in Economic Dynamics, Allen and Unwin, London

Medio, A. (1979) Teoria Nonlineare del Ciclo Economico, Societa Editrice il Mulino, Bologna

APPENDIX

We rewrite here the differential system determining the motion of (y, b) namely

$$\begin{bmatrix} \dot{y} \\ \dot{b} \end{bmatrix} = A \begin{bmatrix} y \\ b \end{bmatrix} + \gamma^* \varepsilon(y) \begin{bmatrix} 1 \\ \omega \end{bmatrix}. \tag{A1}$$

Since we are considering the case when A has complex eigenvalues we denote these as

$$\lambda_1, \lambda_2 = u \pm iv \tag{A2}$$

Time Lags and Nonlinearities in Macroeconomic Models

where i is the complex number,

$$u = \operatorname{tr}(A) = -(\gamma*\bar{\phi} + \mu) + r(\omega\gamma*\beta + 1 - \tau - \mu/r), \quad (A3)$$

and

$$\begin{aligned}v^2 &= 4\det(A) - \operatorname{tr}(A)^2, \\ &= 4r\gamma*\beta(\omega\gamma\ddot{\phi} + \tau) - [\gamma*\bar{\phi} + r(\omega\gamma*\beta + 1 - \tau)]^2.\end{aligned} \quad (A4)$$

The corresponding eigenvectors of A are found to be

$$V_1, V_2 = \begin{bmatrix} \frac{\gamma*\bar{\phi}+\mu}{r\hat{\tau}} \\ 1 \end{bmatrix} \pm i \begin{bmatrix} \frac{v}{r\hat{\tau}} \\ 0 \end{bmatrix}, \quad (A5)$$

where $\hat{\tau} = \tau + \omega\gamma*\bar{\phi}$.

Introducing the matrix

$$P = (V_2, V_1) \quad (A6)$$

it is a known result from linear algebra that

$$A = P^{-1}\Omega P, \quad (A7)$$

where

$$\Omega = \begin{bmatrix} u & -v \\ v & u \end{bmatrix}. \quad (A8)$$

Defining a new set of coordinates (x, a) by

$$\begin{bmatrix} x \\ a \end{bmatrix} = P \begin{bmatrix} y \\ b \end{bmatrix} \quad (A9)$$

The differential system (A1) for (y,b) transforms into the following:

$$\begin{bmatrix} \dot{x} \\ \dot{a} \end{bmatrix} = \Omega \begin{bmatrix} x \\ a \end{bmatrix} + \gamma*y\varepsilon(y) \begin{bmatrix} \nu \\ \omega \end{bmatrix} \quad (A10)$$

for (x, a). Here

$$\nu = [v + \omega(\gamma*\bar{\phi} + \mu)]/r\hat{\tau},$$

and from (A9) y is expressed in terms of x and a as

$$y = [r\hat{\tau}x - (\gamma*\bar{\phi} + \mu a]/v. \quad (A11)$$

The differential system (A10) is most easily analysed by transforming it to polar co-ordinates, $x = \rho\cos\theta$, $y = \rho\sin\theta$. Upon performing this transformation, we find that the differential equation for the radius vector ρ is

$$\dot{\rho} = u\rho + f(\rho,\theta), \qquad (A12)$$

where

$$f(\rho,\theta) = \gamma * y(\rho,\theta) \cdot \varepsilon(\rho,\theta) \cdot (\nu\cos\theta + \omega\sin\theta), \qquad (A13)$$

and $y(\rho,\theta)$, $\varepsilon(\rho,\theta)$ are the expressions for y and $\varepsilon(y)$ in terms of (ρ,θ). We do not write down the differential equation satisfied by the polar angle θ, as we are not concerned with a detailed analysis of the speed of approach towards the limit cycle in the present study.

We analyse the differential equation (A12) for ρ by an application of the method of averaging, which yields a first order approximation to ρ by approximating $f(\rho,\theta)$ with the first term of its Fourier expansion

$$\bar{f}(\rho) = \frac{1}{2\pi} \int_0^{2\pi} f(\rho,\theta) d\theta. \qquad (A14)$$

We do not include all the details of the calculation of $\bar{f}(\rho)$, however these calculations hinge upon the limits of the interval in which $\varepsilon(\rho,\theta)$ is zero. From the definition $\varepsilon(\rho,\theta)$, we have that

$$\varepsilon(\rho,\theta) = \begin{cases} 0, & \dfrac{-\nu y_0}{h\rho} < \dfrac{r\hat{\tau}}{h}\cos\theta - \dfrac{(\gamma*\bar{\phi}+\mu)}{h}\sin\theta \leq \dfrac{\nu y_0}{h\rho}, \\ -\bar{\varepsilon}, & \text{outside this interval,} \end{cases} \qquad (A15)$$

where

$$h^2 = (r\hat{\tau})^2 + (\gamma*\bar{\phi}+\mu)^2. \qquad (A16)$$

Defining ξ and ψ by

$$\sin\xi = \nu y_0/h\rho, \quad \tan\psi = r\hat{\tau}/(\gamma*\bar{\phi}+\mu), \qquad (A17)$$

we find that $\varepsilon(\rho,\theta) = -\bar{\varepsilon}$ within the intervals $\xi + \psi < \theta < \pi + \psi - \xi$, $\pi + \psi + \xi < \theta < 2\pi + \psi - \xi$, and $\varepsilon(\rho,\theta) = 0$ outside these intervals.

After integration, we find that

$$\frac{\bar{f}(\rho)}{\rho} = \frac{-\bar{\varepsilon}}{\pi} \left[\frac{\pi}{2} - \xi + \frac{(1 + 2\beta\nu\rho*)}{h^2} \sin\xi \cos\xi \right], \qquad (A18)$$

which conforms with the general configuration depicted in Figure 9.5.

PART IV

TIME SERIES ANALYSIS AND ECONOMETRICS

Chapter Ten

ITERATIVE FITTING OF A TIME SERIES MODEL

Bruce D. Craven

INTRODUCTION

Economic time series are often not stationary (especially if data are in terms of inflated money), and often do not satisfy the <u>additive</u> assumption that the time series u_t (t = 0, 1, 2, ...) is the <u>sum</u> of a deterministic component y_t (trend, seasonal effects) and a stochastic component z_t (supposed to be stationary). Most of the theory assumes this additivity. Since it usually does not hold, a <u>transformation</u> of the data is needed to ensure approximate additivity. The example given by Chatfield and Prothero (1973), see also Box and Jenkins (1973), shows that the predictive accuracy of a Box-Jenkins fitted model can depend seriously on the right choice of transformation. But this choice is not obvious, especially with limited data - perhaps only 30 to 50 data points. Although it is reasonable to deflate money data by analysing log u_t, and to expect that this transformation will bring the series nearer to additivity, there is no guarantee that the logarithmic transformation is the best for the purpose of prediction.

Desirably, one needs some iterative process in which an initial transformation is estimated and then adjusted to suit the data better. In fact, some iterative model-fitting is also needed in estimating the deterministic component, since the significance of a fitted term is only roughly known in advance of a complete analysis of the stochastic residual z_t.

It is noted further that some methods of analysis restrict the shape of a seasonal component to something like a sine wave, although there seems no reason why a seasonal component should have such a form. For example, the Box-Jenkins method models the seasonal component by a difference equation, and thus restricts its functional form. It is conjectured that a more accurate estimation of the seasonal component would be needed in order to get good prediction. A Fourier analysis (into sine waves) may converge too slowly to be useful.

This paper presents some ideas and approaches for such iterative fitting, using a univariate time series u_t (t = 0, 1, 2,...n). Most parts of the approach are well known, in isolation;

Iterative Fitting of a Time Series Model

the aim is to combine them into a workable package.

INITIAL TRANSFORMATION OF DATA

If the given series shows inflation of money, it should be roughly de-inflated by a logarithmic transformation. If there is any large seasonal component, this should be removed by estimating a seasonal factor (with say monthly data) by averaging all January figures, all February figures, etc., and then dividing by (or maybe subtracting) this seasonal factor. Both these 'pre-transformations' are only rough; they can be adjusted at a later stage of the analysis.

Assume then that there is no large seasonal factor, and no large inflationary trend. The following diagrams illustrate some possibilities (In practice, there would be more data than shown). In Figure 10.1, the 'scatter' is confined to a band of constant width about an apparent linear trend, and there is no obvious need for a transformation. But in Figure 10.2, the 'scatter' increases and additivity certainly does no hold. (The increase is somewhat exaggerated in Figure 10.2, over what might normally be expected, to make the difference clear).

We do not usually know a priori whether the series of Figure 10.2 is 'exploding' in time, or whether the 'scatter' is increasing systematically with increasing mean value, unless we have a theory discriminating between the two cases. We can try to fit the second possibility (scatter increases with mean) by dividing the series into 'chunks' (shown ringed in Figure 10.2), and estimating roughly a mean m and a scatter s for each 'chunk'. The difficulty here is that the u_t may have a large amount of serial correlation. If the 'chunks' are of sufficient time duration, we can hope that there is not too much correlation between successive 'chunks'.[1]

Suppose then that the relation $s = g(m)$ is observed to hold approximately, for some function g. (A plot of s against m would estimate g). Then a suitable transformation takes u_t to $x_t = \psi(u_t)$, where

$$\psi(u) = \int^u dm/g(m).$$

This makes the scatter more nearly constant for the transformed series x_t. This follows from $s_x \cong \psi'(u)s_u \cong (1/g(m))g(m)$, where s_x and s_u denote the respective scatters for 'chunks' of x_t and u_t. This same transformation is often used in analysis of variance, with uncorrelated data; but here we must work with 'chunks'. Often transformations $\psi(u_t) = u_t^a$ or $\psi(u_t) = \log u_t$ will result. This compares with Box and Cox (1964); however, there will not be enough 'chunks' to make a likelihood approach useful.

Iterative Fitting of a Time Series Model

Fig. 10.1

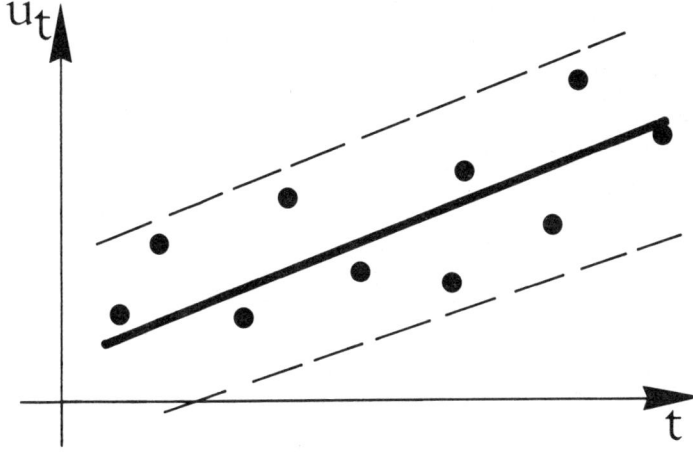

Fig. 10.2

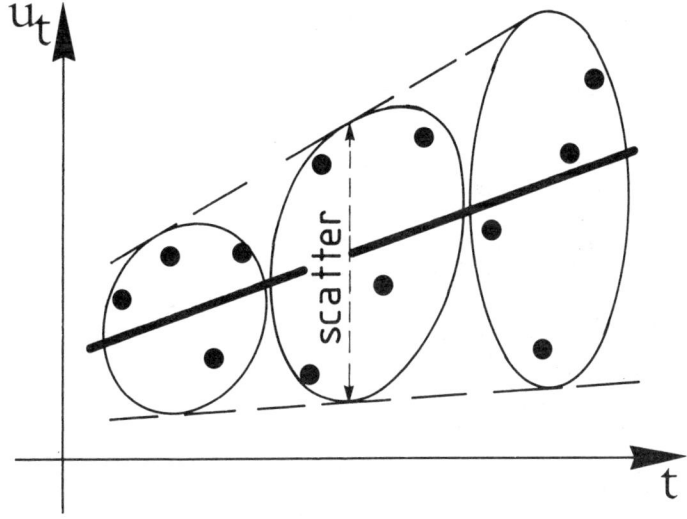

Iterative Fitting of a Time Series Model

SCHEME OF ANALYSIS

(a) Pre-transformation (see previous section)

(b) Estimate the transformation ψ, as in previous section, and thus calculate x_t.

(c) Estimate the deterministic component y_t. This could consist of (i) a polynomial in time t (perhaps only a + bt), (ii) a periodic component (one or several sine or cosine terms), (iii) an exponential $y_t = c^t$; (iv) a sum of several such terms. The coefficients in y_t would be estimated by the usual least-squares regression. Note that least-squares does not find the frequencies for periodic components: either these are known already (particularly an annual cycle for agricultural data), or they may be estimated using Fisher's test for "leading periodic components". These are well known techniques (see Hannan, 1960). Note also that sine and cosine terms will usually not represent seasonal effects very well; but the pre-transformation is assumed to have already accounted for a large part of these effects.

(d) Do a rough test of significance for the terms in the estimate, $\bar{y}_t$ say, of y_t. Note that the (likely) serial correlation of the residuals z_t invalidates the usual regression test of significance; but it is the best which can be applied at this stage. For (i) and (ii), but not (iii), the least squares estimates are asymptotically efficient (Hannan, 1960); but this is not so helpful for small samples. Deleting (apparently) insignificant terms from $\bar{y}_t$, estimate z_t by

$$\bar{z}_t = x_t - \bar{y}_t.$$

Unfortunately this estimate is apt to be biased.

(e) If the $\bar{z}_t$ are significantly dependent, as determined, say, by the test of Durbin and Watson, then a stochastic model is fitted to the $\bar{z}_t$. This would often by an ARMA. If, in particular, an autoregression is fitted:

$$\bar{z}_t = a_1 \bar{z}_{t-1} + a_2 \bar{z}_{t-2} + \ldots + a_p \bar{z}_{t-p} + e_t,$$

where the increments e_t are supposed independently distributed, then for a given p the coefficients a_i may be estimated by regression. One well-known method for estimating p is to fit an initial autoregression for a large value of p, to estimate the residual variance, and then truncate to a smaller value of p which does not increase the residual variance too much. Some computer programs for regression do this. An estimate $\bar{f}(\lambda)$ is then required for

Iterative Fitting of a Time Series Model

the spectral density $f(\lambda)$ of $\bar{z}_t$. This is obtained either by calculation from the fitted autoregression or ARMA, or directly estimated by some 'window' technique (see Hannan, 1960) applied to the $\bar{z}_t$. Note that bias corrections (which may be large) must be applied to $\hat{f}(\lambda)$ from a 'window' technique. Details are given in Hannan (1960).

It may happen that the predictability of the time series x_t is all in its deterministic part y_t. In that case, the $\bar{z}_t$ are likely to show no significant serial correlation; so the stochastic model reduces to independent $\bar{z}_t$, whose variance may be calculated. Otherwise, there will be a residual variance calculated from the autoregression.

(f) The <u>significance of the terms of y_t can now be re-tested</u>. For (i), the residual variance estimate from the least-squares fit is replaced by $2\pi\bar{f}(0)$. For (ii), the periodogram component is divided by $2\pi\bar{f}(\lambda)$ at the appropriate frequency λ, before applying Fisher's test (the Whittle-Walker test). More information can be obtained from Hannan (1960).

(g) Since, in general, (f) will alter the assessed significance of some components of $\bar{y}_t$, it follows that $\bar{y}_t$ <u>can now be re-estimated</u>, retaining those components found significant in (f). Then the calculation is repeated, proceeding to step (e) again. For future reference, a variance, say s^2, is now calculated for the prediction given by the fitted model, including both deterministic and stochastic terms, for one step ahead in time. In principle, the calculation might have to go to another iteration, but most probably $\bar{y}_t$ would reach a steady value after two calculations of (e) and (f).

(h) An appropriate time duration for each 'chunk' in (b) may now be estimated, using the autocorrelogram for the residuals $\bar{z}_t$. Denote by r_τ the autocorrelation with lag τ for $\bar{z}_t$. A possible case is illustrated in Figure 10.3. Also shown is the 'noise band'; for lags $\tau > L$, the autocorrelations r_τ are no longer individually significantly different from zero. Thus L would be an appropriate duration for each 'chunk'. Note that the variance of r_τ is of order $1/(n-\tau)$, for fixed sample size n, and $\tau < n$. Hence b could be taken of order $(1/\sqrt{n})$. If L is greatly different from what was assumed in (b), then the transformation ψ can be re-estimated, using better 'chunks'. This may require subsequent steps to be repeated.

Iterative Fitting of a Time Series Model

Fig. 10.3

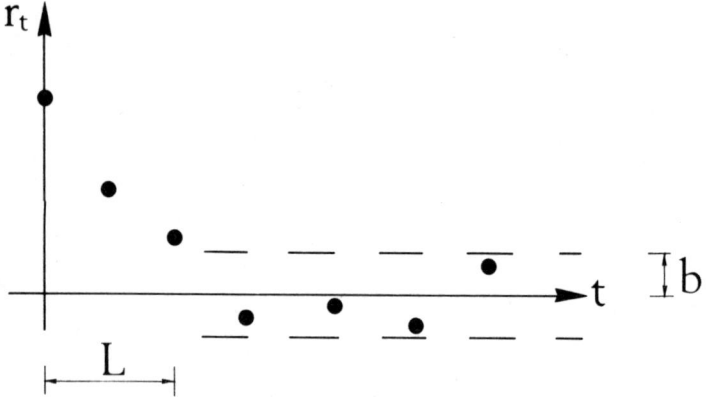

Iterative Fitting of a Time Series Model

(i) The transformation ψ has, however, only been roughly estimated. For definiteness, suppose that a transformation $\psi(u) = u^q$ was chosen. The value of q is then only known approximately. Hence, q could be varied a little, and the prediction variance s^2 calculated as a function of q, over some small interval containing the estimated value of q. Ideally, q could be varied so as to minimize s^2. In practice, s^2 might be calculated for three values of q, and interpolation applied to find a minimizing value of q.

A similar procedure could be adopted if the Box and Cox formula, $\psi(u) = (u^q - 1)/q$, is adopted; this would be suitable if $\psi(u) = \log u$ had been estimated, corresponding to q = 0.

DISCUSSION

This approach is exceedingly rough. But so is any time series prediction from small samples, which is often the case when using economic time series. Computation with actual data will be needed, to ascertain what can be achieved. The proposed approach allows the data, instead of a priori assumptions, to determine the transformation to be used.

Any such transformation introduces bias into the subsequent estimates. Bias corrections could be estimated approximately, but would they be meaningful? It could well happen that the transformed data x_t could have more meaning than the given data u_t, and in that case unbiased estimates for x_t would seem to be more useful. For example, with money data, a model in terms of constant dollars would have more conceptual meaning that a model in terms of inflated dollars. However, the whole question of bias corrections for time series estimates seems to need more enquiry.

Instead of fitting a trend as in c(i), or a periodic component as in c(ii), the Box-Jenkins method could instead be applied. The above discussion of iterative adjustments to such estimates will still apply. However, the method of Box-Jenkins differencing (to fit a seasonal factor) may not be appropriate for some data sets.

In general, $\bar{y}_t = y_t + E_t$, where the error term E_t includes both bias and stochastic terms. At a theoretical level, one may consider a function F, which takes (y_t, z_t, s^2) from one iteration to the next. However, a proof of convergence, together with distributional properties of the limiting results based on properties of the mapping F, has still to be deduced.

NOTES

1. The desired duration of a 'chunk' is discussed later. Figure 10.2 shows, for simplicity, three 'chunks'. With actual data, one would hope for about five 'chunks', with more data points

per 'chunk'.

REFERENCES

Box, G.E.P. and Cox, D.R. (1964) 'An analysis of transformations', Journal of the Royal Statistical Society B 26, 211-243

Box, G.E.P. and Jenkins, G.M. (1973) 'Some comments on a paper by Chatfield and Prothero and a review by Kendall', Journal of the Royal Statistical Society A135, 337-352

Chatfield, C. and Prothero, D.L. (1973) 'Box-Jenkins seasonal forecasting: problems in a case-study', Journal of the Royal Statistical Society A136, 295-336

Hannan, E.J. (1960) Time Series Analysis, Methuen, London

Chapter Eleven

THE STATE SPACE SOFTWARE SARAS FORECASTS BETTER THAN THE BOX-JENKINS METHOD

Keshav P. Vishwakarma

INTRODUCTION

This chapter compares two time series forecasting alternatives. One is the statistical software called SARAS. The other is the well-known Box-Jenkins procedure. A key economic indicator, namely the quarterly gross national product, is used in the study. One year ahead (four quarters ahead) forecasts are prepared by each method, and ten different samples are employed. Correspondingly, ten different forecasts beyond the sample period are obtained. It is found that SARAS performs better than the Box-Jenkins method. SARAS also provides estimates of the seasonal and trend components of the time series. For business and economic planning this information is very useful. Such information is, in contrast, not given by the Box-Jenkins Procedure.

SARAS is based on the state-space approach of modern control theory. It includes various options for data analysis and forecasting. A brief description of SARAS is given in the next section. The forecast evaluation test is then described, followed by the selection of a suitable Box-Jenkins model. Both SARAS and the Box-Jenkins procedure employ stochastic models. They therefore furnish probabilistic forecasts. The probability distributions are designated in terms of the conditional means and confidence intervals. The conditional means are the 'best' forecasts which minimize the variance. Comparison of the conditional means and variances is also discussed.

THE STATE SPACE SOFTWARE SARAS

SARAS is an easy-to-use computer software for the analysis and forecasting of single discrete time series. It is based on the following state-space formulation of modern control theory:

$$x(t+1) = A(t) \cdot x(t) + B(t) \cdot u(t) + C(t) \cdot v(t) \quad (1)$$
$$y(t+1) = H(t+1) \cdot x(t+1) + w(t+1) \quad (2)$$

The symbols in (1) and (2) represent the following:
 x(t) is the n-dimensional state vector,
 y(t) is the l-dimensional observation vector,
 u(t) is the m-dimensional non-random input (control) vector,
 v(t) is the k-dimensional random disturbance (noise) vector,
 w(t) is an l-dimensional random noise vector,
 A(t), B(t), C(t), D(t) are non-random matrices of appropriate dimensions, and
 t is a discrete time index.

The random disturbances v(t) and w(t) are assumed to be independent Gaussian (normally distributed) white noise sequences. Since v(t) affects the transition of the system state over time, it is called the state transition noise. The random sequence w(t) is called the measurement (or the observation) noise. Assuming that the initial state x(o) at t=0 is Gaussian, then the stochastic process x(t) is also Gaussian.

An important feature of the state-space model is that no direct measurements of the state x(t) are made. Instead, a linear transformation of the state corrupted by random noise w(t) is observed as vector y(t).

The filtering and prediction theory relating to the above stochastic model has been discussed in the literature (see, e.g., Aoki, 1967; Astrom, 1970; Jazwinski, 1970; Anderson and Moore, 1979). Let

$$x^*(t) = E[x(t) \mid y(1), y(2),\ldots, y(t)] \qquad (3)$$

$$S(t) = cov[x(t) \mid y(1), y(2),\ldots, y(t)] \qquad (4)$$

$$\hat{x}(t+j) = E[x(t+j) \mid y(1), y(2),\ldots, y(t)], j = 1,2,\ldots (5)$$

$$P(t+j) = cov[x(t+j) \mid y(1), y(2),\ldots,y(t)], j = 1,2,\ldots (6)$$

That is, $x^*(t)$ and $S(t)$ are the conditional mean and covariance, respectively, of the system state x(t) based on the data history up to time t. The well-known Kalman filter facilitates their calculation in a recursive manner (see, e.g., Kalman and Bucy, 1961; Aoki, 1967; Meditch, 1969; Anderson and Moore, 1979).

The conditional mean, $\hat{x}(t+j)$, and the conditional covariance, $P(t+j)$, relate to future system states or forecasts. The conditional mean, $\hat{x}(t+j)$, is the 'best' forecast in the minimum variance sense. These forecasts can also be calculated recursively.

Different estimation problems arise in the context of the above stochastic formulation. One is that of estimation of the system state for a given model. Filtering, smoothing and prediction theory deal with this issue. Estimation of models from given data history is called the identification problem in control theory. Optimal identification using the maximum likelihood criterion has also beeen discussed in the literature (e.g., Sage and Melsa, 1971). Once a model has been identified, forecasts can be prepared.

A given set of historical data is, of course, a particular realization of the observations: $y(1), y(2), \ldots, y(t)$. In the case of univariate time series, the observation process, $y(t)$, is a scalar process. However, the state vector can be multidimensional.

A variety of options is included in SARAS:
1. Trends
   1.1 Constant level (no trend)
   1.2 Linear trend
   1.3 Exponential trend
2. Seasonals (4- and 12- period)
   2.1 No seasonals
   2.2 Additive seasonals
   2.3 Multiplicative seasonals
3. Autoregressive - moving average component
   3.1 First order autoregressive
   3.2 Second order autoregressive
   3.3 Second order autoregressive - first order moving average
4. Noise
   4.1 State transition and observation noise
   4.2 No observation noise (error free measurements)
5. Trend adaptation with memory fade
   5.1 No trend adaptation
   5.2 Trend adaptation with finite memory.

The selection of alternative options for a specific application is simple. Maximum likelihood estimation of desired model(s) is inbuilt. Similarly, the calculation of forecasts is inbuilt. SARAS obtains one-period-ahead predictions over the sample which incorporate successive observations through the Kalman filter. Beyond the sample it calculates true (ex ante) forecasts up to a given lead time. Both the mean level and the 95% confidence interval are obtained. In addition, corresponding forecasts of the trend and the autoregressive-moving average components are given. The predictions can be saved in computer files where necessary, and the stored results can be plotted subsequently on available graphics equipment. SARAS itself does not have graphics capabilities. SARAS is written in FORTRAN and double precision is used for real variables.

A comment on the trend adaptation option is in order. Suppose a sample consists of N historical data, $y(1), y(2), \ldots, y(N)$. Then the most recent M observations, $y(n-M+1), y(N-M+2), \ldots, y(N)$, can be employed to obtain the latest trend estimate. Simultaneously, the sample as a whole is used to obtain estimates of other unknowns in the model. When this option is not invoked, estimation of trend and other unknowns is based on the complete sample.

Forecasting Software SARAS and the Box-Jenkins Method

Some applications of modern control theory in economic forecasting and decision-making have been considered by the author previously (Vishwakarma, 1970, 1974). Other appear in Chapters 2 through 5 of this volume. SARAS represents further work on applications of the state-space methodology (Vishwakarma, 1982).

FORECAST EVALUATION TEST

Time series methods provide useful forecasting information for certain planning and management functions (Chambers et al., 1971). There are several statistical methods for forecasting univariate data. Recently, the Box-Jenkins procedure has become well-known in this field. It is considered to give very accurate forecasts. In this report, therefore, we compare the forecasting performance of SARAS with that of the Box-Jenkins method.

We consider the problem of preparing one year ahead (four quarters ahead) forecasts of the quarterly gross domestic (non-farm) product for Australia. We use a 20-quarter sample period for estimation of both SARAS and the Box-Jenkins models. For example, data over 1966, March quarter - 1970, December quarter are used to obtain forecasts for the 1971, December quarter. We employ 10 such sample periods: the first over 1966, March - 1970, December; the second over 1967, March - 1971, December; and the tenth over 1975, March - 1979, December. Corresponding one-year-ahead forecasts for 1971, December; 1972, December;...; 1980, December are calculatd by both methods. There are thus 10 beyond-the-sample predictions in the test. Since the corresponding actual values are known, the accuracy of the forecasts can be determined. The complete data set therefore consists of 60 observations from 1966, March quarter to 1980, December quarter. We use the official Gross Non-Farm Product data (in billions of dollars) published by the Australian Bureau of Statistics (original, unadjusted data from Seasonally Adjusted Indicators, 1981, p.92).

It is useful to qualify the sample size used. A sample of only 20 quarterly observations might be considered as rather small. However, in real time this sample spans a five year period which is a medium term horizon for many planning situations. Therefore, the sample period chosen represents a significant time interval. Because economic data are scarce and costly to obtain, there are only 20 observations in this period.

Both SARAS and the Box-Jenkins procedure include many alternative models. A specific model from each needs to be chosen for the comparison test. The small sample of 20 observations restricts the choice in that we cannot have models with too many parameters. The presence of seasonal fluctuations in the (original) gross non-farm product data further demands that this variation be included.

In the case of SARAS, a model with exponential trend, multiplicative (4-quarter) seasonals, first-order autoregressive component, and trend adaptation is selected because this is considered to be the simplest model suitable. For trend adaptation, the latest 8 quarters (two years) are regarded as adequate. This is the finite memory period for trend updating. Table 11.1 and Figures 11.1, 11.2 and 11.3 illustrate the performance of this model. The sample period is over 1975, March-1979, December, since this is most recent in the data set. Table 11.1 is part of the printed output from SARAS. It shows one-quarter-ahead forecasts over a part of the sample period and forecasts up to four quarters beyond the sample. The one year ahead entry for 1980, December is $30.372B for the mean. The corresponding 95% confidence limits are $29.97B and $30.769B. The one-interval-ahead forecasting errors average -0.05647 over the sample and their standard deviation is 0.17920. The ratio of the variance of these errors to the time series variance is only 0.26 per cent. These statistics indicate that the fit of the model is satisfactory. The latest exponential growth is estimated to be 2.74 per cent each quarter. Figure 11.1 exhibits the one quarter ahead predictions of the trend level over the sample period. For illustration purposes, the estimated seasonal factors are graphed in Figure 11.2. The 95% confidence intervals of the forecasts during and beyond the sample period are plotted in Figure 11.3.

The selection of a suitable Box-Jenkins model for the comparison test is considered in the next section.

SELECTION OF A BOX-JENKINS MODEL

The Box-Jenkins procedure for the univariate time series is of relevance here. The general form of the autoregressive-integrated moving average models considered in this approach is as follows (Box and Jenkins, 1970; Hull and Nie, 1981):

$$\phi(B).\psi(B^S).(1-B)^d.(1-B^S)^D Z(t) = \theta(B).\xi(B).a(t) \qquad (7)$$

where
- B is a backward shift operator such that $BZ(t) = Z(t-1)$,
- S is the seasonal time period; S = 4 for quarterly data and S = 12 for monthly data,
- d is the degree of non-seasonal differencing,
- D is the degree of seasonal differencing,
- $\phi(B)$, $\psi(B)$, $\theta(B)$, $\xi(B)$ are polynomials in B,
- a(t) is a Gaussian white noise sequence,
- t is the discrete time index, and
- Z(t) is an optional log or power transform of the time series y(t), or the variable y(t) itself.

For a particular application, choices must be made regarding seasonal and non-seasonal differencing, transformation of time series y(t), and the autoregressive - moving average polynomials. The identification and estimation of suitable models has been described in the literature (Box and Jenkins, 1970; Nelson, 1973).

Table 11.1: A Sample of SARAS Output

SARAS Options: Trend - Exponential.   Seasonal - Multiplicative.
Autoregressive (order 1).
State Transition and Observation Noise.
Trend Adaptation with Latest 8 Observations.

Date: 19th May 1982

S. No.	Year	Month/ Quarter	Historical Data	Mean Forecast	Lower 95% Conf Limit	Upper 95% Conf Limit	Trend	AR-MA Part
		* * * ESTIMATION PERIOD - ONE-INTERVAL-AHEAD FORECASTS * * *						
		--- ONLY A SUBSET OF SAMPLE IS PRINTED ---						
17	1979	MAR	23.159	22.827	22.471	23.183	24.024	-0.001
18		JUN	24.032	24.292	23.922	24.661	24.636	0.000
19		SEP	25.431	25.353	24.977	25.729	25.263	0.000
20		DEC	27.526	27.466	27.069	27.863	25.906	-0.000
		* * * PROJECTIONS (FORECASTS) BEYOND AVAILABLE DATA * * *						
21	1980	MAR		25.243	24.887	25.599	26.566	0.000
22		JUN		26.861	26.492	27.230	27.242	-0.000
23		SEP		28.035	27.659	28.410	27.936	0.000
24		DEC		30.372	29.975	30.769	28.647	-0.000

Forecasting Software SARAS and the Box-Jenkins Method

```
ONE-INTERVAL-AHEAD FORECAST ERROR STATISTICS

    MEAN  -0.05647      STANDARD DEVIDATION  0.17920

    AUTOCORRELATION FUNCTION
     0    1.000    1   0.118    2   0.166    3   0.321    4  -0.078

RATIO OF FORECAST ERROR VARIANCE TO TIME SERIES VARIANCE (PER CENT)
    0.26 PER CENT

EXPONENTIAL GROWTH (+) or CECLINE (-)   2.74 PER CENT

MULITPLICATIVE (RATIO) SEASONAL FACTORS
    MAR   0.950
    JUN   0.994
    SEP   1.004
    DEC   1.060
```

Fig. 11.1

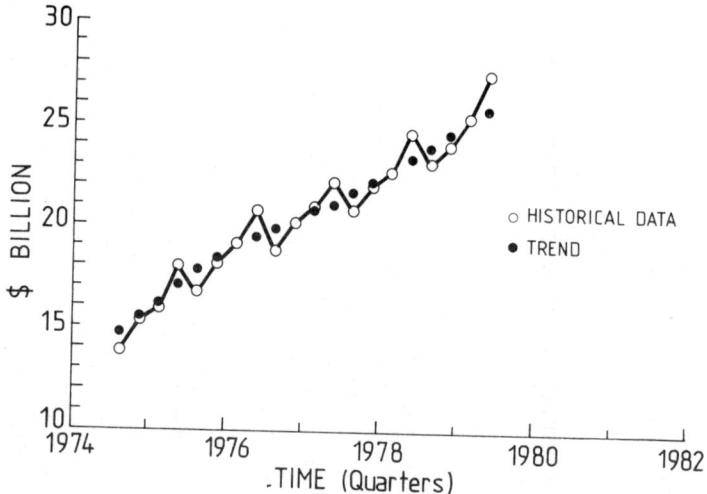

Fig. 11.2

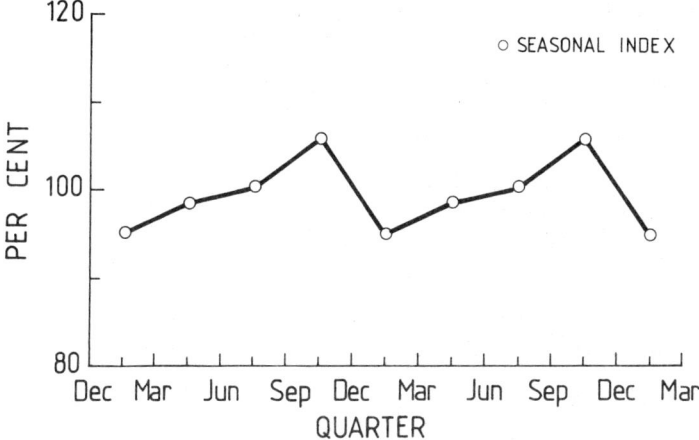

Fig. 11.3

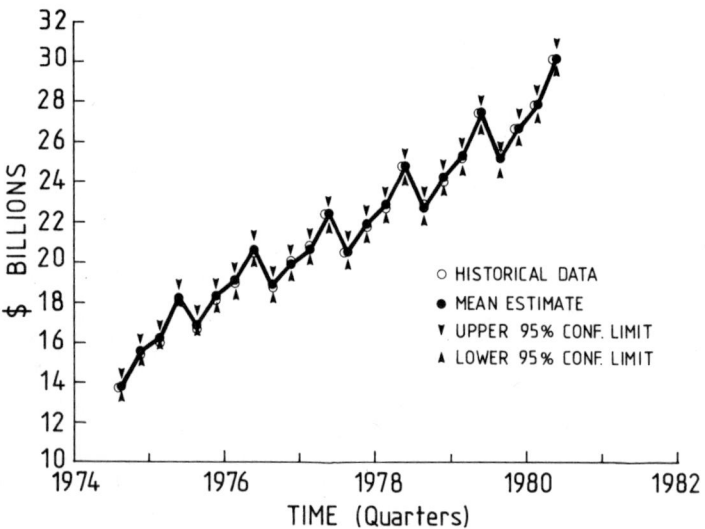

Forecasting Software SARAS and the Box-Jenkins Method

Many computer programs are available which enable selection of such models and preparation of forecasts. For example, the Library of the International Mathematical and Statistical Libraries (IMSL, 1975) includes subroutines for the Box-Jenkins method.

The Box-Jenkins routine contained in the well-known SPSS software (Hull and Nie, 1981) is used for the calculations in this. We employ the most recent sample of 20 observations over 1975, March - 1979, December for selection of a suitable model. Consider the following alternatives:

- I   Log transformation, degree of non-seasonal differencing $d = 1$, degree of seasonal differencing $D = 1$, first order autoregressive with a constant.
- II Log transformation, $d = 1$, $D = 1$, first order moving average with a constant.
- III Log transformation, $d = 1$, $D = 1$, first order auto regressive - first order moving average with a constant.
- IV Log transformation, $d = 2$, $D = 1$, first order moving average without a constant
- V   Log transformation, $d = 2$, $D = 1$, first order auto regressive without a constant.

The seasonal period S equals 4 for the quarterly gross domestic non-farm product data. The seasonal differencing reduces the number of degrees of freedom for estimation by 4. Similarly, each non-seasonal differencing reduces the degrees of freedom by one. As the sample size is merely 20, we are restricted to models with very few parameters. These alternatives were estimated using SPSS which gives various statistics relating to the Box-Jenkins approach.

It is useful to examine the one year ahead forecasts for 1980, December quarter produced by each alternative. These are included in Table 11.2. The entries in this table are in billions of dollars. We see that model V cannot be considered suitable because it gives a confidence interval of more than $11 billion width for a mean forecast of about $32 billion. Model IV produces a forecast confidence interval of $5.8 billion width in contrast to a width of $4 billion given by models I, II and III. Both models IV and V involve non-seasonal differencing of order two. The implication is that a non-seasonal differencing of order more than one worsens the confidence interval forecasts.

These results show that model I gives the narrowest confidence interval forecasts while producing about the same expected value as models II and III. The identification and estimation statistics also support that model I is a suitable choice for our comparison test. To recall, model I involves the log transformation, a seasonal differencing of order one and a first order autoregressive component with a constant.

Table 11.2 One Year Ahead Forecasts for 1980, December Quarter

Model	Mean Forecast	95% Confidence Interval		
		Lower Limit	Upper Limit	Range (Width)
I	30.081	28.144	32.150	4.006
II	30.055	28.109	32.135	4.026
III	30.073	28.132	32.146	4.012
IV	28.492	25.733	31.548	5.815
V	31.817	26.683	37.939	11.256

COMPARISON OF MEAN FORECASTS

The selected SARAS and Box-Jenkins models can be estimated for each of the ten samples mentioned earlier. Each respective software furnishes one year ahead forecasts beyond the sample period. In this section, we compare the expected values of the probabilistic forecasts. The calculated mean forecasts are presented in Table 11.3. The first row shows the forecasts for 1971, December quarter based on the sample data over 1966, March - 1970, December. SARAS gives an expected level of $9.329B and the Box-Jenkins model $9.19B. The actual gross non-farm product was recorded at $9.342B. The other rows in Table 11.3 give similar information for different samples.

We calculate the following descriptive statistics for the two sets of forecasts:

$$\text{mean percentage error} = \left(\sum \frac{\text{actual} - \text{forecast}}{\text{actual}} \right) \times 10$$

and mean absolute percentage error

$$= \left(\sum \frac{|\text{actual} - \text{forecast}|}{\text{actual}} \right) \times 10$$

The results are presented conveniently as follows:

	SARAS	Box-Jenkins
Mean percentage error	0.135	0.575
Mean absolute percentage error	4.523	5.105

We see that in this test SARAS performs better than the Box-Jenkins model on both scores. The small mean percentage error for SARAS indicates that its forecasts were practically unbiased. In contrast, the Box-Jenkins forecasts show a bias of half a percentage point. Similarly, the mean absolute percentage error for SARAS is one half of a percentage point better (smaller). For forecasting

Forecasting Software SARAS and the Box-Jenkins Method

Table 11.3: Comparison of Mean Forecasts (in billion dollars)

Sample Number	Sample Period	Forecast Period	Actual Data	SARAS Forecast	Box-Jenkins Forecast
1	1966,M-70,D	1971,D	9.342	9.329	9.195
2	1967,M-71,D	1972,D	10.408	10.547	10.591
3	1968,M-72,D	1973,D	12.340	11.451	11.449
4	1969,M-73,D	1974,D	15.293	14.161	14.911
5	1970,M-74,D	1975,D	17.998	18.280	19.378
6	1971,M-75,D	1976,D	20.769	21.894	21.585
7	1972,M-76,D	1977,D	22.294	24.977	24.355
8	1973,M-77,D	1978,D	24.659	25.013	23.305
9	1974,M-78,D	1979,D	27.527	26.935	26.292
10	1975,M-79,D	1980,D	32.370	30.372	30.081

Mean percentage error:				0.135	0.575
Mean absolute percentage:				4.523	5.105

Note: M and D refer to March and December quarters, respectively.

key economic indicators like the gross non-farm product figures, such an improvement in accuracy is certainly advantageous.

COMPARISON OF INTERVAL FORECASTS

The second moment of the probabilistic forecasts can also be compared for the two methods. We do this in terms of the 95 per cent confidence intervals. The interval estimates are functions of the forecast variance which in turn depends on the random noise in the models. If the estimated noise is large, the models will give wide intervals.

The type of stochastic models we are dealing with in this chapter are, in general, intended to represent a signal (message) process vis-a-vis random noise. The real-life processes that generate the observation data are of course unknown by assumption; otherwise there would be no modelling and estimation problem. In this discussion therefore, the size of signal and noise is in the context of assumed models. For a given model, wide confidence intervals show that the random noise is large compared to the signal, and narrow intervals indicate that it is small.

In this respect the selected SARAS and Box-Jenkins models differ a great deal. Tabe 11.4 lists the interval estimates for the one year ahead forecasts. To consider one case, we see that SARAS gives an interval from $29.975B to $30.769B for the 1980, December quarter. This is a spread of 0.794B, or nearly $800 million. In contrast, the Box-Jenkins interval is from $28.144B to $32.150B with a width of $4.006b, or more than $4000 million. For forecasting of important economic indicators like the non-farm product, a spread of $4B around the mean forecast of $30B will be regarded as rather inaccurate.

Inspection of Table 11.3 shows that SARAS consistently gives narrower intervals than the Box-Jenkins model in this test. In other words, the estimated random noise in the SARAS model is small compared to the signal, whereas in the Box-Jenkins model it is much larger.

CONCLUSION

To conclude, we summarize the results of the forecast evaluation test. We find that SARAS performs better than the Box-Jenkins model in the test just described. Both the mean percentage error and the mean absolute percentage error of the forecasts are smaller for SARAS. Its confidence intervals are also narrower. In fact, the Box-Jenkins confidence intervals are so wide that they may not be considered very satisfactory for the forecasting of gross domestic product.

As mentioned before, SARAS employs the state-space framework of control theory. A major concern of control and communication theory is with the separation (filtering) of messages (signals) from noise. SARAS is accordingly set up to filter the trend, seasonal and irregular components which are considered typical of business and economic data. Figures 11.1 and 11.2 illustrate this feature. Even visual inspection of graphed economic data is usually enough to discern the trend and seasonals. However, the Box-Jenkins procedure does not provide information on such characteristics of time series. In fact there are several forecasting methods that lack the identification of seasonals and trends in business and economic data. SARAS would be considered preferable to them in this respect, although further testing is advisable before we can reach any general conclusions about the comparative merits of each forecasting technique.

For illustrative purposes, we have employed an economic indicator in this report. SARAS can of course be used for the analysis and forecasting of data other than economic ones.

Forecasting Software SARAS and the Box-Jenkins Method

Table 11.4: Comparison of Interval Forecasts (in billion dollars)

Sample Number	Forecast Period	SARAS Intervals		Box-Jenkins Intervals	
		From	To	From	To
1	1971,D	9.260	9.399	8.879	9.522
2	1972,D	10.483	10.611	10.239	10.956
3	1973,D	11.316	11.517	11.027	11.889
4	1974,D	13.993	14.329	14.095	15.774
5	1975,D	18.064	18.496	18.293	20.527
6	1976,D	21.633	22.155	20.040	23.248
7	1977,D	24.696	25.258	22.727	26.098
8	1978,D	24.597	25.430	21.547	25.207
9	1979,D	26.561	27.309	24.594	28.117
10	1980,D	29.975	30.769	28.144	32.150

REFERENCES

Anderson, B.D.O., and Moore, J.B. (1979) *Optimal Filtering*, Prentice-Hall, Englewood Cliffs, N.J.

Aoki, M. (1967) *Optimization of Stochastic Systems*, Academic Press, New York

Astrom, K.J. (1970) *Introduction to Stochastic Control Theory*, Academic Press, New York

Box, G.E.P. and Jenkins, G.M. (1970) *Time Series Analysis: Forecasting and Control*, Holden-Day, San Francisco

Chambers, J.C., Mullick, S.K. and Smith, D.D. (1971) 'How to Choose the Right Forecasting Technique', *Harvard Business Review*, 49, 45-74

Hull, C.H., and Nie, N.H., Editors (1981) *SPSS Update 7-9*, McGraw-Hill, New York

International Mathematical and Statistical Libraries, Inc. (1975) *IMSL Library*, Houston

Jazwinski, A.H. (1970) *Stochastic Processes and Filtering Theory*, Academic Press, New York

Kalman, R.E. and Bucy, R.S. (1961) 'New Results in Linear Filtering and Prediction Theory', *Journal of Basic Engineering*, 83, 95-108

Meditch, J.S. (1969) *Stochastic Optimal Linear Estimation and Control*, McGraw-Hill, New York

Nelson, C.R. (1973) *Applied Time Series Analysis for Managerial Forecasting*, Holden-Day, San Francisco

Sage, A.P. and Melsa, J.L. (1971) *System Identification*, Academic Press, New York

Vishwakarma, K.P. (1970) 'Prediction of Economic Time Series by Means of the Kalman Filter', *International Journal of Systems Science*, 1, 25-32

Vishwakarma, K.P. (1974) *Macro-economic Regulation*, Rotterdam University Press, Rotterdam

Vishwakarma, K.P. (1982) 'SARAS: A Computer Program for Time Series Forecasting with State Space Models of Control Theory', School of Economics, LaTrobe University, Melbourne

Chapter Twelve

ELECTRICITY DEMAND MODELLING

William A. Donnelly

INTRODUCTION

A prerequisite for the development of an effective energy policy is knowledge of the relative importance of the factors affecting the demand for electricity. Basic economic theory postulates that demand responds to numerous influences, among the more important ones being prices (of the product itself, of substitute goods, and of complementary goods), income levels, plus other social, economic, demographic, and physical factors. When analyzing a derived demand, information about the stock and usage of the products requiring the immediate commodity can be incorporated in the relationship.

It is convenient in demand analysis to divide the economy into separate sectors, e.g. agricultural, commercial, residential, industrial, and government. This approach is justified here because previous energy demand studies have shown that the various sectors respond differently to the factors mentioned above. For example, the industrial sector is generally able to respond more rapidly to changes in relative prices than is the residential sector. This may occur because industry, as a part of normal business activity, regularly monitors economic conditions and has a greater degree of flexibility in modifying operating practices or changing technology. Whereas in the household sector, energy consuming appliances represent a major capital investment with a long life expectancy and the household is only able to offset the cost of replacing or retrofitting these devices against energy savings. This usually entails a long payback period. Therefore changes in the important decision variables would need to be larger and of longer duration in order to elicit a similar level of response from residential consumers as compared with their industrial counterparts.

This paper outlines the formulation of a dynamic model for personal consumption expenditures based upon utility theory. Special attention will be directed toward the determinants of household energy consumption, in particular electricity demand.

A discussion of the data required for estimation is presented. Results of a preliminary single equation model estimated from currently available data are discussed so as to illustrate the potential for an expanded model. Finally, suggestions are made as to alternative modelling strategies that might be effectively developed to address other electricity policy issues.

MODEL FORMULATION

The demand for a product as postulated in the theory of the firm is a function of prices, income, and a set of other factors. The consuming unit chooses its purchases from the basket of available commodities subject to an income constraint. The household's desire to maximize utility means that changes in the relative prices of the commodities will affect the position of the goods purchased. Several modelling strategies might be pursued. First, one might wish to explain both the level of household consumption expenditure as well as the pattern of that expenditure among commodity classes, e.g. household consumption and its component parts: housing, food, clothing, health, education, recreation, and energy consumption. Such an approach requires detailed information about each of the broad categories defined within the market basket. An alternative might be to consider only the allocation of demand among the goods within a particular commodity class, e.g. an attempt to explain the shares of less data, namely information on the relative shares and a price for each of the alternative sources of energy. Still fewer data are required when considering the demand for only a single energy commodity such as electricity. The single equation approach provides insight into the policy factors affecting the demand for the product but not the nature of its interrelationships with other goods within the same commodity class or across classes of goods.

We begin by specifying the household's objective function as the desire to maximize utility subject to a budget constraint. This is denoted:

maximize: $U(X)$ (1)
subject to: $PX \leq y$ (2)

Here U is the household's utility function which comprises the market basket of goods represented by the vector X. The budget constraint, household income (y), is imposed so that consumption expenditure, defined by multiplying the goods purchased by their prices (P), is less than or equal to income. When provided with the utility function, commodity prices, and income, the level of consumption for each item in the market basket can be determined by use of mathemtical programming techniques. The specific form and parameters of the utility function are generally unknowns. In addition, a debate involving both theoretical and empirical questions clouds the issue of deriving an aggregate utility function. One means of avoiding these problems is to assume that the level of total consumption is given and that only the question of the allocation of expenditure among the alternative commodity classes needs to be resolved.

This simplifies the analysis by reducing the data requirements and allows the use of duality theory to derive the parameters of the direct utility function from the estimation of the corresponding indirect utility function. The necessary assumptions needed to invoke the concepts of duality theory are that the aggregate utility function is twice differentiable, monotonic, and quasi-concave. One specification for the utility function is the transcendental logarithmic (translog) form defined by Christensen, Jorgenson and Lau (1975). The translog is a flexible functional form imposing a minimum number of a priori restrictions on the parameters. The translog utility function is of the form:

$$\ln U = \ln \alpha_0 + \sum_i \alpha_i \ln X_i + 1/2 \sum_i \sum_j \gamma_{ij} \ln X_i \ln X_j \qquad (3)$$

As Christensen, Jorgenson and Lau (1973, p.374) explain, the "direct and indirect translog approximations to a given pair of direct and indirect utility functions represent different preferences" unless the utility functions are self-dual. In the case of the translog this requires the functions to be linear logarithmic, i.e.

$$\gamma_{ij} = 0, \text{ for all } i \text{ and } j. \qquad (4)$$

This restriction can be statistically tested as can the equality, symmetry, additivity and homotheticity restrictions. The latter restrictions are required for the function to be 'well-behaved'. The estimation and derivation of the substitution and demand elasticities requires data on each commodity group's share of consumption expenditure and their respective prices. If the utility function is separable, then a multi-stage decision process may be modelled. Separability requires that the marginal rate of substitution between one commodity group and the other groups is independent of the level of consumption of these goods. Various forms of separability can be tested. The existence of a separable function allows the analysis of the shares within a commodity class independently from analysis of the overall share of that class. The general aggregate utility function is denoted as:

$$U = f(S, F, C, H, T, R, E) \qquad (5)$$

The commodity groups included here are: housing (S), food (F), clothing (C), health-care (H), schooling (T), recreation (R), and energy (E). A utility function that is separable in energy expenditures would allow estimation of Equation 6 independent of Equation 5.

$$U_E = g(O, G, W, El) \tag{6}$$

This equation represents an energy utility function comprising the various forms of energy available to the household, i.e. oil (O), gas (G), wood (W), and electricity (El). Estimation of the function would require information on the share of the total energy expenditure that each fuel type represents and the respective prices. Several problems arise. First, in a technical sense the energy sources are not perfect substitutes for one another. Electric motors and lighting require electricity. Cooling and water heating may use either electricity or gas (with perhaps small proportions of solar for water heating and wood for cooking). All of the energy sources may be used for space heating. Since these forms of energy are imperfect substitutes, lighting will not be converted from electricity to some other fuel regardless of the relative price increases in electricity that might occur. Second, wood is only partially a market good. Much of the wood fuel used by households is scavenged or collected from ones own property. Also, much of the recent trend toward wood burning stoves and open fireplaces probably reflects a change in consumer tastes rather than a response to energy prices. Finally, since the demand for energy is derived from the end-uses to which it is a necessary input, information on the stocks and prices of this end-use equipment in the household is needed. Time-series of these data are not currently collected.

If electricity demand is separable from the demand for the other energy fuels, then it is possible to model this demand relationship independently. Such a formulation would be:

$$Q_{El} = h(P_{El}, P_S, P_C, Y, X) \tag{7}$$

The variables in Equation 7 are: the quantity of electricity consumed (Q_{El}), the price of electricity (P_{El}), the price of substitute goods (P_s), the price of complementary goods (P_c), income (Y), and other factors (X). While economic theory does not suggest any specific functional form - the two most frequently estimated forms are the linear and log-linear forms - it does imply what the appropriate algebraic sign for each variable should be. For a 'normal' good, an inverse relationship is expected to exist between the quantity demanded and its price. A similar negative relationship is expected between the demand for a good and other goods consumed in conjunction with it, namely complementary goods. A direct relationship is anticipated with respect to the price of substitute goods. The same relationship is expected with income. The algebraic signs for any other factors affecting the demand relationship depend upon the nature of these effects. For example, severe weather could be expected to increase the consumption of electricity used for space heating or cooling purposes.

The demand for electricity is a derived demand which reflects the uses to which electricity is put rather than the direct satisfaction provided to consumers from the use of the commodity itself. In such an instance, it is often useful to consider the demand of other goods that make use of the commodity in question. Thus, the stock of electricity-using appliances and the intensity of their use are important determinants of the demand for electricity. Unfortunately, only infrequent surveys are done on the stock of household appliances and no information is available on the intensity of their use. Therefore, it is not currently feasible to include a stock of appliances variable in Equation 7. An alternative approach, first applied to energy modelling by Houthakker and Taylor (1970), is to incorporate a lagged dependent variable (Q_{Et-1}) in the explanatory variable set X. One interpretation of this dynamic demand model formulation is that the lagged dependent variable represents a proxy for the stock of appliances and their utilization rates.

THE DATABASE

The data used in the residential electricity demand model are presented in Table 12.1. This analysis is restricted to the annual consumption data published in the reports of the Electricity Supply Association of Australia (ESAA). An annual time-series for average consumption per household in kilowatt hours (kWh) was constructed. While it is recognized that there is a seasonality in the consumption of electricity in the Australian Capital Territory (ACT), it is not possible from currently published data to identify the nature of this variation. Therefore, Q_{Et} is defined as the average annual electricity consumption per ACT household. Because of the simultaneity problem caused by the quantity purchased decision directly affecting the unit price to be charged, a problem first recognized by Houthakker (1951), Taylor (1975) argues that the marginal price of electricity should be used rather than the more easily calculated average revenue per kWh figure. A difficulty arises, however, when using annual data in specifying the marginal price, since billing rates are based upon monthly consumption and those data are not published. It is assumed in this analysis that residential usage is uniform throughout the year. Thus the marginal price was calculated as the price of the next kWh of electricity which would be consumed in excess of the average monthly consumption figure. When the electricity tariff changed during the year, a weighted average of the applicable marginal prices was computed.

A price index for substitute fuels, an unpublished component of the Consumer Price Index for Canberra, was obtained from the Australian Bureau of Statistics (ABS). This series reflects the price of heating oil and kerosene sold in Canberra. It correlates well with the heating oil price series obtained previously from a retail supplier of heating oil. Since the ABS series was

Table 12.1: ACT Residential Electricity

Fiscal Year	Annual Residential Electricity Consumption	Number of Residential Electricity Customers	Average Revenue	Marginal Price
	('000 kWh)		(¢/kWh)	(¢/kWh)
1963-64	106847	19998	1.614	1.500
1964-65	125223	21577	1.597	1.475
1965-66	143893	24380	1.577	1.450
1966-67	165722	26551	1.574	1.450
1967-68	180563	29008	1.576	1.450
1968-69	213668	31969	1.568	1.450
1969-70	235841	35437	1.568	1.450
1970-71	268643	39386	1.541	1.400
1971-72	307255	43010	1.531	1.400
1972-73	333226	47088	1.567	1.4125
1973-74	367587	50604	1.683	1.450
1974-75	456089	55463	1.824	1.550
1975-76	501518	59634	1.974	1.643
1976-77	580752	63732	2.123	1.785
1977-78	625397	66152	2.286	1.950
1978-79	695980	69954	2.399	2.067
1979-80	734588	70529	2.538	2.266
1980-81	793972	72518	2.792	2.615
1981-82	840795	75027	3.322	3.382

Electricity Demand Modelling

Annual Demand Model Data

Household Disposable Income	Fuels Price Index	Consumer Price Index	Degree Days	
			Heating	Cooling
			($12°$ Base)	($23°$ Base)
5620	19.9	92.4	777.2	19.3
5825	19.9	95.2	851.7	14.8
5888	19.9	98.1	781.9	19.0
6201	20.6	100.0	745.1	19.0
6574	20.6	102.6	760.1	73.8
6926	20.3	104.4	901.8	45.3
7067	20.6	107.4	803.9	10.0
7655	20.9	113.0	868.3	20.9
8022	20.9	119.4	877.4	10.6
8855	20.9	126.3	647.3	75.5
10679	21.2	142.7	599.8	21.4
13149	24.0	164.9	789.2	12.0
14329	30.3	187.3	671.8	23.9
14770	34.1	212.9	802.4	33.1
16572	40.9	232.2	727.9	33.4
17081	52.7	251.0	798.5	66.5
19249	79.3	278.0	687.0	41.6
22149	100.0	305.0	624.4	108.4
24566	111.8	337.6	714.3	67.9

available only from 1972-73 onwards, the initial years of the series were backcast using the heating oil price series. No information on the price of complementary goods was included in the analysis because of the lack of data on the stock or usage rates for electrical appliances. A series of household disposable income for the ACT was developed by S. Leung from Taxation Statistics and the Australian National Accounts. This series more accurately reflects the purchasing power of the household than does average weekly earnings of taxpayer disposable income, which both relate to an individual in the household.

As mentioned earlier, a stock of or utilization rate for electricity-using appliances was not available and thus could not be included in the model formulation. The alternative selected was to model a dynamic demand function by inclusion of a lagged dependent variable in the set of explanatory variables. Two climate variables were analyzed in order to determine the affect of severe weather on electricity consumption. The variables tested were a heating degree day (HDD) and cooling degree day (CDD) series, using reference temperatures of 12 degrees Celsius and 23 degrees Celsius, respectively. Although these are both quite gross measures of weather, they were deemed suitable for an annual study.

STATISTICAL RESULTS

The single equation demand model presented in Equation 7 was estimated in several linear and non-linear forms using various subsets of the explanatory variables described above. The statistical results obtained from the linear and log-linear model estimations were quite similar; therefore it was decided to use the Box-Cox (1964) procedure as an attempt to test the functional form. Savin and White (1978) use this procedure with likelihood ratio statistics to test several conditional, general, and joint hypotheses concerning the appropriate functional form, and also for serial correlation. The maintained hypothesis, Ω, is tested against the restricted hypothesis, ω, the null hypothesis, H_0, to yield a "limiting chi-square distribution with q degrees of freedom where q is the number of additional restrictions imposed." (Savin and White, p.6). The test statistic is

$$\theta = 2 [L(\Omega) - L(\omega)] > \chi_{\alpha}^{2} (q) \qquad (8)$$

Various combintions of three restrictions can be tested:
1. $\lambda = 1$ - a linear model,
2. $\lambda = 0$ - a logarithmic model, and
3. $\rho = 0$ - no first-order serial correlation.

The Box-Cox lambda variable transforms all of the regression variables in the extended Box-Cox (BCE) case. The BCE procedure is applied here because the lagged endogenous variable is included in the explanatory dataset and therefore must be transformed by the

Electricity Demand Modelling

same lambda used on the dependent variable. The estimation results of the alternative BCE forms of the electricity demand relationship, along with the relevant elasticities (E_i), are presented in Table 12.2. The hypotheses tested and the chi-square results are presented in Table 12.3. Of the conditional hypothesis tests only the linear model given no serial correlation is rejected at the 0.10 significance level. The unrestricted and joint tests of the linear model are rejected at the 0.25 level of significance. The unrestricted serial correlation test is rejected at the 0.10 level. Thus the Box-Cox procedure rejects the linear formulation. The unrestricted and joint tests do not reject the logarithmic formulation. The absence of first-order serial correlation is not rejected. Because of these results it was decided to report upon the log-linear model shown in Equation 9:

$$\ln Q_{El} = \alpha + \beta_1 \ln P_{El} + \beta_2 \ln P_S + \beta_3 \ln Y + \beta_4 \ln W + \varepsilon \quad (9)$$

where Q_{El} is the average household electricity consumption,
       P_{El} is the real marginal price of electricity,
       P_S is the real price of substitute goods,
       Y is the real income,
       W is the weather term,
       ε is a stochastic error term,
       ln   is the natural logarithm.

The parameter estimates in this formulation are the relevant elasticities indicating the percentage change expected in the dependent variable for a given percentage change in an explanatory variable. These elasticities are constant over the entire range of the demand function, as opposed to the variable elasticities that a simple linear model yields. The imposition of the constant elasticity assumption as a maintained hypothesis is acceptable if, as is the case here, only an indication of the relative magnitudes of consumer response is to be expected from the available data. Owing to the annual nature of the presently available database and the concomitant simplifying assumptions, it seems reasonable to accept this formulation.

An additional variable, lagged consumption, was incorporated into the model as a proxy for the stock of electricity-using appliances and their usage rates. The inclusion of the lagged endogenous variable enables the derivation of both short-run and long-run elasticities. While the definition of the duration of the long-run is imprecise - merely being the time required to achieve a stable demand after a system shock has occurred - it is possible to make a crude estimate of the number of time periods needed to achieve stability from the value of the coefficient of the lagged variable. The estimation results are given in Equation 10:

Electricity Demand Modelling

Table 12.2: Box-Cox ACT Electricity Demand

Model	λ	ρ	$L(\lambda,\rho)$	E_{PE1}	E_{PS}	E_Y	E_{HDD}	Q_{t-1}
linear	1	0	8.00238	-0.33	0.17	0.12*	0.19	0.60
AR, linear	1	0.33	8.56993	-0.34	0.18	-0.17*	0.23	0.58
BCE, log	0	0	9.57310	-0.35	0.19	0.31	0.20	0.55
BCE-AR, log	0	-0.35	10.02221	-0.34	0.17	0.26	0.15	0.56
BCE	-0.04	0	9.57546	-0.35	0.19	0.32	0.20	0.55
BCE-AR	-1.10	-0.65	11.24629	-0.29	0.15	0.43	0.11	0.58

* not statistically different from zero at the 0.05 level.

Table 12.3: Box-Cox Test Results

Null Hypothesis, H_0	χ^2
Conditional tests	
$\lambda = 1 \mid \rho = 0$	3.1462***
$\lambda = 0 \mid \rho = 0$	0.0047
$\rho = 0 \mid \lambda = 1$	1.1351
$\rho = 0 \mid \lambda = 0$	0.8982
Unrestricted tests	
$\lambda = 1$	5.3527*
$\lambda = 0$	2.4482
$\rho = 0$	3.3417***
Joint tests	
$\lambda = 1, \rho = 0$	6.4878**
$\lambda = 0, \rho = 0$	3.3464

* reject at 0.025 significance level
** reject at 0.05 significance level
*** reject at 0.10 significance level

$$\ln Q_{Elt} = -2.94 \; -0.35 \ln P_{Elt} + 0.19 \ln P_{st} + 0.31 \ln P_{Yt}$$

"t" values (-4.273) (-3.873)   (3.487)   (2.413)

FG R^2 0.93   0.83   0.70

$$+ 0.20 \ln HDD_t + 0.55 \ln Q_{Elt-1}$$

(3.607)   (4.625)
0.31   0.96   (10)

$$\bar{R}^2 = 0.990$$
$$D.W. = 2.149$$
$$\text{Durbin's h} = -0.655$$
$$RMSE = 1.8\%$$
$$\text{Theil's U} = 0.366$$

The variables included in the model are: the dependent variable, electricity consumption per household (Q_{Elt}); explanatory variables, the lagged dependent variable (Q_{Elt-1}), the deflated marginal price of electricity (P_{Elt}), the real price of other fuels (P_{st}), real household disposable income (Y_t), and heating degree days (HDD_t). All data have been transformed by taking natural logarithms. The cooling degree day variable was not statistically significant and has been omitted from the regression results. The coefficient of multiple determination adjusted for degrees of freedom, $\bar{R}^2$, indicates that the estimated relationship accounts for 99 per cent of the observed variation.

Collinearity, as measured by the Farrar-Glauber R^2, may pose an estimation problem, being 0.96 for the lagged dependent variable and 0.93 for the electricity price variable. The high level of collinearity is not an unexpected result in a dynamic demand function model specification. In an attempt to assess the potential impact of the collinearity, a series of ridge regressions were estimated. In this approach, the diagonal of the X'X matrix is augmented by some small value k. The selected values for k were between zero and one in increments of 0.1. The results are presented in Table 12.4. The own-price variation is over 45 per cent and the cross-price variation is 40 per cent. The income elasticity range of variation is about 35 per cent and that of the lagged dependent variable is over 80 per cent. The heating degree day elasticities are generally insignificant. A more comprehensive analysis of the impact of collinearity, as recommended by Belsley, Kuh and Welsch (1980), would seem warranted.

The Durbin-Watson statistic value falls within the range of uncertainty. However, Durbin's alternative 'h' statistic suggests that first-order serial correlation is not a problem. The root mean squared error (RMSE) for the equation is 1.8 per cent of the annual electricity consumption levels. The elasticities are statistically significant with all Student's 't' statistics in excess of two.

Table 12.4: Ridge Regression Results

k	EP_{EL}	E_{PS}	E_Y	E_{HDD}	Q_{Elt-1}
0.0	-0.35	0.19	0.31	0.20	0.55
0.1	-0.35	0.21	0.39	0.14	0.45
0.2	-0.33	0.20	0.41	0.09*	0.42
0.3	-0.32	0.19	0.42	0.06*	0.40
0.4	-0.30	0.18	0.42	0.03*	0.38
0.5	-0.29	0.18	0.42	0.01*	0.36
0.6	-0.27	0.17	0.42	-0.01*	0.34
0.7	-0.26	0.16	0.41	-0.03*	0.33
0.8	-0.26	0.16	0.41	-0.04*	0.32
0.9	-0.25	0.15	0.40	-0.05*	0.31
1.0	-0.24	0.15	0.40	-0.05*	0.30

*not statistical different from zero at the 0.08 level.

Table 12.5: ACT Residential Electricity Demand Elasticities

Elasticity	Short-run	Long-run
Own-price	-0.35	-0.77
Cross-price	-0.19	0.42
Income	0.31	0.69
Weather	0.20	0.43

Residential electricity consumption in the ACT is found to be inelastic in the short-run with an own-price elasticity of -0.35 (see Table 12.5). The long-run price elasticity is estimated to be -0.77. This indicates that a one per cent increase in the real marginal price of electricity to the household will induce a 0.77 per cent decline in average consumption. Under a ceteris paribus assumption of all other factors remaining constant, a 90 per cent adjustment to an equilibrium level of consumption will be achieved after four time periods (years) and a 95 per cent adjustment by the fifth year.

The cross-price elasticity of demand has the appropriate positive algebraic sign for substitutes and its value confirms the hypothesis that the goods are not close substitutes. In the long-run, a one per cent increase in the other fuel price would be expected to increase the electricity consumption of the average household by 0.42 per cent. An equilibrium proportionate increase in the price of electricity and of household income would result in a reduction in electricity consumption of roughly 10 per cent of the change. The value of the weather elasticity indicates that a 10 per cent colder winter would be expected to increase electricity consumption by about two per cent. The significance of these log-linear results must be interpreted in the light of the ridge regression which indicated a stability problem.

SUMMARY AND SUGGESTIONS FOR FUTURE RESEARCH

The single equation model results provide an interesting contrast to those reported for previous studies of residential electricity demand (see Table 12.6). While it is difficult to make comparisons among the various model results, some general comments may be made; in particular, the differences between the present results and those in the studies cited are interesting.

Of the other models, only Hawkins (1975) and the three Houthakker papers report larger income elasticities, and the long-run income elasticities from these latter papers are all considerably greater than one. The Brain and Schuyers (1981) income elasticity estimates appear anomalous in that they are quite small, and the long-run elasticity is less that the short-run.

While several of the studies cited indicate that electricity demand is highly price-elastic (i.e. that price elasticity is less than -1), our ACT results do not support this conclusion. The only other Australian estimates of price elasticity provide figures of similar magnitude to ours. Conceivably, overseas responses to price change differ from that in Australia.

Other fuels in the ACT are found to be imperfect substitutes for electricity. The historical absence of natural gas as an alternative fuel may well result in understating the level of potential substitutability to be expected after its large-scale introduction into the residential market. A multi-fuel demand

Table 12.6: Selected Residential Electricity Demand Results

Study	Type	Own-price	Cross-price	Income	Elasticity Weather	Data type	Period	Region	Other
Brain & Schuyers (1981)	SR	-0.23	0.06	0.17	–	TSA	1975-1977	AUS-N	AP
	LR	-0.77	-0.77	0.14					
FEA (1976)	LR	-0.15	–	0.10	–	CS-TSA	1960-1972	US-D	AP
Fisher & Kaysen (1962)	LR	-0.15	–	0.10	–	CS-TSA	1946-1957	US-S	AP
Griffin (1974)	LR	-0.27	–	0.53	–	TSA	1951-1971	US-N	AP,DL
Halvorsen (1975)	LR	-1.00 to -1.21	0.04 to 0.08	0.47 to 0.54	-0.02 to -0.10	CS-TSA	1961-1969	US-S	AP
Hawkins (1975)	LR	-0.55	–	0.93	–	CS	1971	NSW-T	AP
Houthakker (1951)	LR	-0.89	0.21	1.17	–	CS	1937/38	UK-T	MP
Houthakker & Taylor (1970)	SR	-0.13	–	0.13	–	TSA	1947-1964	US-N	AP
	LR	-1.89		1.93					
Houthakker, Verleger & Sheehan (1973)	SR	-0.09	–	0.13	–	CS-TSA	1951-1971	US-S	MP
	LR	-1.19		1.61					
Mount & Chapman (1979)	SR	-0.31	0.16	0.16	–	CS-TSA	1963-1972	US-S	AP
	LR	-1.17	0.61	0.61					
Mount, Chapman & Tyrrell (1973)	SR	-1.14	0.02	0.02	–	CS-TSA	1947-1970	US-S	AP
	LR	-1.20	0.19	0.20					
Wilson (1971)	LR	-1.33	0.31	-0.46	0.04	CS	1966	US-C	AP

Notes: LR = long run, SR = short-run, TS = time series, CS = cross section, A = annual, M = monthly, N = national, D = census division, S = state, T = town, C = city, AP = average price, MP = marginal price, and DL = distributed lags.

model would need therefore to include natural gas as an alternative. Future residential energy demand studies should analyze the household's demand for different forms of energy and explain the shares of these.

Weather changes were found to affect residential electricity consumption in the ACT. The short-run HDD elasticity is however small, indicating that householders do not rely entirely upon electricity to compensate for colder weather. The use of other fuels, including non-market ones, for space heating and behavioural changes (such as the wearing of heavier clothing) must also occur with more severe winter weather. The significance of the weather variable, however, does suggest that its omission from other studies could well result in a misspecification of the demand relationship.

Areas for future research suggested by the analysis are several. A translog model specification including the alternative energy forms might provide further insights into the substitutability among energy sources. Greater temporal disaggregation might better identify the influence of those factors affecting electricity demand, since more accurate measures of the marginal price of electricity and the weather variables might be developed from a monthly or quarterly dataset. Attention to diurnal variations in electricity consumption would provide the means to analyze the potential effects of alternative time-of-day price tariffs. Such analysis would entail a mixed time-series econometric approach. This would allow studying the factors affecting the demand for electric power and determining the most appropriate mechanisms for minimizing peaking problems and smoothing the load curve. However, as with all empirical work, these extensions must await the further development of the necessary data.

SELECTED BIBLIOGRAPHY

Australian Department of National Development & Energy (1981) <u>Forecasts of energy demand and supply; primary and secondary fuels; Australia 1980-81 to 1989-90</u>, Australian Government Publishing Service, Canberra

Australian Bureau of Statistics (1981) <u>Australian National Accounts; Concepts, Sources and Methods</u>, Australian Bureau of Statistics, Canberra

Belsley, D.A., Kuh, E. and Welsh, R.E. (1980) <u>Regression Diagnostics; Identifying Influential Data and Sources of Collinearity</u>, John Wiley and Sons, New York

Box, G.E.P. and Cox, D.R. (1964) 'An analysis of transformations', <u>Journal of the Royal Statistical Society</u>. (B) 26, 211-243

Brain, P. and Schuyers, B. (1981) <u>Energy and the Australian Economy</u>, Longman Cheshire, Melbourne

Christensen, L.R., Jorgenson, D.W. and Lau, L.J. (1973) 'Transcendental logarithmic production functions', Review of Economics and Statistics, 55, 28-45

Christensen, L.R., Jorgenson, D.W. and Lau, L.J. (1975) 'Transcendental logarithmic utility functions', American Economic Review, 65, 367-383

Cumberland, J.H., Donnelly, W.A., Gibson, C.S. and Olson, C.E. (1976) 'Forecasting alternative regional electric requirements and environmental impacts for Maryland, 1970-1990', In Chatterji, M. and van Rompuy, P., (Eds.) Energy, Regional Science and Public Policy, Springer-Verlag, Berlin

Donnelly, W.A. and Leung, E.S. (1983) 'Residential electricity demand', Search, 14, 206-211

Donnelly, W.A., Gooneratne, E.S. and Turnovsky, M.H.L. (1982) 'The residential demand for electricity in the ACT', Working paper HE/WP1, Centre for Resource and Environmental Studies, Australian National University, Canberra

Donnelly, W.A. and Saddler, H.D.W. (1982) 'The retail demand for electricity in Tasmania', Working paper R/WP63, Centre for Resource and Environmental Studies, Australian National University, Canberra

Fisher, F.M. and Kaysen, G.S. (1962) The Demand for Electricity in the United States, North-Holland, Amsterdam

Griffin, J.M. (1974) 'The effects of higher prices on electricity consumption', Bell Journal of Economics and Management Science, 5, 515-539

Halvorsen, R. (1975) 'Residential demand for electricity', Review of Economics and Statistics, 57, 12-18

Hawkins, R.G. (1975) 'The demand for electricity: a cross-section study of New South Wales and the Australian Capital Territory', The Economic Record, 51, 1-18

Houthakker, H.S. (1951) 'Some calculations of electricity consumption in Great Britain', Journal of the Royal Statistical Society, 114, 351-371

Houthakker, H.S. and Taylor, L.D. (1970) Consumer Demand in the United States, Harvard University Press, Cambridge, MA

Houthakker, H.S., Verleger, P.K. and Sheehan, D.P. (1973) 'Dynamic demand analyses for gasoline and residential electricity', Mimeo

Mitchell, B.M., Manning, W.G., Jr. and Acton, J.P. (1978) Peak-Load Pricing, Ballinger, Cambridge, MA

Mount, T.D. and Chapman, L.D. (1979) 'Electricity demand, sulfur emissions and health: an econometric analysis of power generation in the United States', In Norhaus, W.D. (Ed.) International Studies of the Demand for Energy, North-Holland, Amsterdam

Mount, T.D., Chapman, L.D. and Tyrrell, T.J. (1973) 'Electricity demand in the United States: an econometric analysis', Oakridge National Laboratory, Oakridge, TN

Pindyck, R.S. (1976) 'International comparisons of the residential demand for energy'. Working paper MITEL 76-932, Massachusetts Institute of Technology, Cambridge, MA

Saddler, H.D.W., Bennett, J., Reynolds, I. and Smith B. (1980) 'Public choice in Tasmania: aspects of the lower Gordon river hydro-electric development proposal', Monograph No.2, Australian National University, Centre for Resource and Environmental Studies, Canberra

Saddler, H.D.W. and Donnelly, W.A. (1982) 'The demand for energy in Tasmania with particular reference to electricity', In Official Hansard Report, Senate Select Committee on South-West Tasmania, Government Printer, Canberra, pp.150-212

Savin, N.E. and White, K.J. (1978) 'Estimation and testing for functional form and autocorrelation', Journal of Econometrics. 8, 1-12

Taylor, L.D. (1975) 'The demand for electricity: a survey', Bell Journal of Economic and Management Science, 6, 74-110

Taylor, L.D. (1977a) 'Decreasing block pricing and the residential demand for electricity', In Nordhaus, W.D. (Ed.) International Studies of the Demand for Energy, North-Holland, Amsterdam

Taylor, L.D. (1977b) 'The demand for electricity: a survey of price and income elasticities', in Nordhaus, W.D. (Ed.) International Studies of the Demand for Energy, North-Holland, Amsterdam

U.S. Federal Energy Administration (1976) 1976 National Energy Outlook, U.S. Government Printing Office, Washington, DC

White, K.J. (1978) 'A generalized computer program for econometric methods: SHAZAM', Econometrica, 46, 239-240

Wilson, J.W. (1971) 'Residential demand for electricity', Quarterly Review of Economics and Business. 11, 7-19

CONTRIBUTING AUTHORS

David F. BATTEN, Commonwealth Scientific and Industrial Research Organisation and International Institute for Applied Systems Analysis

John M. BLATT, School of Mathematics, University of New South Wales

Carl CHIARELLA, School of Mathematical Sciences, New South Wales Institute of Technology

Bruce D. CRAVEN, Department of Mathematics, University of Melbourne

Glen J. CROUCH, Department of Mathematics, University of Queensland

Peter B. DIXON, Institute of Applied Economic and Social Research, University of Melbourne

William DONNELLY, Centre for Resource and Environmental Studies, Australian National University

George LEITMANN, College of Engineering, University of California, Berkeley

Paul F. LESSE, Commonwealth Scientific and Industrial Research Organisation

Janislaw M. SKOWRONSKI, Department of Mathematics, University of Queensland

Keshav P. VISHWAKARMA, Department of Economics, LaTrobe University

AUTHOR INDEX

Adams, D.M., 69
Aizerman, M.A., 17
Allais, M., 130
Allen, P.M., 7, 71
Ananev, B.I., 16
Anderson, B.D.O., 164
Anderson, A.E., 7
Andronov, A.M., 149
Aoki, M., 6, 164
Arrow, K.J., 4, 6
Astrom, K.J., 15, 42, 164

Barmish, B.R., 18, 19
Batten, D.F., 6, 7, 71
Baumol, W.J., 2
Belsley, D.A., 189
Bertram, J.E., 16
Black, F., 38
Blatt, J.M., 6, 39, 41, 42, 43, 132
Blinder, A.S., 131, 132, 141, 147
Botman, J.J., 47
Boulding, K., 3
Box, G.E.P., 8, 155, 163, 166, 167, 185
Brain, P., 191
Breinl, W., 19
Bromilow, F.J., 47
Bucy, R.S., 164

Carroll, R.L., 16
Cass, D., 6
Chambers, J.C., 166
Chatfield, C., 155
Chiarella, C., 6, 149
Chow, G.C., 6

Christ, C.F., 131
Christensen, L.R., 181
Cigno, A., 7
Clark, C.W., 88
Corless, M., 16, 17, 19, 20, 26
Cournot, A., 4
Cox, D.R., 185
Craven, B.D., 8
Crouch, G.J., 7

Day, R.H., 2, 7
Dixon, P.B., 6, 120, 128, 129
Doman, E., 2
Donnelly, W.A., 8
Dorfman, R., 5
Dornbush, R., 131

Flippov, A.F., 92
Forrester, J., 8, 69
Frisch, R., 149

Gale, D., 5
Galperin, E.A., 91, 107
Goodwin, R.M., 132, 149
Gray, M.R., 131
Grujic, Lj. T., 16
Gutman, S., 16, 17, 19

Hadjimichalakis, M.G., 131
Haken, H., 7
Hannan, E.J., 8, 158
Harrod, R., 2
Hawkins, R.G., 191
Haynes, R.W., 69

Hicks, J.R., 4, 132, 149
Hirsch, M., 7
Hotelling, H., 4
Houthakker, H.S., 183
Hull, C.H., 167, 173
Hosteland, J.E., 71

Infante, E.F., 131
Intriligator, M.D., 4, 6, 7
Ito, K., 38, 41, 43, 44

Jazwinski, A.H., 164
Jenkins, G.M., 8, 155, 163, 166, 167
Johansen, L., 6, 119, 120, 121, 122, 123, 124, 128, 129
Johansson, B., 7
Johnson, C.D., 16

Kaldor, N., 132, 133, 136, 149
Kalecki, M., 5, 132, 149
Kalgraf, K., 69, 70
Kalman, R.E., 16, 164
Kendrick, D.A., 6
Kerner, E.H., 98
Khaikin, S.E., 149
Koopmans, T., 6
Krasovskii, N.N., 15
Kreisselmeier, G., 16
Kuh, E., 191
Kuhn, H.W., 7
Kushner, H.J., 15

Lau, L.J., 183
Leitmann, G., 6, 16, 17, 18, 19, 25, 26, 27, 31, 33, 112
Lessee, P.F., 6, 7, 73
Letov, A.M., 16
Levack, H.H., 69
Lindorff, D.P., 16
Luenberger, D.G., 7, 90, 91, 98, 107
Lujanen, M., 47
Lurie, A.L., 16
Lyapunov, A.M., 7, 16, 18, 27, 62, 63, 66

Makarov, V.L., 6
Malinvaud, E., 5
Malthus, T.R., 1, 2
Marx, K., 2
May, R.M., 9, 69
Medio, A., 132, 147, 149
Meditch, J.S., 164
Melsa, J.L., 165
Merton, R.C., 38, 39
Molander, P., 16
Monopoli, R.V., 15, 16
Moore, J.B., 164
Morishima, M., 6
Morse, A.S., 16
Mullick, S.K., 166
Murphy, R.E., 6

Narendra, K.S., 16, 107
Nash, J., 7
Needleman, L., 47
Nelson, C.R., 8, 167
Nelson, R.R., 2, 7
von Neumann, J., 2, 5, 6
Nie, N.H., 167, 173
Nitecki, Z., 7
Nomura, I., 69

Okuguchi, K., 131

Palmor, Z., 17, 19
Parmenter, B.R., 120, 128, 129
Peterson, B.B., 16, 18
Pitchford, J., 6
Poincare, H., 7
Pontryagin, L.S., 7
Porter, B., 16
Prigogine, I., 7
Prothero, D.L., 155
Pyatnitskii, E.S., 17

Ramsey, F.P., 4, 6
Randers, J., 69
Rhodes, I.B., 7
Rubinov, A.M., 6

Sage, A.P., 165
Salukvadze, M.E., 16
Samuelson, P.A., 4, 5, 6, 37
Savin, N.E., 185

Schieve, W.C., 7
Scholes, M., 38
Schumpeter, J., 2, 3, 8
Schuyers, B., 191
Shell, K., 6
Shubik, M., 7
Simaan, M.A., 88
Skowronski, J.M., 6, 7,
 65, 66, 73, 81, 88, 90,
 91, 92, 105, 107, 113
Smale, S., 7
Smith, A., 1
Smith, C.W., 38
Smith, D.D., 166
Sobel, M.J., 7
Solow, R.M., 2, 5, 131,
 132, 141, 147
Stein, J.L., 131
Stenberg, L., 69
Sutton, J., 120, 128, 129
Swan, T., 2
Szego, G.P., 7

Takayama, T., 88
Taylor, L.D., 183
Theocharis, R., 9
Thom, R., 7

Thorp, J.S., 18
Tinbergen, J., 2, 5
Tsukui, J., 6
Tucker, S.N., 47
Turnovsky, S.J., 6, 131

Valavani, L.S., 16
Varian, H.R., 6
Vincent, D.P., 120, 128,
 129
Vincent, T.L., 7, 88, 92
Vishwakarma, K.P., 6, 8,
 166
Vitt, A.A., 149

Wan, H.Y., 31, 33
Welsch, R.E., 189
White, K.J., 185
Wiener, N., 38, 39, 41,
 43, 44
Winter, S.G., 2, 7

Yukutake, K., 69

Zeeman, E.C., 7

SUBJECT INDEX

adaptive control, 6, 15-33
adaptive economics, 7
admissible control, 87
anti-target set, 106
asymptotic stability, 17, 33, 56
autocorrelation, 159
autoregression, 158-159
autoregressive-integrated moving average models, 167

balanced growth, 2, 97
bifurcation theory, 7
bio-economic model, 88
Box-Cox method, 156, 159, 185-188
Box-Jenkins method, 155, 161, 163-178
Brownian motion, 39
budget constraint, 132, 180
building industry operated by sole owner, 52, 57-68
with an open access, 52-57

capital accumulation, 5
carrying capacity, 71, 105
Caratheodory function, 17, 25, 33
catastrophe theory, 7
chaotic behaviour, 9

Chi-square distribution, 185
closed loop control, 42-43
comparative statics, 1
complementary goods, 185
composite control, 87, 106
control theory, 6, 8, 15-68
cross-price elasticity of demand, 189

development, 2, 3
differential
 games, 6, 47, 87-115
 topology, 7
diffusion coefficients, 105
discontinuity manifolds, 33
disequilibrium, 2, 7
duality theory, 181
Durban-Watson statistic 189
dynamic
 adaptive observer theory, 90
 econometric models, 69
 macroeconomic models, 119-149
 programming, 43

econometric forecasts, 8
economic dynamics, 1-4

202

efficiency coefficient, 106
electricity demand modelling, 8, 179-194
Euler's method, 129
evolutionary theory, 2, 7-8
exchange rate dynamics, 131
exploitation of mineral resources, 119

feedback
 control, 15, 20, 42-44
 loops, 8
Filippov solutions, 100
filtering theory, 162-165
Fisher's test, 158-159
fluctuation, 2, 3
Fokker-Planck equation, 42
forest sector models, 69-82
Fourier
 analysis, 155
 expansion, 152

game theory, 5, 6-7, 87-115
Gaussian white noise, 164
general equilibrium theory, 1, 120, 128
government budget constraint, 132

Harrod-Domar model, 2
harvested production, 87
harvesting
 effort, 89
 games, 7, 87-115
 power, 89
 rate, 78, 87, 105
household
 disposable income, 185
 size, 49
housing market, 47

import parity pricing for oil, 119
industrial instability, 47

innovation, 2
integro-differential equation, 42
I-stability, 58, 65

Johansen method, 120, 123, 129
 extended, 120-129
Juglar cycle, 3

Kalman filter, 43, 164, 165
Keynesian demand stimulation policies, 119
Kitchin cycle, 3
Kolmogorov equation, 42
Kondratieff cycle, 3
Krylov-Bogoliubov method of averaging, 132, 144

Lagrange multipliers, 4
leading periodic components, 158
least-squares regression, 158
limit cycles, 132, 137, 144, 147, 152
linear
 activity analysis, 2
 differential equations, 131
 feedback strategies, 18, 58-68
 games, 107
 models, 5, 182, 185
 oscillator, 19
 programming, 5
 rotation strategy, 82
logistic growth, 71, 88
log-linear model, 182, 186
log-normal distribution, 39
Lotka-Volterra model, 88, 98
Lyapunov
 equation, 18
 function, 17, 18, 25, 27, 62, 63, 66, 98, 113
Lyapunov theory, 7, 16

macroeconomic models, 6, 31, 119–149
marginal
  price of electricity, 194
  rate of substitution, 181
Markov process, 40–41
mathematical economics, 4–8
maximum likelihood estimation, 165
minimax theorem, 6
multisector growth model, 5, 6
multi-stage decision process, 181

Nash
  competitive game, 91, 105
  equilibrium, 100
natural
  regeneration, 70
  thinning, 70
neoclassical growth models, 2
von Neumann growth model, 2
Newton's laws of motion, 40
non-equilibrium statistical mechanics, 39
nonlinear
  accelerator principle, 149
  difference equations, 8, 131
  dynamical systems, 7
  feedback, 18
  modelling, 5, 7–9
  theory of adaptive identifiers, 7, 105
  zero sum game, 91, 107

observer theory, 91
open loop controls, 89
optimal
  control, 37–45, 70
growth theory, 5
ORANI model, 119–129

Pareto-cooperative fishing, 107
payback period, 179
periodic
  component, 158, 161
  path, 132, 147
phenomenological theory, 7
planting rate, 78
playing region, 87
Poisson distribution, 37
Pontryagin
  function, 113
  structural stability analysis, 7
price index for substitute fuels, 183
product cycle theory, 7

quadratic cost function, 54–55

random
  noise, 174
  walk process, 37
rate of
  construction, 49, 51, 57
  depreciation, 57
  government spending, 133–135
  interest, 133
reaction function, 4
recursive programming, 7
renewable resource management, 7, 69–82, 87–115
ridge regressions, 189, 191
rotation strategy, 79, 81

SARAS model, 163–178
seasonal factor, 156
self-organizing models, 7
serial correlation, 158, 185–186, 189
servomechanisms, 8
set theory, 5
spectral density, 158
speculative market, 37

stability analysis, 7, 51-68
stabilisation policy, 47, 133
stable
 cycles, 9
 points, 9
state-space model, 164
stochastic
 differential equation, 42
 model, 6, 158
storage
 function, 97
 interactions, 96
supplied consumption, 87
sustainable yield, 70-71, 78
synergetics, 7
system dynamics models, 8, 70

tariffs, 119-127, 183, 194
taxpayer disposable income, 185
technical progress, 2
technological change, 2
temporary equilibrium, 2, 5
thinning rate, 78
time-series analysis, 6, 8, 155-178
Tobin monetary growth model, 131
transcendental logarithmic utility function, 181, 194
turnpike theorem, 5, 6

unbalanced growth, 97
utility
 functions, 180-182
 theory, 179

Volterra function, 98
volumetric density, 70

Walrasian general equilibrium, 4
white noise, 37-45
Whittle-Walker test, 159
Wiener
 -Ito theory, 41-44
 process, 37-38
world commodity prices, 119